The Berlin Police Force
in the Weimar Republic

The Berlin Police Force
in the Weimar Republic

HSI-HUEY LIANG

UNIVERSITY OF CALIFORNIA PRESS

Berkeley · Los Angeles · London · 1970

University of California Press
Berkeley and Los Angeles, California
University of California Press, Ltd.
London, England

Copyright © 1970 by The Regents of the
University of California
SBN 520–01603–3
Library of Congress Catalog Card Number: 74–85452

Designed by James Mennick
Printed in the United States of America

TO MY FATHER

the late Dr. Lone Liang,
Chinese Chargé d'Affaires in Berlin
1928–1934

Preface

THE STUDY OF modern German history requires that attention be given to the rules of German historiography. In addition to the factual information, we must be familiar with the way in which Germans have explained and periodized the events in their past and, above all, know what expressions they have employed and what assumptions they have made. The best foreign contributors to the subject have normally drawn heavily on the intellectual pattern of German scholarship, and where they have not, they have often missed the essential point. They have borrowed not simply because the German historians were the pioneers in this field, but because the materials of modern German history until the middle of the twentieth century have to a large extent demanded an interpretative approach of their own. Unlike the English historians with their pronounced emphasis on constitutional procedure, and the historians of France who concentrated on national politics, German historians found their idiom in abstract—sometimes even speculative—historical propositions. It was probably the only way to give coherence to the oscillating and disjointed history of their people. The alternative would have been unmanageable bulk. It did, however, create a tendency toward dogmatic generalizations.

The German school of historical writing can present some difficulties to the student unfamiliar with German social customs and the German cultural idiom. A succession of theoretical or simply colloquial concepts interpose themselves as barriers between him and the object of his studies. To provide a remedy for this difficulty, there have been repeated calls for a stronger emphasis on German social history, especially in regard to the twentieth century.[1] Conventional studies of Germany's political and economic condition since 1918 seem particularly inadequate either to convey the horror of the Hitler regime, or the confusion and indecision of the period preceding it. Consequently, playwrights have tried their hand at political subjects, elder statesmen at personal memoirs, and scholars have turned to social history in the hope that the private and prosaic, when paired with national public events, would give rise to a new credibility.[2]

Social history, in turn, has called attention to the need for more city history. The narrow focus of such studies allows for precise examples and detailed accounts, and for indulgence in those paradoxical circumstances that, on a higher plane of historical analysis, are too often dismissed as the irrelevant product of chance.

It is true that some of the city history of modern Germany has also been written in monumental abstractions. There exist bulky volumes described as "Kultur- und Sittengeschichte" which purport to weave "symphonic images" out of the customs and mores of entire periods. Then again, city history has taken the form of parochial chronicles devoutly compiled by local *Heimatforscher*. To the English-speaking public, the former approach can be irritating because of the subjectivity of its sweeping conclusions. Local narratives, on the other hand, have the disadvantage of antiquarian accounts too obviously intended for local consumption.

This does not deny the possibility of reform. Thus, while the historiography of Berlin contains bold interpretations of the city's changing personality over the centuries[3] and any number of anecdotal compilations centered on its older quarters,[4] there are also monographs that go far beyond the fancy of local patriots without losing themselves in subjective impressions.[5] Some very good novels have been written on Berlin which express ideas and concerns that reach far beyond the locality.[6] Sociological works at the turn of the century, studies in municipal government during the 1920's, and the investigations sponsored by the Berliner Historische Kommission since the end of the Second World War, have shown that well-selected topics in the history of one city can lay the basis for a fresh look at the social history of modern Germany.[7]

Berlin offers many advantages for such an undertaking. It cannot, of course, claim to be the obvious or even the best choice of a German city for English-speaking students to study.[8] No such choice could ever be perfect in view of the diversity of Germany's social and cultural scene. But Berlin is a feasible, and I would like to think, a good choice to make. A city as young and as uninhibited as Berlin is particularly susceptible to the changes brought with each successive period in modern German history. Its versatile population of immigrants has nearly always moved in step with the times.

It is also true, of course, that Berlin rarely succeeded in wholly absorbing the innovations that came with each stage of modern Germany's political and cultural development. Many of these stages, after all, have been little more than short episodes. Karl Scheffler's much quoted observation, that "Berlin is a city forever in the making and destined never to be"[9] consequently threatens to disqualify Berlin as too singular a phe-

nomenon on Germany's sociohistorical map. If this limits the
usefulness of our undertaking, it applies with equal force to
any other German city.

On the other hand, it is compensated by Berlin's determin-
ing influence in the course of Germany's history from 1871 to
1933. For the story of modern Berlin is not of uniform historical
value. In the seventeenth, the eighteenth, and during the first
half of the nineteenth century, Berlin was by and large the passive object of larger historical forces in Prussia and Northern
Germany. The historian can find in its chronicles little more
than samples from life in one of Germany's many royal residential towns. And if, jumping two generations, we turn to Berlin's
history during the Third Reich and the years since 1945, we are
dealing with materials best suited for a symbolic interpretation
of Germany's twelve years of dictatorship and Europe's ideological division after the Second World War.

There remains the period from 1871 to 1933. For just over
sixty years, Berlin was truly Germany's administrative and political capital, the focal point of its economic life, and after 1900
the scientific and cultural center of the nation as well. During
the Second Empire and the Weimar Republic Berlin was much
more than a passive associate to its hinterland: the newly-born
metropolis nearly engulfed the old militaristic Prussia; its
dynamic growth affected the entire Reich.[10]

This study proposes to present one episode from Berlin's
time of greatest historical impact: the story of its police service
during the Weimar Republic. The significance of this topic will
be explained in the Introduction. But it should be stressed at
this point that research on Berlin history for the 1920's and the
early 1930's is urgently needed now, since many documents
were lost in the Second World War and those in East German
archives are not readily available to Western scholars. To com-
pensate for gaps in the written record, the historian must appeal
to the memory of elderly residents whose testimonials need to
be recorded and sifted as long as they are still available.

Much of the information for this study was gathered during the fall of 1962 in West Berlin by personal interviews with veterans of the police force. These interviews varied in length from half an hour to an entire afternoon. My informants did not speak of their personal experience exclusively—some of them preferred to comment only on the general condition of police service in the twenties and shunned details such as salaries and promotions. All were interviewed with the prior understanding that they would not be asked about their activities after January 30, 1933. Their cooperation was indispensable as a source for innumerable items of information, suggestions for interpretation, and hints for further lines of inquiry. A list of my informants and the subjects they discussed will be found in the Appendix. I am particularly indebted to Polizeimeister Hermann Artner and Inspektionsleiter F. Gediehn for their patient and detailed testimonials; to Polizei-Hauptkommissar Willi Lemke for entrusting me with the unpublished manuscript of his autobiography; and to Amtsrat Heinz Thiel, Kriminalmeister Teigeler, Kriminaldirektoren Lehnhoff and Togotzes, and Kriminalrat Hoberg for their illuminating introduction to the world of the criminalist. I acknowledge my indebtedness to Commander Hans Ulrich Werner and Deputy Commander Gottfried Miczek of the Schutzpolizei, to Oberrat Finger and Oberkommissar Hollstein at the police school in Spandau, and to Leitender Kriminaldirektor Wolfram Sangmeister for enabling me to talk freely to their subordinates.

Above all, I must thank Police President Georg Moch who, as Deputy President in the fall of 1962, gave me permission to hold all my interviews.

To all the officials formerly or currently on the staff of the police force in West Berlin who have helped me in my endeavor I would like to express my sincerest thanks. This book could not have been written without their encouragement and assistance, even though its interpretation may not always agree with their own views on the subject.

The technical literature on Prussian police ideas and police methods in the Weimar Republic was made available to me through the courteous assistance of the librarians at the headquarters of the West Berlin Police, at the headquarters of the criminal police in Schöneberg, and at the police school in Spandau. The unpublished documents concerning individual police officials, including court cases, were put at my disposal at the Berlin Document Center, the Federal Archive in Koblenz, the archive of the Landeskriminalgericht in Berlin-Moabit, the Landesarchiv Berlin, and the former Prussian Secret State Archive in Dahlem. I was unfortunately not allowed to use police documents presently located in East German archives. The background material on Berlin history was obtained at the Senatsbibliothek, the Landesarchiv, and the university library of the Free University in Berlin. Nearly all the photographs were supplied by the Landesbildstelle Berlin.

The preliminary research in the fall of 1962 was undertaken during a semester's sabbatical leave from Bard College. The main bulk of the work was done with the assistance of a fellowship of the Alexander von Humboldt Foundation between October, 1967 and July, 1968, during which time Professor Dr. Dr. h. c. Hans Herzfeld of the Free University in Berlin acted as my benevolent mentor.

I would finally like to express my gratitude to Miss Kathryn Pennypacker, my student assistant at Vassar College in 1965–66, who proofread the early drafts of some chapters, and to Mrs. Shirley Warren of the University of California Press, who painstakingly edited the final manuscript. My warmest thanks go to my friend Professor Donald J. Olsen who improved my English and encouraged my interest in city history, and above all to my wife Francette Liang who made writing this book a pleasure.

Contents

List of Illustrations

The Schlosskaserne
Mounted police guarding the Reichstag, 1930
Police restraining crowds on Hindenburg's birthday
Police escorting Communist May Day Parade
Police escorting Nazi parade
Communist insurgents
Police attacking Communists
Schupos intercepting Communist agitation team
Armored police car
Police protecting S.A. demonstration
Main Communist headquarters
Funeral of Horst Wessel
Monument to Police Captains Anlauf and Lenck

MAPS

Abbreviations

NOT EXPLAINED IN THE TEXT

I. *Ranks in the Schutzpolizei*

Kdr:	Kommandeur (Commandant, General of Police)
PO:	Polizei-Oberst (Police Colonel)
POL:	Polizei-Oberstleutnant (Lieutenant Colonel of Police)
PM:	Polizei-Major (Police Major)
PH:	Polizei-Hauptmann (Police Captain)
PL:	Polizei-Leutnant (Police Lieutenant)
PHWM:	Polizei-Hauptwachtmeister (Sergeant Major)
POWM:	Polizei-Oberwachtmeister (First Sergeant)
PWM:	Polizei-Wachtmeister (Sergeant)
PUWM:	Polizei-Unterwachtmeister (Constable)

II. *Ranks in the Detective Force (Departments IA and IV)*

ORR:	Oberregierungsrat (Assistant Commissioner)

RR: Regierungsrat (Government Councillor)
KD: Kriminaldirektor (Police Director)
KPR: Kriminalpolizeirat (Police Councillor)
KOK: Kriminal-Oberkommissar (Chief Inspector)
KK: Kriminal-Kommissar (Detective Inspector)
KBS: Kriminal-Bezirkssekretär (Detective Sergeant)
KS: Kriminal-Sekretär (Detective)
KA: Kriminal-Assistent (Assistant Detective)

III.   *Abbreviations in Reference Notes*

Vossische Zeitung (M): morning edition
Vossische Zeitung (A): evening edition
Vossische Zeitung (S): Sunday edition
Berlin Document Center:
    ORPO: Ordnungspolizei (Order Police)
    RUSHA: Rasse- und Siedlungs-Hauptamt
           (S.S. Central Bureau for Questions
           of Race and Resettlement)

Introduction

BERLIN in the twenties was a national clearinghouse. Neither its position as the Reich's foremost industrial city nor as its chief communications center was as exciting and novel as the fact that it had become Germany's gigantic stock exchange for ideas and experiments in almost every field of endeavor.[1] To be sure, most innovations after 1918 assumed radical dimensions on reaching Berlin. But this, contemporaries thought, only served to enhance Berlin's usefulness as a starting point for an inquiry into the nation's current condition.[2] They had no use for an average town. "The truth must be uncovered by studying its extremes," wrote S. Cracauer in the introduction to his sociological analysis of Germany's office workers in 1930, which he based largely on what he found in her capital.[3]

Extremes, however, when joined together without coordination, often produce conflict. The many dynamic impulses at work in Berlin created the illusion of a powerful metropolis, while in fact much of the intellectual and material potential at hand was frittered away in mutual competition. As a result, Berlin, whose claim to leadership since 1871 had evoked much resentment in Imperial Germany, became in the twenties the universal scapegoat for a plethora of national grievances.

> They talk about [Berlin] as of an outside calamity that has befallen them through other people's fault, even through malevolence or conspiracy. . . . When something goes wrong in politics, economics, in Germany's social order or cultural life . . . of course Berlin! When a province, a section of the population, a social class, or a clan nurses an imaginary grievance: it is the fault of Berlin. When foreigners make derogatory comments: Berlin's to be blamed.[4]

The city's political importance was not in dispute, only its ability to offer the defeated nation the rallying point it demanded. And indeed, life in Berlin offered a remarkable sample of Germany's uneasy posture during the *"Zwischenreich"* between a renunciation of the monarchical past and conflicting conceptions of a democratic future. This can be illustrated by a simple observation. Nearly every important turn in the history of this city—its rise from an obscure fishing village seven centuries ago to a pretentious world metropolis by the 1890's, as much as its demotion to a frontier post of Western Europe in 1945—all this had come together with a remarkable transformation in the city's external appearance. But not the republican era of 1918 to 1933. Apart from a number of isolated modern building projects, the 1920's offer comparatively little material to the historian of architecture and city planning.[5] Quite a number of contemporaries have, instead, testified to a feeling of unreality living as they did among the stone monuments of an old order whose everlasting endurance, once taken for granted, had vanished in the course of a single afternoon. Wolfgang Schadewaldt, a Berlin writer, recalls that before the First World War his mother would take him for walks between Leipziger Platz and Gendarmenmarkt, and on the way instill in the boy something akin to a "secular reverence" for his hometown.[6] The war disrupted this sense of kinship between the Berliner and his city.

> In the Berlin of 1921 everything seemed unreal. Big-bosomed valkyries stonily supported the facades of houses as before. The lifts worked, but there was hunger and cold in the flats. The conductor courteously helped the *Geheimrat's* wife out of the tram-car. The tram-routes remained unchanged, but no one knew the routes of history.[7]

The city, by all accounts, had lost its former bearings. Contemporary novelists used a clipped staccato to convey the average Berliner's fragmented impression of each fleeting moment of the day. Theirs was a literature from an unreal world, whose essential instability, Ernst von Salomon said, found its appropriate expression in psychological studies of personal experiences.[8] Social critics liked to speak of the cynicism of the post-war generation, of its easy excitability, and of its indiscriminate search for new values and a new faith.[9] "Ah! what must we expect from these sixty millions of empty minds, in which the good and the bad, the true and the false can be instilled with equal facility. . . ." wrote Henri Béraud after his visit to Berlin in 1926.[10]

The existence side by side of radically opposed ideas within a city of four million inhabitants caused anxiety in the minds of many a contemporary. At social gatherings,

> arch conservative noblemen stood besides Socialist members of Parliament; a wild little anarchist conducted a heated argument with a bemonocled officer; even an unshakable anti-Semite fell momentarily silent when a well-known Jewish attorney drew near.

There was much tolerance on the surface. "But where would the conflicts find their ultimate resolution?"[11]

Not everything was arrested development hovering on the brink of disintegration. Berlin shared many of the trends that

historians of other cities in other countries have described as
the hallmark of progress in the twenties. There was the growth
of modern motor traffic, the new industry of moving pictures,
much popular interest in English sports and American dance
music, the rising importance of white-collar workers and of
women in professional and business life. No social trend, however, could claim an overriding influence in shaping the future.
The historian who does not want to isolate one fragment of
Berlin's social picture from the vaster panorama of change—for
example by describing only the milieu of Berlin's prominent
writers, artists, and theatrical personalities, as so many of them
have done—must laboriously account for the activities of scores
of public figures and social groups: professions, commercial en-
terprises, institutions, classes. One possible solution for him is to
study the police service in Berlin. This topic has the following
advantages to offer.

The jurisdiction of the police extended to the entire area of
Greater Berlin, not to one portion of this territory alone.

The police in the twenties assumed an unprecedented
amount of responsibility for the security and welfare of the inhabitants in this city and drew a proportionately large amount
of public attention.

Its performance in Berlin between 1918 and 1932–33 was
important for the physical security of the republican government of Prussia and the German Reich.

Between the end of the First World War and the beginning
of the Hitler period, the police was the backbone of public order
in Berlin. This was a novel situation for both the public and its
law-enforcing agents. Under the Empire, the royal constabulary
(Königliche Schutzmannschaft) had been overshadowed by
the prestigious Imperial Army. The police was only the internal
instrument of the Prussian state, whose political and social system antagonized a large portion of its own people, while the

soldiers stood for Prussia's military renown abroad and for the recent triumph of Germany's national cause. Visual impressions mattered too. The guard regiments with their colorful parades made a deeper impression on the imagination of the people than many other elements in Berlin's social life however important they were. Walther Kiaulehn, half-mockingly, has suggested that the working-class movement was often underrated in the Empire merely because Socialists wore no uniforms.[12] Even the blue-clad police played a junior role to the army in the popular mind of the time.[13]

After the collapse of the monarchy in 1918, it was the army's turn to recede into the background of the daily scene in Berlin. Patriotic holidays, court festivities, and military pomp became a memory of bygone days; army barracks and war memorials acquired the patina of historical relics—a contributing cause, some people thought, to Berlin's declining attraction for foreign tourists.[14]

With Germany's major problems shifted from foreign affairs to internal security, the police had become the government's principal and most visible symbol of authority, its chief support in a time of widespread domestic lawlessness.[15] All the branches of the Berlin police were enlarged and modernized. Detachments of the new security police provided armed protection for public buildings, stood by at countless open-air demonstrations, and staged massive raids in areas of high criminality. The Schutzpolizei's ubiquitous presence on the public scene astounded foreign visitors as much as its novelty irritated disgruntled residents.[16] Novelists of different political shades revealed their colors as they praised the smart turnout of the traffic cop or attacked the policeman as a heavy-handed disciplinarian. To some the Schupo was the agent of order and security in the midst of threatening chaos, to others the last defense of an indecisive regime.[17] No one ignored it. "The his-

tory of the Republic," wrote Carl Severing in 1929, "is insepar-
able from the history of the Police."[18]

Even the plainclothesmen received their share of publicity.
Everyone knew that the Prussian political police, which had
been disbanded in the Revolution of 1918, had promptly been
resuscitated—in tenfold numbers, so the journalist Adolf Stein
claimed—to protect the new regime against conspirators on the
right and left. According to him the agents of what in the twenties became known as the Police Presidium's Department IA[19]
covered every nook and corner of Greater Berlin, searching for
secret stores of arms, violating the privacy of letters, and infil-
trating clubs and associations.[20] Their names were even mentioned in the daily news columns reporting on political street
fights and brawls at party assemblies. Publicity offered the leaders of the Weimar police an escape from their dilemma of having
to choose between their democratic conscience, which abhorred
secret police methods, and their political common sense, which
told them to watch their enemies' machinations.[21] In 1928, Deputy Police President Dr. Bernhard Weiss wrote a popular book
presenting the case for a political police, which sought to dispel
the public's suspicion toward Department IA.[22] But if *Polizei
und Politik* like other semiofficial publications of the time succeeded in creating the appearance of frankness in matters of
domestic espionage, it also confirmed the general view that the
Weimar Republic, compared to the Prussian monarchy, had
vastly extended the sphere of police surveillance.[23]

Not that Berliners necessarily disliked the police. The ordinary detective force, for example, benefited from the contemporary wave of interest in criminal affairs of all sorts. Few
descriptions of Berlin in the twenties fail to include stories of
dope peddling and prostitution, of homicidal maniacs and notorious robbers. Memoirs recounting the great days of Hotel
Adlon and other fashionable establishments invariably include

anecdotes of gentleman burglars and international swindlers.[24] Hans Fallada's novel *Wer einmal aus dem Blechnapf frisst,* and Alfred Döblin's *Berlin-Alexanderplatz* are pictures from the milieu of professional crooks, while Erich Kästner's best known children's stories *Emil und die Detektive* and *Pünktchen und Anton* deal with criminal methods whose novelty and success were then a matter of current concern.[25]

True, the average man in the street showed little inclination to assume the role of a lay criminologist. His curiosity about crime, however, was easily extended to include the work of some outstanding detective inspectors of the criminal police whose names and achievements had appeared in the press. There was the courageous Albert Dettmann, who personally laid hand on some of Berlin's most dangerous burglars in the early twenties. There were the commissars Werneburg and Lissigkeit, whose rapid work in solving a number of robberies attended with murder won public acclaim. Otto Busdorf's name made headlines in the Haas-Schröder affair of 1926, and Kriminalrat Ernst Gennat helped to establish the Berlin Kripo's international claim to excellence. If a generalization may be ventured at this point it would be this: that the twenties were the one period in Berlin's modern history when a number of outstanding detective inspectors enjoyed great popular renown.[26]

Police sports, police concerts,[27] and progress in the development of police science were all reminders that the German government after the war sought to fulfill many of its multifarious tasks through the wideflung organization of its police. The enormous routine work of the administrative police—from registering the inhabitants and running Germany's new unemployment insurance to the enforcement of fire laws and the licensing of public houses—is too vast to be recounted here. "There is no other administrative authority that can rival the competence of the police," wrote an official in Berlin as early as 1919. "There

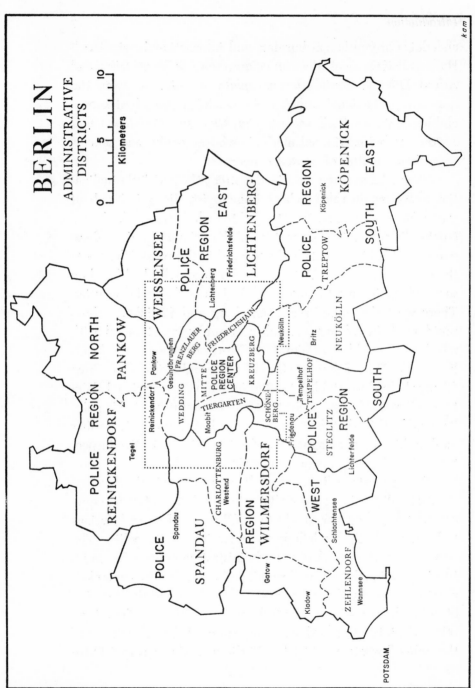

The dotted lines indicate area covered by detail map, pp. 12–13.

will soon be nothing left which does not fall under its jurisdiction."[28] A decade later, Police President Menzel of Magdeburg confirmed this prognosis when he wrote:

> Generally speaking, the interest of the state and of its citizens does not allow for any curtailment in the police's range of activities. On the contrary, this area must be constantly enlarged in accordance with the changing conditions of life. . . . Growing complexity in living conditions calls for growing complexity in policing. In every part of the world, the twentieth century is and will be an age of revolutionary tensions. . . . The calm and deliberate work of social reform, so necessary for the relief of these tensions, makes political isolators imperative if short circuits— read revolutions—are to be averted and the reforms secured. The most important isolator of all is the security police.[29]

Since the end of the war, the police, not surprisingly, was filled with a heightened sense of importance. Dr. Weiss noted somewhat complacently in *Polizei und Politik:* "Every political party and every party politician wants to capture the soul of the police."[30] Yet the problem of policing the territory of Greater Berlin was becoming increasingly complex throughout this period.

The area controlled by the police president of Berlin covered 552 square miles of tenement houses and factories, of shopping streets and railway yards, of residential quarters, schools, and government buildings. Four million people fell under the jurisdiction of a police machine employing 14,000 uniformed security guards, 3,000 detectives, 300 agents of the political police, and 4,000 administrative officials.[31] The amalgamation in 1920 of what previously had been eight independent municipalities, fifty-five suburban districts, and twenty-three estates into one Greater Berlin had necessitated a parallel integration of the police service in this area.[32] The old "Landespolizeibezirk Berlin," which had consisted of five separate police presidiums, was abolished, and so were eight rural police districts in the surrounding countryside. Their place was taken by a single authority under the direction of the police president of Berlin, who in turn was directly responsible to the Prussian Minister of Interior. The police apparatus thus created in 1920 was the largest of its kind in Prussia and Germany.[33]

Berlin was an integral metropolitan expanse within the limits of the city's circular railway (Ringbahn) from Seestrasse in the north to the town-hall of Steglitz in the south. Yet the task of the police varied considerably from district to district and from one neighborhood to the next. There were "riot-prone wards" *(Krawallreviere)* and easy wards, depending on the social composition of the local residents, their political views, and their attitude toward law and order. These differences mattered the more since the police leaders of the Republic, anxious to manage their public relations at the precinct level as much as in the Prussian Diet, had decided to shed the pompous image of the prewar constable (whose waxed mustache and martial saber had spelled "Keep your distance!") for the benevolent motto "The Police, Your Friend and Assistant." To realize the ideal of a "People's Police" was not easy in the face of the people's traditional suspicions of the police however anxious they were otherwise to be "controlled in all things."[34]

> A Berlin constable who intercedes, arranges, supervises the public scene (and let us admit that the postwar cop is doing his best) ... must always struggle against the local temper, the local element. He is called on to be an everyday hero whilst a policeman in Paris, London, or Vienna can be a public darling any time.[35]

To complicate matters, the local temper in this city of millions lacked a common denominator.

There was, to begin with, the government district in Mitte and Tiergarten. During the twenties, the entire area to the north and south of Unter den Linden was in decline as the wealthy moved to the western suburbs and left the symbolic streets of Imperial Berlin to travel agencies and sight-seeing tours in motor coaches.[36] To the dismay of conservatives, Marxist demonstrations were regularly allowed in the Royal Pleasure Grounds (Lustgarten), and shop windows in the Friedrichsstrasse could be seen displaying the Crown Prince of Meiningen side by side with "Documents of Feminine Beauty"—a grotesque "synthesis of Byzantinism and pornography."[37]

Mitte and Tiergarten had seen much fighting in the months immediately following the end of the war, but the time when Karl Liebknecht and Rosa Luxemburg were taken to their death from Hotel Eden were almost forgotten before half a decade had passed.[38] A section of this area was now declared a forbidden zone (Bannmeile) for all political demonstrations.[39] "Men and events are classified and screened before they are allowed [into Wilhelmstrasse]. Chaos cannot rage here, and if it does, the ban has been violated and this has the smell of civil war."[40] Which is not to say that anyone really believed that all was well as long as the government districts were sealed off from the contamination of political extremists.

It was a false security, just as the glamour and wickedness attributed to "the Kurfürstendamm" in the Roaring Twenties were false. The Kurfürstendamm, once the fashionable avenue of Berlin's prosperous middle class, now gave its name to an ill-defined concept of civilization supposedly in the region centered on Kaiser Wilhelm Memorial Church.[41] To Hermann Ullmann and Paul Marcus, the Kurfürstendamm was a gathering place for Germany's most promising intellectual and artistic talent.[42] To Friedrich Hussong and Adolf Stein, it was the spiritual home of a shiftless Bohemia and a vulgar class of *raffkes*—people of means who, to use Calvin B. Hoover's apt definition, "did not by culture and moral standards properly belong to the propertied class."[43] To the Nazis, the Kurfürstendamm was the representative street of international Jewry: nomadic, cynical, and parasitic, and therefore the appropriate stage for anti-Semitic riots.[44]

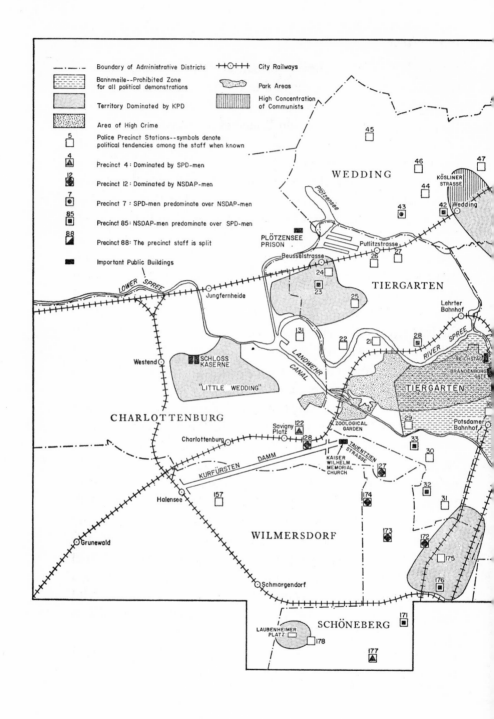

Boundary of Administrative Districts

Bannmeile--Prohibited Zone for all political demonstrations

Territory Dominated by KPD

Area of High Crime

5 — **Police Precinct Stations**--symbols denote political tendencies among the staff when known

4 — **Precinct 4:** Dominated by SPD-men

12 — **Precinct 12:** Dominated by NSDAP-men

7 — **Precinct 7:** SPD-men predominate over NSDAP-men

85 — **Precinct 85:** NSDAP-men predominate over SPD-men

88 — **Precinct 88:** The precinct staff is split

— **Important Public Buildings**

City Railways

Park Areas

High Concentration of Communists

WEDDING

TIERGARTEN

TIERGARTEN

CHARLOTTENBURG

WILMERSDORF

SCHÖNEBERG

LOWER SPREE

Jungfernheide

Westend

SCHLOSS KASERNE

"LITTLE WEDDING"

Charlottenburg

Savigny Platz

KURFÜRSTEN DAMM

Halensee

Grunewald

Schmargendorf

PLÖTZENSEE PRISON

Beusselstrasse

Plötzensee

Putlitzstrasse

Lehrter Bahnhof

RIVER SPREE

REICHSTAG

BRANDENBURG GATE

Potsdamer Bahnhof

ZOOLOGICAL GARDEN

LANDWEHR CANAL

TAUENTZIEN STRASSE

KAISER WILHELM MEMORIAL CHURCH

KÖSLINER STRASSE

Wedding

LAUBENHEIMER PLATZ

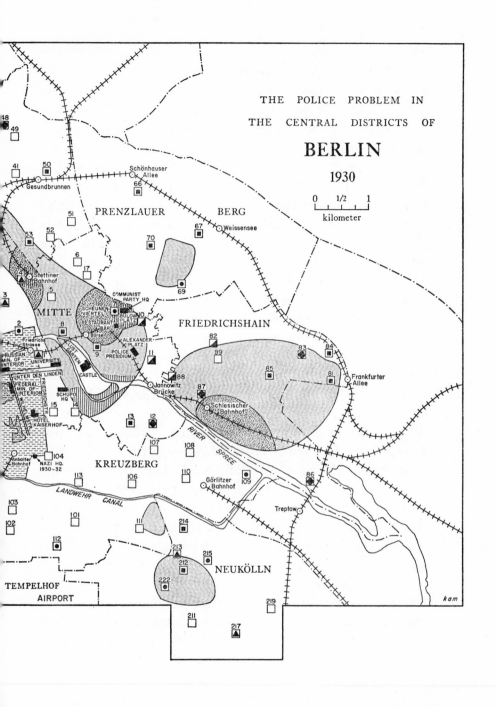

THE POLICE PROBLEM IN

THE CENTRAL DISTRICTS OF

BERLIN

1930

0   1/2   1

kilometer

48
49

41   50   Schönhauser
Allee
Gesundbrunnen   66

51   PRENZLAUER   BERG

53   52   67   ○ Weissensee

6   70

17

53   ○ Stettiner
Bahnhof   5   69

3
MITTE   COMMUNIST
PARTY HQ

2   8   SCHEUNEN-
VIERTEL   BÜLOW NO.   FRIEDRICHSHAIN
RESTAURANT   PLATZ
○ Friedrich   BAR   82
Strasse   Borse   89   83   84
PRUSSIAN   ALEXANDER-
MIN. OF   9   PLATZ   85   81
INTERIOR   UNIVERSITY   POLICE   11
PRESIDIUM   88   Frankfurter
FEDERAL   CASTLE   Jannowitz   Allee
MIN. OF   Brücke   87
INTERIOR   SCHUPO   Schlesischer
15   HQ   14   Bahnhof
HOTEL
KAISERHOF   13   12

Anhalter   104   107
Bahnhof   NAZI HQ.   108   RIVER
1930-32   SPREE
KREUZBERG   113   106   110
LANDWEHR   CANAL   Görlitzer   109   86
Bahnhof
103   Treptow
102   101   111   214
112   213   215
212   NEUKÖLLN
TEMPELHOF   222
AIRPORT   219
211
217

kam

Flashy nightclubs, sensational crimes, and intermittent assaults on pedestrians by Nazi thugs kept the Kurfürstendamm in the headlines of the boulevard press. But that would not warrant calling it a zone of serious police insecurity. The permanent residents were sober and law-abiding burghers,[45] and the metropolitan glitter of this avenue was valued as a financial asset for the city: the Berliners, who were wont to see romantic nocturnes in colored electric advertisements, elevated city trains rushing between tenement houses, and limousines mirrored in gleaming asphalt,[46] thought of the Kurfürstendamm as their star attraction for foreign visitors. "Another city arises in the glare of its street lights, a city more noisy and furtive, to which the white gloves of the Schupos add the air of a gala event."[47]

Minutes away from the former imperial residence and from Berlin's metropolitan center, the police faced major zones of common crime and political rebellion. The most extensive and dangerous area began immediately east of the Bannmeile and from there skirted the northern edge of Friedrichsstadt. It extended from the historical quarters of Alt-Kölln south of Alexanderplatz to the lower part of Wedding. Twisted lanes like Friedrichsgracht, Spreestrasse, Molkenmarkt, and Krögel— their slum dwellings evidence of municipal indifference toward historical sites[48]—offered excellent hiding places to lawless elements of all kinds. This was one of the territories of the notorious gang of the "Immertreu," while the restaurant "Zum Nussbaum" (1517) served as a hangout for local Communists.[49] Fugitives in this area were seldom tracked down by the police.

Leaving to one side the heavily-guarded Police Headquarters at Alexanderplatz, this danger zone continued on the northern side of the Royal Castle. Bülowplatz was in a perpetual stage of tension throughout the Weimar period. The central offices of the German Communist party were located here, and Detachment "Mitte" of the Red-Front Fighting League (Rot Frontkämpferbund or RFB) at the "Bär" restaurant in Dragonerstrasse was battling with Nazi storm troopers for control of this neighborhood from 1926 on.[50] Police station 7 in Hankestrasse was caught in the cross fire of the two antagonists. Mutual threats and armed clashes between police and Communists at Bülowplatz culminated in the shooting of police captains Anlauf and Lenck on August 9, 1931, in what probably was the most notorious murder of uniformed policemen during the Weimar Republic. The Schupo's elite troops of police inspection 21 ("Alexander"), equipped with armored cars, were stationed at Kleine Alexanderstrasse to meet any major emergency.[51]

The security problem of Bülowplatz was aggravated by the latter's proximity to the city's worst criminal district. The Scheunenviertel was Berlin's equivalent to London's Whitechapel or Hamburg's St. Pauli.[52] Jerrybuilt tenements and uncounted flophouses dating from the Founding Years of the Second Empire harbored the greatest concentration of prostitution, crime, and poverty in Berlin. Many destitute Jewish immigrants from Eastern Europe were housed here by the authorities. The Municipal Loan Office and the Central Employment Office in Münzstrasse and Gormannstrasse were assembling places for rioters in times of acute distress.[53] Police officials spoke with dread of streets like Mulackstrasse where tenements like the "Ochsenhof" with its dozen entrances and twenty stairways defied systematic searches, and where in times of troubles the street lights went out and no patrolman would venture alone.[54]

We must finally include in this principal zone of insecurity the southern reaches of Wedding district between Hussitenstrasse, Kösliner Strasse, and Wiesenstrasse, where three days of street fighting took place in May, 1929. There may have been much crime in this area too, but the major reason for trouble was the existence of organized Communist masses side by side with small but aggressive elements of Nazis clustered around the Kriegervereinshaus. The propinquity of the two enemy camps was underlined by the not infrequent instances in the early thirties of local Communists and Nazis switching their party allegiance.[55]

Because the danger belt from Fischerkietz to Kösliner Strasse bordered directly on the government district, it was the most important security problem for the police in Berlin. But it was not the only region of lawlessness in the city. An ingrained area of high crime covered the environs of Schlesischer Bahnhof (now Ostbahnhof) in Friedrichshain, where the police in 1928 conceded that it was incapable of wresting control from the local crime syndicate of the Immertreu.[56] Even the precinct police who always patrolled in pairs could not win the acceptance of the local inhabitants. "Fraternization with these people was out of the question," recalled Hermann Artner, who in 1928 served at police station 88 in Andreas Strasse. "Their squalor was too repulsive!" To protect the precinct police against acts of personal retaliation, riot policemen of the Second Emergency Brigade in Köpenickstrasse were frequently called in as substitutes.

In contrast, the so-called Karpathen region in Neukölln was again a center of political unrest. Until 1929, the largest RFB detachment in all Berlin, numbering some 2,000 men, was stationed here. Neukölln and adjoining Kreuzberg experienced numerous political street fights between members of this unit and pugnacious Brownshirts at the banqueting halls of "Neue Welt." During the May Day uprising in 1929, "Communists poured from the tenement houses in this quarter like rats out of holes."[57]

Not all the working-class districts were centers of political strife. The economic consequences of war, defeat, and inflation had leveled some traditional class barriers between artisans, small traders, and white-collar employees. Among some workmen, the lean postwar years even brought to the surface the rural attitudes of Silesian and Pomeranian farmhands with all the conservative connotations that this entailed.

Economic dislocation had come as a greater shock to the lower middle class than to the workers. In Steglitz and Friedenau, local retailers in the late twenties began to display the same goods at the same prices as those in the proletarian north and east of Berlin. The apartment houses carried the same smell of poverty though their poverty was new and still embarrassing. The men here wore hats instead of peaked caps and the young people "dreamt not of Soviet Russia but of the Third Reich, not of socialism but of overseas travel or being successful inventors."[58] The large number of Nazi sympathizers among the residents might have caused tensions but for the absence of a dissenting working class and the concurring sentiments of many local policemen.

Other bourgeois quarters had enclaves of political unrest. The territory of police station 156 in Wilmersdorf, otherwise a quiet beat, suffered recurring clashes in and around the Spichern meeting halls. Schöneberg owed many of its troubles to the Sportpalast and the "Red Island" around Anhalter Bahnhof. Charlottenburg had its "Little Wedding"—a stronghold of the underworld gang "Libelle" and a "terrorist zone" of the Communists until 1933. Policemen here were instructed to carry their pistols in their coat pockets as an additional measure of safety. Not far from the respectable Hansaviertel, Tiergarten had an industrial settlement around Beusselstrasse, Turmstrasse, and Sickingerstrasse, whose Communist inhabitants were at war with the Nazis in Hebbelstrasse and the Hohenzollern banqueting rooms. Even Friedenau developed a danger zone around Laubenheimer Platz by 1932, though the opposition was not between Communist and Nazi workers, but between leftist intellectuals and artists on the one side and members of the veterans' organization Stahlhelm on the other.[59]

Endemic crime in some quarters and political violence bordering on revolt menaced the public peace in the capital throughout the Weimar Republic.

Berlin was in a state of civil war. Hate exploded suddenly, without warning, out of nowhere; at street corners, in restaurants, cinemas, dance halls, swimming baths; at midnight, after breakfast, in the middle of the afternoon. . . . In the middle of a crowded street a young man would be attacked, stripped, thrashed and left bleeding on the pavement; in fifteen seconds it was all over and the assailants had disappeared.[60]

The issues were often confused by the intermixture of political and common crime, ordinary police problems and emergency situations. The Berlin police, intent on setting an example of democratic tolerance and respect for the law, tended to interpret its obligations in a restrictive manner even at the risk of letting the situation get out of hand. In the midst of virtual civil war, it gave priority to the task of prosecuting the person or persons responsible for individual breaches of the peace while hesitating to apply sweeping measures for the restoration of public order.[61] Political parties that openly sought to destroy German democracy were protected as long as the number of their adherents gave them some claim to "democratic" support. "At no time . . . did I believe in or defend the dangerous fallacy of opposing or suppressing a popular movement by police force," recalled Police President Albert Grzesinski in 1939.[62] But costs could not in the long run be ignored with such homilies as "Everything in this world is ruled by money—everything save emergency operations by the police."[63] The price of an extravagant deployment of police resources was eventually paid in 1932, when the federal government under Chancellor Franz von Papen divested the Prussian state of its police powers on the grounds that it had failed to maintain order and security within its territory.

The question has often been raised whether the Prussian police—and this concerns the Berlin police in particular—could and should have fought in defense of the Prussian government on July 20, 1932.[64] Yet the answer has long been clear: nearly every important figure on the Prussian side has affirmed that the police was neither legally obliged nor entitled to resist the move of the federal government. All of them furthermore have thought that armed defiance would have been utterly futile. With the Prussian government of that time unwilling to move, the question—what countermeasures the local police might have taken —must be considered pointless from the beginning.

But there is another question that the historian still needs to clarify: had the Prussian police in Berlin truly failed in its appointed task as a security force, and, if so, how had it failed, and why? In historical retrospect, spokesmen for the Republic have explained the death of German democracy as a tragedy beyond the control of the local police and even beyond its legal jurisdiction. Were they not forgetting the vast areas of responsibility that the police so confidently had claimed in the early days of the Weimar Republic?[65] If Carl Severing was right in thinking that the majority of the police was loyal to the Republic as late as the summer of 1932, why could the Nazis six months later use the selfsame police to consolidate their antidemocratic regime?[66]

The police departments examined in this study are the security police, the criminal police, and to some extent the executive branch (Aussendienst) of the political police in Berlin. They were the most conspicuous instruments of the law in the German capital and the agents in closest touch with the daily affairs of the average Berliner. Since we cannot, as city historians, take up larger national issues, our attention will have to focus on the police agents in the streets rather than the politicians at the Police Presidium and the Prussian Ministry of Interior. The work of the administrative police, which in Germany included many routine tasks of state administration as a matter of simple convenience, will be left out entirely as inconsequential to our inquiry.

1 | The Historical Legacy of the Schutzpolizei

The Importance of Traditional Police Doctrine

Postwar Berlin made unprecedented demands on its police, both in the extent and in the nature of the work it called for. The Weimar period consequently saw many changes introduced in the three main executive branches of the Police Presidium. But while the criminal police simply expanded its staff and modernized its equipment, and the old Prussian political police—Department VII—gave way to Department IA,[1] the uniformed street police proved to be more cumbersome to transform into a republican institution. Conscious of its role as the principal executor of state authority at home, the constabulary could not follow the example of the detective force in ignoring the political changes at the end of the war. Its size, furthermore, ruled out a speedy overhaul in staff and organization as in the case of the political police. But above all, its reform was inhibited by the existence of a long historical tradition that the Schutzpolizei of the twenties was not prepared to relinquish.

To be sure, the existence of a considerable historical legacy need not in itself have made for rigid conservatism. The record of the royal constabulary in the nineteenth century contained sufficient instances of mistakes and failures to justify drastic recommendations for reform. Yet the fact remains that publications sponsored by the police or written by high police officials of the Republic were much inclined to dwell on historical precedent. More, they usually denied that the events of 1918 and 1919 constituted a major turning point in the history of the uniformed police.[2] The definition of modern police functions, as formulated in the Prussian Law Code of 1794, for example, was pronounced to be as valid after the First World War as it had been at the end of the eighteenth century.[3]

The historical consciousness of the uniformed police must be explained by its experience in the fall and winter of 1918. When the monarchy came to a sudden end, the Schutzmannschaft faced a public deeply distrustful of all representatives of the defunct order. Political turmoil further added to the bewilderment of the police officials who sensed that yesterday's service instructions were obsolete, but dared not rely on the orders of the revolutionary government. To keep some measure of authority—indeed, to survive the attacks of would-be rivals to their public functions—the policemen could neither resort to force nor exert political influence. Their one recourse, in fact, was to public persuasion. The inhabitants and the new government had to be told that to disband the established police corps would be an act of political vandalism. They had to be convinced that the constabulary was Berlin's best hope for peace and order because of its demonstrable service to state and society over the last two centuries.

The issue here is not whether these claims were historically justified, or whether such arguments did ensure the survival of Berlin's professional police. What does matter is that after 1918, when the police could have remolded itself in keeping with a new political era in Germany, it proclaimed itself to be neutral and retreated behind long-established police ethics and police principles, and that this professionalism eventually forced the police into the camp of conservatism. For police ethics could command respect only on the basis of their longevity, in other words, on their ostensible merit during earlier periods of absolute and autocratic government. The contention that the republican police possessed a tradition of selfless public service had to be supported by the record of its predecessors. Before long, the postwar police found itself compelled to excuse, and often to justify, the authoritarian performance of its colleagues under the monarchy.[4]

This is not to say that royal police service since the eighteenth century was uncritically praised by police historians of the Republic. Nor would it be correct to suggest that the historical rules and principles of Prussian police doctrine were necessarily incompatible with the demands of popular sovereignty. They were far too general to apply to concrete political situations. But their very ambiguity made them well suited to the political uncertainties at the end of the First World War.

Official theory stipulated that the ultimate task of the police was to safeguard the public order. The public order, however, was broadly defined as an overall social and cultural condition prevailing at a given moment in history. The protection of this civilizatory condition went before the enforcement of statutory laws since code books depended on the people's moral will to "turn them to beneficent effect."[5] Therefore, every policeman must be well acquainted with contemporary mores and notions of justice, and with the salient traits in the people's character.[6] Bill Drews called on the police to uphold

> The norms underlying all acts of commission and omission, and of every relationship which, according to current opinion, is indispensable to the continued existence of fruitful human and civic life. . . . [The task of the police] goes far beyond a mere enforcement of existing laws and includes the suppression of

everything offensive to the dominant views on ethics and social conduct.[7]

The purpose of the police could then be shown as essentially unchanging through time, no matter what alterations in legally prescribed police procedure accompanied the movements in the political and social environment. One could even speak of a positive obligation of the police to adjust to every historical change as it occurred.[8] Therefore, if the Revolution of 1918 was interpreted as the product of basic social and cultural developments, the republican regime was a new form of public order fully deserving police protection.

But it was also possible to interpret the Revolution of 1918 as a public disturbance bordering on anarchy. In that case, other principles of police doctrine could be cited to justify rigorous intervention against the trend of events. Assuming still that police work was more than merely enforcing existing laws— "formal expressions to ideas matured in a preceding age"—it does not always follow that the anonymous masses in society could alone provide laws with an effective meaning. For

> It is the state's obligation to study and observe the source of all ideas, and to shape them and *influence their further growth* [italics mine].[9]

According to police doctrine, the state had a cultural task to fulfill, and the police was one of its chief instruments to this end. The moral guidance that the state and its subsidiary organs had to provide at all times could go as far as to cast the police in the role of "custodians of the public conscience."[10] The authoritarian implications that this conception entailed for the functions of the police may be assessed in the following statement by Ernst van den Bergh (1926):

> The assembled crowd is but a temporary and multifarious entity brought together by chance. It dissolves [as quickly] as it comes

into being. While it can thus give rise to collective emotions and to the most elementary spiritual energies, it cannot produce a sense of responsibility. . . . The police . . . is also a composite entity filled with strong collective impulses. [But the impulses of the police] are derived from the amalgamated egoism of both the nation and the state and are aimed at the undisturbed preservation of the life functions of the whole. Consequently, the sense of responsibility, so easily lost to the crowd, finds its strongest development in the police. It penetrates [into the heart of] every single official and gives him a moral and spiritual superiority over each individual in the crowd. Once the crowd has learned to recognize in every policeman a carrier of state authority as well as of the people's conscience, the mere appearance of police should suffice to evoke ideas contrary to those inspired by brutish personal egoism and its attendant mental aberrations.[11]

We cannot, of course, dismiss the contradictions involved in these two views of police functions as simple doctrinal inconsistency.[12] We must remember that police doctrine had evolved from the experience of the eighteenth and nineteenth centuries. During some of this time at least it had been possible to think of the police as an intermediary agent designed to bridge the separate interests of "society" and "state." That some principles possessed a potential democratic meaning while others clearly affirmed the virtue of state authoritarianism did not raise difficulties until placed in the context of twentieth-century politics. And we must remember that police theoreticians after the First World War were not primarily concerned with discovering political truths pertinent to their age. They wanted to uphold the prestige of traditional police doctrine, and with it the authority of their establishment.

If the doctrine had to be preserved for reasons of immediate expediency, but its teachings were ill-suited to the new times, then the least that could be done was to offer a historical explanation for its rationale. And given a careful historical presentation, it might even be possible to show that classical police principles, far from being impractical, had merely been thwarted over the past two centuries by adverse circumstances beyond the control of the police.

The Official Interpretation of Prussian Police History

The most interesting presentation of Prussian police history written in the Weimar Republic is to be found in Ernst van den Berghs *Police and Nation—Spiritual Bonds* (1926). His was the first volume in a popular series edited by Wilhelm Abegg and designed, like the Great Police Exhibition in Berlin of that same year, to improve the public image of the Prussian police. The second volume in this series was a *History of the Police* by Dr. Kurt Melcher, but Melcher's factual narrative barely touched the ideological issues so forthrightly expounded by van den Bergh.[13]

According to van den Bergh, the eighteenth century had been a time when the Prussian police successfully fulfilled its dual purpose as an instrument of the state and a servant of the people.[14] It is true that in the reign of Frederick II, strategical circumstances compelled the Prussian monarchy to build a rational state structure founded on the bureaucracy, the army, and the police.[15] But in view of the political immaturity of Prussian subjects two hundred years ago, a system of local self-policing, as in England, had been out of the question in any case. On the contrary, the government still had to teach the inhabitants the rudiments of civic responsibility and self-reliance. Under its enlightened police tutelage—certainly never as capricious as the French police system of the ancien régime—public safety and economic prosperity steadily improved until the people "learned to understand the necessity and usefulness of subordinating personal to common interest." The people's gratitude to the state, by the end of the century, extended also to the police, "to whom it owed the essence of all these achievements."[16]

To defend the performance of the Prussian police in the nineteenth century was more difficult. Van den Bergh conceded that monarchical absolutism, however benevolent, could no longer be justified after the wars of liberation. In 1813 the people had shown by their patriotism that the educational work of the preceding decades had not been in vain. Henceforth the congenial relation of police and pubilc was liable to suffer under a policy of continued state tutelage. But while van den Bergh regretted the collaboration of the Prussian police with the monarchy during the Metternichian era, he nevertheless justified it with the people's inability to produce an alternative basis of state authority from below. Transforming Prussia into a constitutional state depended on the efforts of the people as much as the monarchy, he argued, and it was the failure on both sides that left the police with no choice but to abide by its alliance with the latter.[17]

The last fifty years before the First World War were portrayed by the author in somber colors. As he saw it, the royal police was caught in a growing dilemma as the two opposite poles in Prussia's political spectrum moved farther and farther apart. The hidebound bureaucracy of the Prussian state could not cope with a phenomenon such as metropolitan Berlin. Large-scale industrialization created social problems that conventional police methods could never solve.

> The previous tension between ruler and ruled in the state was now transferred to the sphere of economic life. . . . This was no longer a question of power, of the need to assure effective authority on the one hand and civic freedom on the other. What now mattered was financial success. Money and not the police was the ultimate basis of power. State tutelage had been replaced by economic exploitation.[18]

The government followed a policy that vacillated between

attempts at suppressing workers' associations and halfhearted relief measures for the poor. It failed to recognize in socialism an elementary historical force impervious to all efforts at administrative containment. Nor did it understand that its unwillingness to interfere in the economic struggle meant, in effect, sanctioning the existing capitalistic order. The consequences of all these blunders had to be borne by the police, who

> lost much standing in the eyes of the common people, to whom it only appeared as an agent of the state. . . . Within the body of the population, one segment stood in opposition to the state and the police. Another [the middle and upper classes] demanded protection by the police but refused to grant it any moral support.[19]

Van den Bergh's rather smooth apology for the old Prussian police is remarkable for nearly omitting two important historical topics: writing for a public who in 1918 had witnessed the breakdown of the royal constabulary, the author obviously hesitated to dwell on the behavior of the Prussian police in the Revolution of 1848. The irresolute stand of the police in both crises could easily expose it to the charge of habitual political opportunism. He also neglected to discuss the relations between the Prussian police and the army. There was enough talk in the twenties of rampant militarism in the Schutzpolizei. The Revolution of 1848 and the rivalry between police and army, however, were treated in great detail in Paul Schmidt's *The First 50 Years of the Royal Constabulary in Berlin*, which was published in 1898.[20]

Writing in the heyday of the Second Empire, Schmidt saw no reason to conceal the fact that the police in 1848 had at first offered its collaboration to the revolutionaries, only to turn against the revolution when the king's army regained the upper hand. Had not the civic guard by then demonstrated its utter incompetence as a guardian of public peace? Schmidt had every intention of casting the police in the role of an important pillar of the triumphant Prussian state of the sixties and seventies. He conceded that the street police of Berlin, reorganized under the name of Königliche Schutzmannschaft in July, 1848, promised to be a civilian force founded on democratic principles. "Far from intending to curb the liberty of citizens or to restore the pusilanimous tutelage of the police state," he quoted from a contemporary proclamation, it would henceforth recruit its members solely from "reputable, able-bodied and honest men" among the local people—a concession to the current fear that a police force of veteran soldiers would, as in the past, serve as the tool of absolute monarchy. Yet with obvious satisfaction, Schmidt next proceeded to list various technical reasons why the Schutzmannschaft was turned into a paramilitary organization after all, not the least being the discovery that local recruitment turned up "too many worthless elements."[21]

Schmidt measured the success of the constabulary on its approximation to the army in appearance and function, rather than on its effectiveness as a peacekeeping force. Indeed, his account suggests that the royal constabulary was sometimes moved by a desire to match the prestige of the army at the expense of other considerations. He cheered the introduction of spiked police helmets in 1850, because similar helmets were also relatively new in the army. Schmidt agreed that styles of uniform or official salutes were mere matters of external form. "But they carried much weight in the eyes of those concerned, especially during the countless occasions when the Schutzmannschaft had official dealings with military personnel."[22]

Schmidt presumably spoke for the Schutzmannschaft too when he expressed his disappointment that the uniformed police was never made an integral part of the armed forces. The police, unfortunately, was in no position to enforce its claims to parity with the soldiers. It was indebted to the army for its "friendly attitude toward the Schutzmannschaft" in the unfortunate episode of 1848. It had not shared in Prussia's military victories between 1863 and 1871. During the subsequent decades, the police even relied on the military to stand by for police functions in the event of serious domestic troubles. There was a trace of jealousy in Schmidt's presentation of the relation of policemen to soldiers in the first two decades of the Second Empire:

> The Corps [of the Schutzmannschaft] performed absolutely the same duties as the gendarmerie that belonged to the army. It daily confronted the enemy too, that is the world of criminals. . . . In case of mobilization, the capital could not do without the Schutzmannschaft, who gave it protection and military cover. Because of its knowledge of the local area and its inhabitants, it could even achieve more in this respect than could the ordinary garrison.[23]

The historical legacy that the uniformed police refused to discard in 1918 was laden with the memory of unfulfilled wishes conceived in a predemocratic age. As the political situation returned to relative stability in the middle twenties, the initial attempt to use history as a defense of established police principles was not abandoned and became a cult of police traditions in general. These chronicles in turn were potential carriers of antiquated police ideas tainted with disdain for the mob, suspicion of the government, and jealousy of the army. They could be potent in a police force whose shaken self-confidence after 1918 called out for a vindication of its record, and who, with the army defeated in war, was suddenly offered a chance to establish its cherished equivalence with the military.

II | The Background of Fear and Irresolution, 1918-1920

The War and the Armistice

The frustrated military pretensions of the Berlin Schutz-mannschaft before 1914 were not alleviated by its experience during the war. While the army imposed its rule over the entire country, the uniformed police declined not only as an instrument of law enforcement but also as an institution with vested interests to defend.

The Schutzmannschaft in Berlin did not escape the general attrition in enthusiasm for the war which spread behind the front as privation and hardship increased. By 1917 more than half its officers had been drafted, and the younger elements in the rank and file had volunteered for the front.[1] The staff of the remaining force was considerably overage, poorly equipped, and untrained in the execution of large-scale police actions that might become necessary at any moment.[2]

Police morale had suffered under the burden of extra work duties accompanied by reductions in real income. Young munitions workers were resented for being better paid and better fed than police sergeants with many years of service.[3] It is significant that the police union movement, much frowned upon by the higher echelon and unable to make headway before 1914, rapidly gained adherents during the war. By 1915 the leading police officials thought fit to permit the creation of a union of Berlin policemen (Verband der Schutzleute des Landesbezirks Berlin). In 1917 this association succeeded in establishing open contacts with police forces in other Prussian towns.[4]

The Bolshevik Revolution in 1917 may well have caused this revision of policy in high quarters. The events in Russia caused many a policeman to think of his future should the German Empire go the same road.[5] The war had failed to inculcate the Schutzmannschaft with either the patriotic fervor of elite troops at the front or with a strong commitment to Germany's wartime regime. The illusion of potential national importance, which the police had nourished at the outset of hostilities, had three years later turned into general resentment at the country's indifference to its services.[6]

When the war ended amid large demonstrations in Berlin, the Schutzmannschaft, along with the local garrison, forgot its past declarations of dynastic loyalty and refused to fight. It offered no resistance to the masses who, on November 9, 1918, marched on City Hall, the Reichstag, important railway stations, and other strategical points in the capital. Not far from the Police Presidium at the Alexander Barracks, the famous Naumburg Rifles defected to the revolutionaries. Other regiments followed suit. The Police Presidium also surrendered without a shot.[7] To contemporaries the swiftness with which the imposing facade of the Prussian military and Prussian officialdom collapsed was astounding.

> A week ago you still had a military and civilian administration whose machinery was so intricate, so intertwined, and so deeply entrenched that its survival seemed assured in the face of all changes time could bring. The gray automobiles of army officers

roared through the streets of Berlin and the policemen stood like pillars of authority in the public squares. . . . Yesterday morning, all this was still here. Yesterday afternoon, nothing was left.[8]

The prompt capitulation of the uniformed Schutzmannschaft remained a source of evident unease to the police for years afterward. Very few details concerning what happened at headquarters on November 9, 1918, were revealed by police officials either then or later. Explanations intended to justify the absence of decisive police action took the place of factual accounts. On August 9, 1919, an article in a police newspaper admitted that the police, on November 9, had acted contrary to an explicit order to fight the insurgents "to the last man." But this article, like so many others, placed its main emphasis on finding plausible excuses for what in fact had been insubordination.[9] Some officials asserted that the police had been moved by a desire to avoid needless bloodshed. Others argued that the police had been forced to yield to the superior numbers of the crowd. Ernst Schrader of the policemen's union placed the entire blame on the revolutionary authorities who, he claimed, extorted a pledge of political neutrality from the armed constabulary by threatening it with dismissal.[10]

Perhaps the most widely accepted stand among police officials was that taken by Dr. Heinrich Lindenau. In an essay that caused much comment in 1919, Lindenau denounced the incompetence of the police leaders whose nerves, he said, had failed them in that moment of crisis. The old police president, Matthias von Oppen, had absconded. His successor, Emil Eichhorn, "only gradually revealed his identity as a Spartacist," a member of the far left in the workers' movement. In any case, all effective armed power had fallen into the hands of the Volksmarinedivision and other revolutionary units.

What could the former Schutzmannschaft be expected to do [Lindenau wrote], decimated as it was by the war and disarmed with the consent of the government?[11]

But recriminations against leading officials could not clear the police of the stigma of weakness any more than could pleas of *force majeure*—not if the narration of the event was thereby left to the pen of political opponents like Emil Eichhorn. City councillor Eichhorn was actually the emissary of the Independent Socialists (USPD) who entered the besieged Police Presidium to negotiate terms of surrender on November 9.[12] In his reminiscences, which came out the following year, he related that the building had been well provided with machine guns and that its normal garrison had been reinforced by a battalion of riflemen plus a detachment of infantry. But in spite of its strength, the police never thought of offering any resistance.

> The growing size of the mob in the streets and its . . . agitation not only deprived the police of its remaining courage, but also of its good sense. Bad conscience [and] the memory of past assaults on Berlin workmen must have inspired it with a paniclike fear of retributon. Police sergeants and officers tore off their sabers and revolvers as fast as they could. . . . The policemen actually were never disarmed. They disarmed themselves. Nor were they chased away. The policemen left the presidium on their own accord and made their way through the surrounding crowd as quickly as possible.[13]

Eichhorn's disdainful report in 1919 was undoubtedly colored by his recent experience as Berlin's chief of police. He was inclined to see in career police officials men who were anxious to save their skins first and their jobs second.[14] But his opinion should not surprise us in light of his subordinates' wavering allegiance to him during his short tenure as People's Commissar of Public Safety.

The Eichhorn Episode

Eichhorn's career as police chief scarcely lasted two months. His vindication of his conduct of office, published not long after his fall from power, bore all the marks of political pamphleteering in revolutionary times. But his candid commitment to the cause of the Socialist revolution contrasted favorably with the timidity of his subordinates.[15] The latter hesitated among monarchism in the name of loyalty to the king, democracy in the name of loyalty to the nation, sympathy for the right because of their affinity with soldiers, and political neutrality based on the ethics of public servants. In fact, even senior police officials seemed undecided.

The editors of *Die Polizei,* a weekly paper that generally reflected official police attitudes,[16] entered the period of Germany's democratic experiment with a grand display of political evasiveness. In the first issue to come out under the rule of Emil Eichhorn, six pages were taken up with a reprint of Immanuel Kant's "Metaphysical Principles of Jurisprudence," Goethe's poem "The State," and brief announcements of orders and decrees by the Council of People's Commissars. This was followed by an article on the reform of the law on licensed public houses and items of administrative news. Very much at the end came a curt notice to the effect that Emil Eichhorn had assumed command of all the police forces in Berlin. It also proclaimed the end of censorship and the extension of the police curfew to eleven-thirty at night. Police and firemen were to remain at their posts.[17]

This last point was of great concern to the men of the royal police. The executive committee of People's Commissars had originally decided that all police officials of the defunct regime were to be discharged at once. But prompt remonstrations from the Police Association had produced a temporary modus vivendi between police and revolutionary authorities.[18] On Sunday, November 10, 1918, the following posters went up throughout the streets of the capital:[19]

WORKERS, SOLDIERS, CITIZENS!

The entire Schutzmannschaft of Berlin has placed itself at the disposal of the Workers' and Soldiers' Councils. [The constables] are commissioned to resume their service in the interest of public order and security on Monday. They will go on duty side by side with soldiers, wearing their old uniform plus red armbands, but without weapons.

People's Commissar for Public Safety

EMIL EICHHORN

All officials of the Schutzmannschaft of Greater Berlin are hereby ordered to report to their posts on Monday, November 11, at 8 o'clock.

SCHRADER, *Chairman of the Policemen's Association*
FRÖHLICH, *Police Major*
MURCHE, *Chairman of the Police Sergeants' Union*
EICHHORN, *People's Commissar of Public Safety*

As it turned out, many police officials did not immediately resume their duties. Some of these men took leaves of absence, among them Police Major Fröhlich who had signed the above proclamation.[20] But as time went by an increasing number of seasoned policemen of the lower ranks returned to their posts in apparent acceptance of the Revolution and its representatives.[21] Their endorsement of the new regime seemed complete.

On November 13, 1918, there was a gathering of lower-ranking Prussian police officials in Berlin. They passed a resolution that is worth quoting in full. Its tone of humble submissiveness certainly contrasted sharply with the language that police officials were to adopt a few months later:

In view of the collapse of the old system and the abdication of the Kaiser, and the fact that the Schutzmannschaft has thereby been released from its oath of allegiance, [we are determined] to do everything in our power to aid the new government in re-establishing and maintaining public security and order. All police sergeants and policemen will constantly strive to avoid petty harshness in their dealings with fellow citizens and to conduct themselves in a spirit of courtesy and tolerance. The old system that always kept us apart from our fellow Germans [Volksgenossen] shall give way to a new course so that a better relationship, based on mutual trust, will henceforth prevail between security officials and the public.

Our special and heartfelt request goes to our fellow citizens of Greater Berlin: May they forget everything that divided us in the past and support us in the performance of our difficult duties so that in the future no unpleasantness will ever recur between security officials and citizens.[22]

The proclamation was not unique in its apologetic note. It was matched, for example, by Police Inspector Eiben's essay on "The Executive Police of the New Times," which *Die Polizei* published on November 19, 1918. Eiben first claimed that the Schutzmannschaft had fought for the old order "to the point of physical exhaustion." But "with its [the old order's] distintegration, and as we realized that it had become antiquated and that the majority of our fellow Germans were demanding a new order, we unanimously accepted the reality of things. . . ." He went on to say that the traditional virtues of the police—obedience and political impartiality—should be accepted as tokens of its continued ability to be of good service, for these very soldierly qualities provide for adaptability. Consequently, there exists no reason why the present staff of the police should be replaced.

Our state used to be a state based on class distinctions (see paragraph 130 of the Penal Code). The new state is meant to be different. . . . The rich and the socially prominent have often been treated with undue consideration. This must have been a matter of habit, not of ill-will. Now this must cease. The officials of the executive will have no difficulty in changing their practice in favor of more equality. . . . Their former attitude was dictated by the instructions of superiors . . . [and] . . . had often caused much unease.[23]

Eichhorn had not demanded that much repentance from the old staff. He appeared satisfied with its consent to serve under his command and to abide by its pledge of political neutrality. He did not encourage the minority of radical policemen who wanted to imitate the revolutionary soldier's councils.[24] To be sure, officials who had chosen to stay at their posts "even under the changed political circumstances" were reminded that they now owed obedience to a different government. But they were assured of absolute political freedom when they were not on duty.[25]

During the closing weeks of 1918, Eichhorn's attempts to democratize the police drew no protests from his subordinates who, incidentally, made ample use of their new freedom of association and speech. Eichhorn did away with the military formations of the Schutzmannschaft. He abolished military salutes. Police ranks were made to conform with those in the civil service, and members of the public (mostly workmen) were invited to sit in at all police stations as "precinct assistants" (Revierbeisitzer). Most important, Eichhorn set up a new security guard, the Sicherheitswehr, numbering 1,800 armed men. They were stationed throughout Berlin and patrolled the streets side by side with local officials of the old police.[26]

The main body of the Schutzmannschaft accepted these changes with a remarkable show of patience. The officials were aware of the widespread hostility that the public harbored toward all uniformed agents of the former regime. As long as moderates and radicals in the Council of People's Commissars quarreled over the permanent settlement of Germany's future, and as long as they were allowed to continue at their posts, these men were willing to be reduced to the position of an "order police." The Sicherheitswehr represented an incursion into the prerogatives of the Schutzmannschaft; but in view of Eichhorn's avowed intention to use his police powers on behalf of the Independent Socialists, was it not better to let the new militia incur the whole risk of fighting for an uncertain cause? Its soldiers lacked the training for normal police duties anyway and could be expected to withdraw as soon as the situation returned to normal.[27]

Indeed, most of Eichhorn's reforms were regarded as temporary improvisations. It was evident that the "precinct assistants" were a transitory institution. It was also known that Eichhorn was experiencing difficulties with his new Sicherheitswehr. The security guard had quickly acquired a corporate interest of its own and was successfully defying Eichhorn's attempts to purge it of criminal elements.[28] The old cadres within the police could therefore afford to bide their time, even to engage in some mutual rivalry while awaiting the outcome of current political conflicts.[29]

If the rank and file of the Schutzmannschaft anticipated difficulties for their chief, their prognosis was certainly correct: Eichhorn did lack sufficient experience to succeed in his task. He wasted an enormous amount of time on petty details like uniforms and service rules.[30] But the policemen remained entirely passive and looked to their immediate commander, Police Major Fröhlich, and to the senior officials in the Ministry of Interior to prepare his eventual defeat.[31] As a result of disagreements that arose over the manner in which the provisional German government—the Council of People's Commissars—had put down the mutinous Volksmarinedivision, the USPD members in the government resigned on December 29, 1918. Their colleagues in the Prussian government followed their example a little later. On January 1, 1919, the moderate Majority Socialists in the government began a press campaign against the only Independent Socialist who still held a post in the Prussian government. Eichhorn was charged with abuses ranging from the illegal distribution of arms to civilians to embezzlement of public funds. *Vorwärts* asserted that he drew pay from Bolshevik sources in Petrograd. Two days after the campaign began, he was called to the Ministry of Interior and asked to submit his resignation. When he refused, the Ministry ordered all officials at the Police Presidium to renounce their obedience to their chief.[32]

The tide was clearly turning against Eichhorn, in spite of the fact that the USPD, the Revolutionary Shop Stewards, and the Spartacists called the workers into the streets on January 5, 1919, ostensibly on his behalf. Their real purpose was to overthrow Friedrich Ebert's provisional government. But the revolution lacked organization. Even the Sicherheitswehr abandoned Eichhorn after a few days' hesitation, having been bribed with promises of monetary rewards by the government and intimidated by the prospect of an encounter with army troops.[33] The Schutzmannschaft, however, continued to act with the greatest of caution. The uniformed officials heeded the injunction of the Ministry by staying away from headquarters, but they refrained from committing themselves openly to the government before Eichhorn's defeat was a fait accompli. In the battle for possession of the Police Headquarters at Alexanderplatz, January 13, 1919, the professional police again took no sides.

Die Polizei also was slow in repudiating Emil Eichhorn. On January 16, 1919, it still praised his achievements in reducing crime in Berlin.[34] On February 13, however, it referred to him as "Herr Eichhorn: the man on the wanted list" and blamed him for interfering with the police's fight against crime.[35] On March 13, 1919, when the Eichhorn episode had long been superseded by newer events, it came out with a vicious and quite pointless personal attack against the fallen chief:

> President Eichhorn was a neurasthenic of the highest order— a weak and blurred face, thin, mangled mustache, nervous gestures of his fingers, restless tripping to and fro. He was visibly flattered when addressed as "Herr Präsident." He invariably called the Soldiers' Councils "my government councillors."[36]

But the end of the Eichhorn affair still left the uniformed police with the need for restoring its previous authority and prestige. In *Die Polizei* recent court decisions were used to provide retroactive justification for renouncing obedience to Eichhorn. Thus the Workers' and Soldiers' Councils which had appointed Eichhorn to his office were declared usurpers without legal claim to public authority.[37] The existing government, on the other hand, was endorsed as the legitimate successor to the Council of People's Commissars that "at one point" had been the de facto agent of sovereign power in Germany.[38] Another article in *Die Polizei*, May 22, 1919, on the right of public officials to go on strike, laid down that state officials were not guilty of insubordination when their employer (the government) instructed them to abstain from duty as a way of defeating Bolshevist and Communist subversion.[39]

Of course, theoretical vindications of its change in allegiance carried an uncertain weight as the police faced its next task of dealing with the number of armed units performing policelike functions in the capital.

Rivalry with Military Forces

In the first months of the Revolution, the constabulary had been reduced to virtual inaction, performing only some administrative and patrol duties under the protection of Eichhorn's Sicherheitswehr. But while the Sicherheitswehr was dissolved in March, 1919, other policelike units were still performing security tasks in Berlin independent of the Police Presidium.

There were, for example, the Einwohnerwehren, raised by the Reichswehr authorities and whose members were chiefly recruited in the conservative, middle-class districts of Berlin.[40] Their purpose was to defend private property against marauders. To be sure, these home guards were never very efficient and, in spite of some friction, did not represent a threat to the prerogatives of the professional police.[41]

More important than the home guards was the Republikanische Soldatenwehr under the command of Otto Wels. Its mission, according to Defense Minister Gustav Noske, was to ensure public safety pending the reestablishment of an effective, normal, police service. Though the Republikanische Soldatenwehr was subordinate to the military commander in Brandenburg, it aspired to be an independent power rivaling Eichhorn's Sicherheitswehr for supreme police authority in Berlin. It even possessed a detective force of its own. But like the home guards, it was undisciplined and susceptible to political influences.[42]

The most effective challenge to the authority of the professional police came from the members of the free corps.[43] These units of volunteers—mostly recent frontline soldiers—carried the main burden of fighting the Spartacist workers during the winter and early spring of 1918—19.[44] The Schutzmannschaft could not match them in combat experience. Subsequent publications by the police were therefore inclined to grant the free corps retroactive recognition as de facto auxiliaries who ostensibly had acted under the auspices of the Ministry of Interior and in close liaison with the uniformed police. Both the republican Sicherheitspolizei of 1919 and the Schutzpolizei after 1920 claimed the free corps as their own direct predecessors since many free corps men later joined the regular police.[45] After the end of the Second World War, Lothar Danner still objected to critics who

> described the free corps as reactionary bands of mercenaries. Had they been no more than that, they could hardly have been welded into that instrument [the republican uniformed police] which prevented the violent overthrow of the Weimar Republic ... to the last day.[46]

Another author, Paul Riege, spoke of the courageous and forceful action of the free corps—"and the new Sicherheitspolizei"—as the main reason for the "astoundingly rapid" return of order in Germany in 1919. The free corps, he concluded, "were the best police force any country could ask for."[47]

While historians of the police can tell us the attitude in official quarters, they are less reliable as reporters of actual events. Between the Eichhorn episode and the formal establishment of the Schutzpolizei in 1920, the military units and the old police staff had not exactly been allies. During these months of tension, the Berlin police had anxiously wondered when it would be restored to full strength and feared that soldiers might be appointed to take its place.

The police cautiously reasserted its claims to authority when the Spartacist threat abated in the spring of 1919. On February 13, *Die Polizei* printed an essay by Dr. Haaselau in which he praised the prewar record of the Berlin police as superior to the achievements of its colleagues in Paris and New York.[48] In April, Police Inspector Eiben came out with an essay entitled "The Police in a Democracy." In contrast to his article in November, 1918, this one was written in a confident tone. Eiben demanded that the Berlin police be immediately restored to its previous position and reminded his readers that every civilized society required law enforcers with professional experience. The problem of democratization in the police was to be solved by a simple expedient: all that was needed, according to Eiben, was for the superior officers of the police to draw up new instructions for their men.[49]

But there was divided opinion concerning the future organization of police service in Berlin. Recent experience had convinced the Federal Ministry of Interior and the Reichswehr of the need for a reliable combat force in case of more armed disorders. They therefore favored the creation of a military arm as a permanent addition to the regular police. Together with the Federal Ministry of Defense and the commanding officers of the Garde-Kavallerie-Division in Berlin, preliminary plans were worked out to absorb the military units on security duty—

mainly the free corps—into the police and to make them the bulk of a special police army, trained for house-to-house fighting, under the name of "Sicherheitspolizei."[50]

The Berlin "Sipo" was to have nine divisions (Abteilungen) of at least 1,000 men each. Every division would be divided into six general service companies (Hundertschaften) and one technical company (technische Hundertschaft) armed with machine guns, trench mortars, and flamethrowers. An aerial detachment with ten planes was designed to increase the military potential of this force. Sipo soldiers were to be dressed in Jäger-green uniforms and live in barracks. They were to have exclusive responsibility for the security of Berlin. The old constabulary would be confined to administrative and criminal duties. By the beginning of June, 1919, a draft proposal for the new security force was made public in the pages of *Die Polizei*.[51]

To the vast majority of the Schutzmannschaft, the Sipo was a formidable menace to its vested interests. Assurances by the Ministry of Interior that the former free corps men "would not deprive them of their jobs" were unable to calm the officials.[52] They were disturbed by the prospect of seeing older policemen forced into early retirement and the rest relegated to the secondary functions of an "order police."[53] At a protest meeting of the police union, Dr. Lindenau told an alarmed audience that under the proposed plan the Schutzmannschaft would be reduced to 3,600 men, or about half its current size, and that two-thirds of the staff in the local police stations would be eliminated. The Sicherheitspolizei, in contrast, would reach an eventual strength of 10,000.[54]

The time had obviously come to dispel the public impression that the old police had been impotent in the turbulent half year since the end of the war. A number of official reports in the summer of 1919 tried to prove that the police had by no means remained idle between November 9, 1918, and June 1, 1919. Armed encounters between robbers and policemen were recounted in statistical figures.[55] The names of individual policemen who were killed during the insurrection in March, 1919, were given special citations.[56] Sometimes the daily press lent its assistance to demonstrate that soldiers made poor substitutes for schooled professionals, as in this news item in the *8-Uhr Abendblatt* of July 12, 1919:

> In one of the many instances of store looting, by now a daily (or rather nightly) routine, the police for once is promptly alerted. It does arrive in time to corner the burglars, who defend themselves with a volley of shots. A crowd gathers, the excitement reaches fever pitch—when a military patrol arrives at the scene. Following the old and tried procedure of authoritarian systems, [the soldiers] immediately go into action against the public. They push back the crowd and cordon it off with such élan that the police is also driven to the rear and the burglars escape. In the end, the poor policemen have no choice but to disarm the leader of the hussar patrol, who was drunk, and to take him to the Kommandantur. Playing at policeman in a big city is not as easy as some people think![57]

In the eyes of the police, the first and most obvious fault of the Sicherheitspolizei was that it was planned without consulting the experts. The Police President of Berlin, Eugen Ernst, was not even asked his opinion before the details of the plan were divulged to the public.[58]

The Sipo was also objectionable on theoretical grounds. Lindenau found it "unthinkable" that "young N.C.O.'s in putties and carrying hand grenades" were to assist the public in a metropolis. Army lieutenants, he explained, intimidate the average man in the street and cannot grasp his valid complaints. "Surely we all have seen enough to know the terrible consequences when military ways of thinking and acting are transposed to the sphere of politics and state administration."[59] Another author, Kriminal-Oberwachtmeister Füth, predicted that a barracked and militarized police could never establish close contacts with the public, and the population, in turn, would always regard it as an instrument of authority and compulsion.[60] Dr. Kurt Wolzendorf, of the law faculty of Halle University, argued that the creation of the Sicherheitspolizei was contrary to the historical trend away from military conceptions of police functions. Even the suppression of internal strife, he believed, would in the future call for men schooled in the techniques of the civil police rather than those of the army.[61]

The police, finally, also used political arguments against the Sicherheitspolizei. The police union warned the government that the reactionary reputation of the military officers who helped draft the project would compromise the new force at home and abroad.[62] Captain Waldemar Pabst of the Garde-Kavallerie-Division came under its special attack. Did Pabst question the efficiency of the professional police? Had his men spied on the Schutzmannschaft and presumed to pass judgment on its performance? Did not he and other army officers simply resent the established police corps because the latter had successfully: (1) avoided a blood bath on November 9, 1918; (2) adopted the non-military approach to police work; (3) remained neutral in recent political conflicts; and (4) demanded its share of civic liberties under the new Constitution?[63]

The vehemence of the police campaign against the army in the summer of 1919 reached the point where the military was directly accused of having helped to bring Germany to her current impasse. Admittedly, the police had recently languished because of forced inactivity. But then the internal security of the country since 1914 had rested with the army and not the police. And the army, far from fulfilling its task, had actually supplied the shock troops of the Revolution.[64]

The massive protests of the Schutzmannschaft could not have prevented the formation of the Sicherheitspolizei had not other events interceded in time. Toward the end of September, 1919, Sipo recruits were already in training at the Westend Barracks in Berlin-Charlottenburg. An official communiqué announced that the first units of the Sipo would be ready for duty in Berlin-Mitte and Berlin-Neukölln by January 10, 1920.[65] The younger men in the Schutzmannschaft were beginning to see the futility of resistance and sought admittance to the ranks of the green police.[66] As to the government, it was fully confident of success since on August 28, 1919, it predicted that the Allied powers, whose consent still had to be sought, would surely bow before the practical arguments in favor of creating a German police army.[67]

But the Allies objected. As early as July, 1919, at a conference held at Spa, the Allies had demanded that all paramilitary organizations in Germany be abolished. On June 22, 1920, they demanded that the Sicherheitspolizei be dissolved within three months.[68] The Sipo thereupon disbanded and many of its men joined the old constabulary to form a new civil police, the republican Schutzpolizei.

The Sicherheitspolizei had nevertheless lasted long enough to permit some doubts about its value in protecting the internal security of the Republic. In the six months of its existence, the Berlin Sipo was put to only one serious test of political loyalty. But in the Kapp putsch of March, 1920, it proved to be no more dependable to the lawful regime than the royal constabulary had been to the monarchy in November, 1918.

The Kapp putsch arose from discontent in the army over the projected German disarmament, the change of the national colors to Black-Red-Gold, and various other reforms. Under the leadership of Wolfgang Kapp, one of the founders of the Fatherland Party in 1916, a plot was hatched to replace the government with a national dictatorship. The government, forewarned, relieved Lieutenant Commander Ehrhardt of his command of a naval brigade at Döberitz (outside Berlin) and also General von Lüttwitz of his command in Berlin. But before the orders could take effect, Ehrhardt's brigade marched on Berlin. When it entered the city in the early hours of March 13, 1920, the units of the Sicherheitspolizei quietly withdrew. Before the morning was over, most of them had sided with the insurgents. The federal and the Prussian governments, who had relied on the army and the Berlin police to protect the city, were dumbfounded.[69]

The bureau in charge of the Sicherheitspolizei at the Prussian Ministry of Interior was headed by Ministerialrat Doyé who regarded the Sipo as his personal creation. In March, 1920, he belonged to the inner circle of the conspirators.[70] But he alone could not have ensured the swift adherence of the Berlin Sipo to the military dictatorship of Wolfgang Kapp. Many Sipo officers came forward spontaneously to offer their support to the rebels. In the First Division of the Sipo, Commander Walther Stennes of the Eighth Company Special Task Force immediately went over to the new rulers.[71] At the police barracks of the Seventh Company in Karlstrasse, Captain von Wederstedt assembled his men and told them that the republican regime was ended. After reaffirming his loyalty to the House of Hohenzollern, he hailed Kapp and Lüttwitz as "excellent men," and announced that he was placing his unit at their disposal. Whoever refused to change his allegiance was free to report to the paymaster's office and collect his papers. Anyone who wanted to quit later would be shot.[72]

The men of the Sipo did not necessarily share the political views of their officers. But they were mostly former soldiers selected because of their dependability and discipline. Obediently they stood guard outside government buildings, went on street patrol, and manned roadblocks on behalf of the usurpers. In Lankwitz they stormed the local gasworks that was held by 500 workmen. Armed clashes with soldiers of the Erhardt Brigade did not take place.[73]

There was nevertheless uneasiness in the ranks. It was apparent that the Sicherheitspolizei was not bowing to superior force as the Schutzmannschaft had in November, 1918. This

time the security police had field guns and armored cars. Nor
was it a matter of accepting a fait accompli endorsed by the
majority of the people. The population was evidently deeply
split in this crisis and there was a general strike. In the Tiergarten, passersby cheered a detachment of Sipo men and offered
it cigarettes. In the working-class streets of Prenzlauer Berg,
the same patrol met a solid wall of hostility. All was quiet in the
western suburbs, but on March 18, at Kottbuser Tor, fighting
broke out between police and civilians. This was not impartial
police duty in the interest of public order and safety. It was
armed support of a political faction.[74]

Uncertainty and dissension spread within the ranks of the
Sicherheitspolizei. One Sipo unit that had orders to tear down
anti-Kapp posters in a working-class district wavered at the
sight of angry crowds. An officer ordered the men to shoot but
they fired their machine guns into the air.[75] Another patrol took
offense when a group of pedestrians jeered them as "Noske-
men." To show how little they cared for the deposed government, they took the hecklers to a police station for a beating.[76]
At the barracks in Karlstrasse, on the other hand, an armored
car carried a chalked declaration of loyalty to the Ebert government. Its crew was placed under arrest.[76]

The performance of the Sicherheitspolizei during the short
rule of Wolfgang Kapp—he fled Berlin on March 17—gave rise
to a wave of self-justification as soon as the Ebert-Bauer regime
was restored in Berlin. The Sicherheitspolizei published an article on March 31 in its official organ under the title "A Crime
Against the German People." The essence of its argument was
that the police had never disobeyed the instructions of the legitimate Prussian government. "It would be unfair to say that the
Sipo had not loyally performed its duties during these difficult
days." True, some of its officers must be reproached for having
supported the putsch, but these individuals would now be taken
to account. Indeed, the Sipo deserved credit for reinstating all

the men discharged earlier because they would not serve the Kapp government.

> We have thereby shown the population that notwithstanding the pressure from some quarters, the officials of the Sicherheitspolizei will not be misled into breaking their sworn loyalty to the lawful government.[78]

Ministerialrat Doyé went into hiding. Colonel von Schönstedt was replaced by Major Kurt von Priesdorff as commander of the Sicherheitspolizei.[79] The Ministry of Interior undertook an investigation into the political performance of the armed police and ordered all Sipo officials to renew their oath of allegiance.[80] But that was all. Captain von Wederstedt stayed at his post. Stennes was promoted to captain. (He was later even put in charge of the Schutzpolizei's special task force assigned to support the political police.)[81] As Grzesinski remarked two decades later in reference to disloyal army officers in 1920: "The republic, always tolerant towards its enemies, did not find it necessary to punish these officers. . . . In mitigation it may be said that the republican government had no loyal troops at its disposal. It had no other alternative than to avail itself of the services of its enemies."[82] His comment applied with equal force to the Sipo.

In conclusion, we should note that the Berlin constables dropped their criticism of the Sicherheitspolizei as soon as the government under Allied pressure agreed to replace it with a civilian security police. When it became clear that the police troops of the Sipo were to join them as fellow comrades in the enlarged body of the Schutzpolizei, the old guard rallied to the defense of its erstwhile competitors. The Police Union defended the conduct of the Sipo during the Kapp putsch in the following words:

> The reliable segment in the Sicherheitspolizei, to which we count most of the subaltern officials, decidedly rejected all attempts to

make the police serve political ends. When the threat of counter-revolution had been eliminated, it conducted an assiduous political purge [within its ranks] and gave evidence of a manly forthrighteousness toward the Republic. [These men] could only be misled for a short moment. Housed in barracks, they had been isolated from the people.[83]

High-ranking officials shared in the efforts to vindicate the posthumous reputation of the Sicherheitspolizei.[84] Its official dissolution on October 4, 1920, was accompanied by laudatory words for its "great services to state and nation."[85] And an illustrated police publication at the end of the twenties carried this caption below a photograph of street fighting in Berlin:

> *Insurrection!* Let us hope that the times are gone when this call reverberated throughout the Germanic world. . . . We stand in reverence at the graves of the brave men of the Sicherheitspolizei, the "Sipo" of those by-gone days, who gave their lives so that Germany might live![86]

III | The Berlin Schutzpolizei, 1920-1932

Organization, Physical Training, Equipment

The Schutzpolizei of the twenties stood alone in protecting public order in the streets of Berlin. Except in national emergencies, it could not rely on the Reichswehr for support and refused the assistance of paramilitary organizations who were anxious to fill the role of nineteenth-century civic guards.[1] Conscious of this responsibility, the leaders of the police gave priority to matters of technical efficiency. In 1920 they set out to build a new security force from the main stock of the Schutzmannschaft and the remains of the Sicherheitspolizei. This police force had to conform to the Allies' concept of a civilian police and yet possess the striking power to guard against organized insurrection. To achieve this goal a host of legal, administrative, and budgetary questions had to be settled in the shortest possible time. New rules had to be drafted concerning salaries, promotion, and retirement benefits. There was need for modern equipment, new training centers, and a revised police code. It also meant that there was little opportunity to consider how the new dispositions might affect the political climate inside the uniformed ranks. While most of the technical questions were resolved between 1920 and 1923, their ideological implications were left unexplored.

The numerical strength of the Schutzpolizei during the twenties stood at from 14,000 to 16,000 men, including over 500 officers.[2] The Schupo Kommando was located at Oberwallstrasse 56, Berlin-Mitte, and was headed by a commander (Kommandeur) invested with the rank of a general of police.[3] The commander was assisted by a police major who acted as his permanent deputy and took charge of the routine work of internal administration. Greater Berlin was divided into six police regions (Polizeigruppen)—West, Center, South, North, East, and South-East—whose regional commanders met in staff conferences with the commander of the security police about every other week.[4]

The task of coordinating the daily operations of the executive personnel—riot brigades (Bereitschaften) and precinct police (Revierpolizei)—took place on a level subsidiary to the police regions: the police inspections (Polizei-Inspektionen). There were twenty-one police inspections all told, each headed by a police major or a police lieutenant-major (Polizei-Oberstleutnant). Their territorial boundaries varied with the need for police protection in different parts of the city. Thus police inspection 4 ("Friedrichshain") covered Friedrichshain, Lichtenberg, and Weissensee. On the other hand, no less than two police inspections—P.I. 1 ("Linden"), and P.I. 21 ("Alexander")—were in charge of the smaller but highly sensitive district of Berlin-Mitte.[5]

Below the inspections came the police precincts. Berlin had 161 police precincts in 1925, and 166 by 1933. Each was controlled by a police station with a police captain acting as precinct head (Reviervorsteher) and a police master (Polizeiobermeister) as his deputy. Precinct heads of the same inspection met about twice a week to discuss local developments and plan concerted security measures. Since the police stations also ran part of the local public administration and accommodated subaltern agents of the criminal police, they may be regarded as the eyes and ears of the police in Berlin.[6]

The men who went out on the beat belonged to the "external staff" of the precincts. They were sergeants and sergeant majors with at least five to seven years of service and schooling. Though they had by then advanced to solitary duty (Einzeldienst), they were still ready to act as reserves for the riot brigades in large-scale operations (geschlossener Einsatz), should ever the need arise.[7]

Their training for military combat had preceded their assignment to precinct duty. From 1923 on, every Berlin rookie spent his first year of service at the newly opened police school in Brandenburg (Havel). There he received intensive arms drill in addition to instruction in theoretical subjects. For the next four to six years, he served as probationer with one of the riot brigades where he was subjected to the discipline of barracks life and received further instruction in fighting techniques. Until he completed another four-month course at the police school and was ready for promotion to precinct work, a rookie was not allowed to marry so that he could "serve the state and nation free from the burden of family obligations."[8]

There were forty-two riot brigades distributed among Berlin's twenty-one police inspections.[9] They maintained their own dormitories—usually former army barracks—and local police posts (Bezirkswachen). Each brigade had a total of about 120 men divided into three platoons (Züge). The platoons took turns spending one-third of their period of duty on guard, one-third awaiting duty, ready to turn out at three minutes' notice for transport in trucks to the scene of a disturbance, and one-third at rest. During the period of awaiting duty they were given physical training and drill.

Because service in the riot brigades was meant to prepare the young Schupoman for later precinct work, the riot brigades sent their men as substitutes for precinct patrolmen on sick leave and local reinforcement in case of trouble. They helped direct traffic, guarded important buildings, and staffed the motorized flying squads (Ueberfallkommandos) that were introduced in Berlin in 1921. But their chief mission was readiness for civil emergencies.[10]

Making all officials begin their careers in the riot brigades must largely account for the good trim of the Berlin Schupo after the First World War. The men who now entered the police service were not superannuated professional soldiers (Kapitulanten) as under the monarchy, but young men between the ages of twenty and twenty-two. They were selected by a rigorous test of physical fitness[11]—in 1931, forty out of sixty applicants for training at the police school in Brandenburg were rejected on medical grounds[12]—and scheduled for discharge when they were about thirty-two.

Emphasis was placed on the budding "police sports movement." A special Academy for Physical Training (Polizeischule für Leibesübungen) was founded in Berlin-Spandau in 1920 to train sports instructors for the uniformed police corps.[13] The activities of local police sports associations were supported by subsidies from the Ministry of Interior.[14] The government apparently hoped to promote the popularity of the Schupo through the sportsmanlike appearance of its uniformed personnel and through public performances by police athletes.[15] The early twenties, after all, were a time of general interest in outdoor sports. Some young men applied to the Schupo principally because they enjoyed bodily exercise.[16] The government may have hoped, furthermore, that police sports clubs would encourage more camaraderie across service ranks during off-duty hours.[17]

Naturally the police sports movement had its military significance as well. But whether or not the police leaders of the

Weimar Republic deliberately intended this is not certain.[18] What is certain is that physical training among the young recruits went hand-in-hand with training for combat. At the police school in Brandenburg the rookies were encouraged to compete for the German gymnastic and sports medal (Deutsches Turn- und Sportabzeichen) which, "by order of the Prussian Ministry of Interior, had to be earned anew every year by passing a physical endurance test in full uniform. The test consisted of a cross-country run of 3,500 meters, the long jump, and grenade-throwing."[19]

Much of the police training at Brandenburg was identical to army drill; a reporter in 1928 charged that it equaled in harshness anything that the old Prussian army had to offer before the war.[20] Willi Lemke, who entered the police school in 1932, described his arrival at Brandenburg in the following words:

> From the first hour we were left in no doubt as to the manner in which we would be treated. Before we had time to change into uniform, we were made to practice roll call to the sound of whistle blows. . . . This was repeated a dozen times. . . . None of us could collect his thoughts in the hurry and bustle accompanied by the inevitable screams of the instructors. We were constantly ordered to do new things. I guess the idea was to break our individual will right from the beginning.[21]

The official arms manual of the Prussian Schutzpolizei expressly called for a thorough training of the uniformed police in the practical use of arms. "Theoretical knowledge [alone] cannot help to overcome the psychological strain of street combat."[22] In support of this policy, *Die Polizei* during the twenties published article after article on police tactics in house-to-house fighting, storming barricades, and quelling riots.

The personal arms of the Schutzpolizei normally consisted of the police truncheon and either the 9 millimeter "o/8" or the 7.65 millimeter Parabellum pistol.[23] Truncheons were in use since the Revolution of 1848, when the civic guard had first introduced "peace batons" on the theory that they represented more democratic implements than sabers and firearms. The republican police after 1918, however, found truncheons just as provocative to civilians and nearly as dangerous because of the internal injuries they could cause. Truncheons also had the drawback that they could only be used at close quarters. Should they fail to disperse an unruly crowd, policemen could not rapidly switch to guns without endangering one another's lives.[24] In 1930 water trucks were introduced in the hope that they would be more effective than truncheons as well as safer for all concerned.[25]

Carbines, submachine guns, heavy machine guns mounted on armored cars, and hand grenades were issued in major emergencies. According to the Allied terms of 1920, the German police could issue every uniformed policeman one bayonet, one pistol, and one hand grenade. Every third policeman could have a rifle or carbine; every twentieth, one machine gun; and for every thousand men the police was allowed one armored car with two heavy machine guns.[26] The heavy arms of the security police were concentrated in the riot brigades for use in close combat formations. The supreme weapon was the "special car" (Sonderwagen), or armored car, whose menacing appearance was intended to demoralize unruly elements in the street before fighting broke out. It had serious drawbacks as a fighting instrument: though the vehicle was specially designed for use by city police in 1924, its machine guns could not reach snipers on rooftops unless the target was more than a hundred meters away. It could not overrun simple obstacles placed in its path; a wooden barricade would stop it. It also took too long to prepare for action. According to rules, it had to be stripped of guns and ammunition when not in use and jacked up to save tires and springs. Finally, the vehicle was difficult to operate, and trained drivers were in short supply.[27]

Fast means of communication made up for shortcomings

in weaponry. Police trucks gave the riot brigades their much vaunted mobility throughout the city.[28] Teletypes were introduced in the late twenties to replace the obsolete Morse telegraph.[29] By 1929 the Berlin Schupo used nine radio transmitters to exchange messages between the six police regions and the outlying police inspections. In that year, the use of aircraft by the police, banned by the Allies in 1921,[30] was permitted in conjunction with the Communist uprising in May. As on former occasions when the police wanted to circumvent foreign restrictions on a police flying corps, a privately-owned aircraft was chartered for police use.[31] It flew reconnaissance missions and maintained direct radio contact with the Kommando post of the Schutzpolizei. In 1932 two planes of the Berlin "Luwa" (Luftpolizeiwache, or air police guard) flew over a Nazi rally at Frankfurt an der Oder. The Nazis even claimed that police pilots were training for bombing missions against the S.A.[32]

The National Socialist government after 1933 scorned at what it called the self-deceptive attempt of the Republic to maintain the fiction of a "civil" security police. Calling companies "detachments of hundreds," brigades "police inspections," regiments "training units," and armored cars "special cars" could not hide the fact that Prussia possessed a military police arm.[33] Under the Nazi government, therefore, the Schutzpolizei was made a branch of the regular army, serving in green uniforms, with steel helmets and infantry weapons in place of the blue dress, leather shako, and truncheon. But then the Nazis could not be expected to sympathize with the Republic's efforts to teach its police officials democracy, if need be through the medium of service designations and operational procedure.

Social Background, Material Compensation, Police Unions, Discipline

The security of Berlin depended on the organization and

striking power of its street police. The government therefore
had to make sure that the Schutzpolizei would remain loyal in
the event of serious internal unrest. Some sort of political education was obviously needed. But it was difficult to devise a program that suited the men who in the Republic joined the police.

In selecting its recruits, the Schutzpolizei, as we have seen,
observed very high standards of physical fitness for combat
duty. As a result, the majority of patrolmen during the 1920's
was drawn from the Prussian countryside. It is true that the
postwar police was more diverse in social composition than had
been its predecessor. The general improverishment after the
war induced a number of former students, commercial employees, and professional men to seek careers in the police, so
much so that salary scales, systems of promotion, and training
programs were sometimes ill-matched to the educational and
social background of the men.[34] It would nevertheless be wrong
to infer that the Schutzpolizei represented a cross section of
German society or was moving in the direction of a "people's
police." The number of urban recruits always remained low.

There was no deliberate policy to broaden the social basis
of the police. In the first two years of the Republic, a few suggestions were made to strengthen the social-democratic element
in the police by enlisting organized workers from the labor
movement. In 1920 Police President Richter and the Prussian
Minister of Interior Severing both voiced their support for more
unionists inside the Schupo. But capable workmen proved to be
hard to get.[35] Berlin workers felt little inclination for police
work; they would not exchange their tools for weapons, or their
class-conscious politics for public service. Besides, their health
could not match that of country lads from Silesia or East Prussia.[36] There were three Berliners among the twenty-one veteran
patrolmen interviewed for this study, but none could be said to
represent the city's working-class movement: Erich Jahn's father
was a school porter who raised his children with the strictness

of a subaltern public servant; Bruno Schirmer's father was with the Tenth Uhlan Regiment in Berlin; and Otto Krause, who called himself a metalworker by trade, was the son of a farmer in Oberbarnim. His career in Berlin industry was limited to four months with the electrical firm of Siemens and Schuckert.[37]

The personal stories of Kurt Fleischer, F. Gediehn, and Hermann Artner, three men who joined the Berlin police in 1920, are by far more representative of the average patrolman's background in the Weimar Republic. Born in the last two years of the nineteenth century, they were all destined for a traditional trade in their native villages before the war. Gediehn and Artner were apprentice wheelwrights, one near Königsberg, the other near Frankfurt an der Oder. Fleischer was apprenticed to a master carpenter in Thuringia. Their experience at the front between 1914 and 1918 had the effect of tearing them from their provincial roots. After the armistice, none of the three men wanted to pick up his former life, realizing that hardened soldiers make poor apprentices. Fleischer and Gediehn tried their luck with the free corps, and Artner joined the border patrol (Grenzschutz). By then, soldiering was the only skill they had to sell. But while the political issues after the war left them largely indifferent, they did worry about their own future once Germany had returned to internal peace. Army service did not attract them, because "professional soldiers have few prospects after a lost war." To these ambitious youngsters, service in the security police seemed like the best answer. The police needed experienced fighters and promised them steady employment and the amenities of life in a modern city. "If you come from a small place, Berlin interests you," was Fleischer's explanation for his decision to join up. And to Artner, "the Berlin Schupo was something different from agriculture. I never did this before."

The Schupomen who enlisted in the latter half of the twenties were not former soldiers like the three men just described.

They had to be trained in the use of arms on the parade ground of the police school and in the riot brigades. But most of them still hailed from the rural districts of Prussia.[38] They had no more political motive for joining up than had the rookies in 1920. There were, however, thousands of jobless young men in the country to whom police service was a good way of getting off the dole.[39] "It was the mark of a young man's uprightness and of his serious intent in life, if he preferred the rigors of a policeman's career to an idle existence," recounted Max Jachode, whose period of service in Berlin dated from the time of the inflation. His opinion was echoed by Willi Lemke who chose the policeman's lot in the midst of the depression in 1931. "Every man with a sound mind and some self-respect either tried to get a position with the police or the Reichswehr," he recollected. Lemke's ambition was to raise his social standing from agricultural laborer to public official. Teacher's training was too expensive and the army only offered public posts after twelve years of service. This left the police. Though policemen were not well paid and not much liked among the peasants, Lemke wrote in his later memoirs, they still represented officialdom and were respected accordingly. Eventually there was the chance of becoming a Landjäger with several villages to control. "That would make me king in my own territory."

Once taken into the force, few security policemen left the service before their normal twelve years were up. Artner attributed this to their esprit de corps, but he agreed that, more important still, policemen had no material incentive to wish for other employment. A good constable was even unwilling to be transferred to police duty outside Berlin, where fringe benefits were smaller and the work dull. Eduard Kolbe, who was in charge of personnel affairs at police inspection Prenzlauer Berg between 1929 and 1931, recalled instances of policemen who were dismissed for disciplinary reasons, but none where a man resigned of his own accord.[40]

To be a policeman in the twenties meant belonging to a comparatively secure income group. Unlike most Berliners of comparable social origin, a patrolman was sheltered from the drastic consequences of the inflation and the depression. He was not well paid, but he was exempted from the salary cuts planned under the government's economy program in 1931 and 1932, and material security mattered more than affluence.[41] An unmarried rookie who received his room and board from the state was considered very well off for a man of his age and social background, and eagerly sought after by traveling salesmen and shop girls alike. In contemporary novels, the policeman is therefore depicted as the object of economic envy on the part of the unemployed. The hero in Hans Fallada's *Little Man What Now?*, an unemployed salesclerk, felt provoked by the Schupo's well-fed and well-clothed appearance.[42] In Heinz Rein's novel *Berlin 1932*, Martin "knew that he would seethe at the sight of the . . . smug, and just a trifle arrogant face [of the cop] . . . the shiny black helmet with the black-red-golden insignia, the calm, self-confident air of the man with prospects for an old-age pension."

"You people can make a living and will always make a living. You always think it isn't all that bad. So far no one has starved to death you think. You will never understand us. That's why you have the gall to run around as policemen and to use your truncheons to . . ." "All right," the policeman interrupted him. "And now, just move along."[43]

In 1919 the starting wage of a patrolman was 160.33 marks per month.[44] During the inflation, the men were paid as often as five times a day. In the depression, Lemke considered himself very fortunate to receive 86 marks per month plus room, board, and clothing. Krause, who served with a riot brigade in the heart of Berlin, earned between 117.50 and 125.00 marks per month in the years 1929 to 1931. He paid for his meals at the mess hall, but after deducting his expenses for food and other essentials, he still had over 70 marks in spending money every month, of which he normally saved half. The concensus of the police veterans interviewed for this study was that policemen in the Weimar Republic made a frugal but decent living and that most of them were well satisfied. "It was not done for policemen to complain about salaries. It was no use bargaining for more pay anyhow. Salaries were fixed by rules."[45]

There were fringe benefits to take into consideration, too. They ranged from the prospect of improved housing for married policemen toward the end of the twenties, to medical and social welfare services free of charge.[46] The most important of these benefits, however, was the severance pay for retiring policemen or, as an alternative, a sinecure in the local civil service.

The republican Schutzpolizei had to take care of its men differently from the royal Schutzmannschaft because they were younger, and many of them had to start a new career after their discharge. The police offered its patrolmen vocational training during off-duty hours, the Polizeiberufsschulen performing much the same service as the Kapitulantenschulen of the old Imperial Army had for soldiers. These schools also offered general education courses on the elementary and secondary school level with the possibility of making the Abitur.[47] A severance pay of 2,400 marks was given to departing patrolmen to help them take charge of the family farmstead, or set up a grocery store, a tobacco shop, or more frequently a pub. This bonus could be increased to several thousand marks more if the retired policeman did well in his new occupation.[48]

In lieu of monetary settlement, a departing sergeant could ask for the "police maintenance claim" (Polizeiversorgungsschein). According to the police code of July 19, 1922, this certificate entitled the bearer to seek appointment of intermediary rank in the civil service branch of his choice. It did not exempt him from having to meet the requirements of other civil service candidates, but it protected him from "arbitrary rejection" of his application.[49] Many policemen applied to services closely associated with their former work, such as air traffic control, administrative police, the customs service, or the internal administration of the Schupo itself.

These rewards for faithful police service were worth seeking in the twenties, in spite of some discouraging stories of retired policemen failing in business or waiting for months for an opening in the civil service.[50] In 1926 Sergeant Karl Gäde of police inspection Steglitz invested his severance pay in a small factory making screws and bolts. When this enterprise went out of business, he worked in a bicycle shop for a while. By 1929 he had 450 marks in debts and drew a weekly dole of 6.55 marks. Though his wife had a small income, the couple and their two children rarely could afford hot meals.[51] Retired officers sometimes fared no better. To name an illustrious example, Hugo Kaupisch, the commander of the Berlin Schupo from 1920 to 1926, was forced to earn his living as a journalist and later as an employee in a Jewish business firm after Severing had dismissed him for political reasons—a painful experience for an officer of the old imperial school.[52] Both the sergeant and the colonel, incidentally, became supporters of National Socialism during their years of hardship. But the well-known hazards of the free economy only strengthened most policemen in their desire to hold on to their posts as long as they could.

Material security for at least twelve years helped to keep the Schupomen honest. The only complaint heard in the twenties concerned a minority of younger patrolmen who were tempted by persuasive tradesmen to live well beyond their means. Traveling salesmen for a time were allowed to solicit business inside police barracks, offering suits of clothing, radios, and bicycles on the installment plan. Some thirty Berlin Schupomen were reported to have committed suicide in 1925 on account of debts. In his New Year's address in 1929, Police

President Zörgiebel warned against the repeated instances of young police officials borrowing sums that they could never hope to repay from their regular earnings.[53] The problem did not, however, affect the performance of the Schutzpolizei at large. When eight Schupos were arrested on June 16, 1926, for accepting gratuities from nightclub owners in Friedrichsstadt, the *Vossische Zeitung* dismissed the incident with the remark that eight corrupt policemen in a force of 20,000 were no cause for alarm.[54]

What dissatisfaction there was among the uniformed men did not concern their material compensation. It was more likely related to the slowness of promotion in individual cases and to the wish of older men for relief from the physical strain of street patrol. The policemen's union as early as 1919 asked that seasoned policemen be transferred to administrative work as a matter of routine,[55] and many applied for desk jobs when they were up for reassignment after ten years on the force.[56] The Nazis in 1933 won some sympathy because they ordered an immediate curtailment of street patrols.[57] But personal danger and hardship also induced in many policemen a professional pride. Lemke wrote in his private memoirs: "It never occurred to us to count our work load. We were police officials doing our duty to the people. The concept of overtime pay was unknown to us." Policemen were taught to stand above personal interest, to regard themselves as different from private employees or civil servants in office jobs. The campaign of the Schutzpolizei to revive the traditional code of Prussian officialdom must account for the good discipline in its ranks.[58]

To illustrate the interplay of material interest and professional consciousness, we must turn to a brief survey of the police union movement in the Weimar Republic.[59]

The police unions had come into their own at the end of the war. By the middle of the twenties, nearly every police official and police employee in Prussia was organized—a remarkable state of affairs if we remember how difficult it was to organize public servants under the monarchy. In January, 1919, a German police convention (Deutscher Polizeitag) in Berlin summed up its view of the new situation in the following resolution:

> The old state is broken and a new political structure is about to emerge. In the political state of the future, the individual will be powerless; only organized groups will be heeded and will determine the course of events. . . . If we police officials want our wishes, proposals, and demands to be heard, we must cover Germany with a network of policemen's unions representing lower- and higher-ranking officials, and have a managing committee in Berlin constantly prepared to undertake steps on our behalf.[60]

By far the most important police union in postwar Berlin was the local branch of the Association of Prussian Police Officials (Verband Preussischer Polizeibeamten), popularly known as the "Schrader-Verband," after its founder and first chairman of many years, Ernst Schrader.[61] Officially established in 1923, the origins of the Schrader-Verband went back to 1915, when the police chiefs in the capital had grudgingly allowed the formation of the Verband der Schutzleute des Landesbezirks Berlin.[62] Ten to twelve years later, after amalgamating with similar unions in other Prussian townships and enlisting the support of some middle-ranking and higher-ranking officials, the former organization of Berlin constables had grown to a membership of more than 60,000 throughout Prussia, making it the largest police union in Germany.[63] There were subsections catering to the particular interests of Schupo officers, police detectives, administrative police, and, in the countryside, the Landjägerei. A special group devoted itself to the study of police science.[64] On the national level, the Schrader-Verband was affiliated with the Reichsverband der Polizeibeamten Deutschlands and the Deutscher Beamtenbund.

The importance of the police unions in the twenties will be

more apparent, when we consider that besides Schrader's Association of Prussian Police Officials, there existed the General Prussian Police Association (Allgemeiner Preussischer Polizeibeamtenverband, often designated as the "Betnarek-Verband"), the Association of Security Police Officials of Prussia (Verband der Schutzpolizeibeamten Preussens, or "Josupeit-Verband"), an association catering only to middle-ranking police officials (the Verband der mittleren Polizeivollzugsbeamten, or "Murche-Verband"), and the Prussian Police Officers' Association (Vereinigung Preussischer Polizeioffiziere). It is not surprising that Dr. Bernhard Weiss was wont to complain that a police president's lot had grown much harder since 1918. While a police chief of the Empire had ruled as absolute master in his own house, he said, his republican successor had to contend not only with parliamentarians and journalists, but with organized grievance committees and union delegates.[65]

His remarks specifically referred to Police President Zörgiebel, whose disagreements with the Schrader-Verband led to a brief rupture of relations between the president and the union in 1930. But Zörgiebel's angry rebuke was as futile as Severing's temporary boycott of the Prussian Police Officers' Association a year later.[66] Neither police presidents nor ministers of interior could afford to ignore the police unions very long.

For the police unions, in particular the Schrader-Verband, enjoyed considerable political weight. In 1918 it was the Schrader-Verband that had negotiated the truce between the insurgent authorities and the rank and file of the Berlin police. It was the Schrader-Verband, too, which appealed to the local inhabitants for continued confidence in the Schutzmannschaft.[67] Concerned with the growing anarchy in Berlin, the Schrader-Verband in 1919 even went so far as to ask the National Assembly in Weimar for help.[68] To be sure, no police union ever challenged the fundamental principle that the police was an executive organ of the government, bound to obey its orders and to submit to its disciplinary sanctions. But since most politicians realized the usefulness of having the police associations on their side, and consequently were willing to pay them some courtesies—for example by personal attendance at their formal events[69]—the unions enjoyed a certain amount of leverage. A Severing who in 1931 denied the right of police unions to offer or withhold their confidence in his leadership obviously did so only because in this instance the Police Officers' Association had challenged his judgment in a disciplinary case.[70] Severing did not reject a vote of confidence by the Schrader-Verband or the Betnarek-Verband when they endorsed his appointment as Prussian Minister of Interior in 1926 and again in 1930.[71] These two associations, after all, could be relied on always to support the government even when they disagreed with some of its policy decisions.[72]

No doubt the Schrader-Verband, because of its large and diversified membership, was compelled to concentrate much of its effort on bread-and-butter issues: salaries, social security, intercession on behalf of individual members in matters of appointments, and so forth. But beyond that, it claimed to further a definite professional mission.[73] This mission was not the attainment of a bloated sense of importance, of course: "that would be offensive." Police unions should rather seek to enhance the popular prestige of the police through constant and active work in rendering more effective the authority of the state. Disagreements with decisions by the Ministry of Interior or the Police Presidium were admissible only if they genuinely arose from considerations of the public interest. "A good deal can be achieved by idealism alone. . . . This is why we have not to this day succumbed to the laws of economic competition, have not become victims of the cult of self-interest."[74]

As a practical example of the Schrader-Verband's concept of union rights, we may cite its position on the right of police officials to strike:

A public official . . . does not conclude a service contract with his employing agency in a civil-legal sense. The right to strike can therefore not be recognized as long as the strike is intended to result in an improvement of earnings and service regulations.

It may be argued that an official may want to claim the right to strike for political and not for self-seeking reasons. He may thus try by such action to protest against measures of the government which threaten the foundations of officialdom—so indispensable to the community—or against measures which emanate from a government to whom all the officials, or some of them, are opposed. It would then appear as if the public interest would be served and not harmed by the right of officials to go on strike.

It is true, that under such conditions matters would be different. . . . But strikes by public officials over questions of principle will always be rare, and must not be confused with strikes where the public cause serves as a mere pretext for private interests. . . . To establish the true circumstances must be left to a disciplinary inquiry whenever a strike by public officials—which is not allowed in principle—has taken place.[75]

The aims of the Schrader-Verband, in other words, went beyond material issues and sought to strengthen the corporative standing of the police within the general structure of Germany's legal society. It preferred a state police to a communal police, and a Reich police to a state police. It advocated democratization within the police corps in the sense of breaking down the vestiges of a castelike distinction between officers and men. It proposed that police presidents be professional law enforcers and not political appointees.[76] In the political quarrel between the parties, however, it steered a carefully neutral course.

During most of the twenties, the Prussian government had no reason to worry over the Schrader-Verband's politics.[77] The inadequacies of its general principles became evident only when German democracy entered a stage of acute crisis at the turn of the decade.

After 1930 studious impartiality in the conflict of parties

had become an untenable position to maintain. A policeman who was suspected of Nazi affiliations and defended himself by saying: "I support the principles of the Constitution. I have been a member of the Schrader-Verband for some time,"[78] could not count on much political credit. The time had come for the Prussian police to rally more specifically to the prevailing Social Democratic regime in Prussia. In May, 1931, the Association of Prussian Police Officials therefore fused with a smaller but politically less ambiguous police association, the General Prussian Police Association (Betnarek-Verband).[79]

The Betnarek-Verband was organized in 1927 on the principles of the "free trade union" movement, and was consequently regarded as an associate of the Social Democratic party.[80] Among its supporters were Minister of Interior Grzesinski, State Secretary Abegg, Ministerialdirektor Klausener, Ministerialdirigent van den Bergh, Deputy Police President Weiss, Schupo Commander Heimannsberg, and numerous deputies of the Prussian Diet.[81] The amalgamation of the Schrader-Verband and the Betnarek-Verband in 1931—the largest union and the union with the clearer democratic goal—meant, in the words of Carl Severing, "a tight consolidation of nearly all the officials of the police executive in one radical, republican organization."[82]

But was it enough? The body of Berlin's police officials did not necessarily follow the leadership of the Association of Prussian Police Officials in its forthright endorsement of Prussia's Social Democratic regime. Traitors to the government could still be found in the ranks of the Schrader-Verband after 1931.[83] The militant elements in the police corps were organized in smaller but more political unions. But only one of these unions stood firmly behind the established regime.

In February, 1928, chairman Ernst Schrader of the Association of Prussian Police Officials had attended the first meeting of a new Union of Republican Police Officials (Vereinigung

republikanischer Polizeibeamten).[84] At subsequent meetings of
this union, police officials of all ranks sat together and listened
to lectures on the legal position of state officials in a democracy,
or on the Republic as the protector of integral officialdom.[85]
How close the meetings of the Vereinigung came to resemble
the current political rallies in Berlin can be seen in an incident
on March 30, 1931, when fifty to sixty young Nazis in the audience provoked a full-scale brawl with beer bottles and chairs
as weapons—an unheard of occurrence in the history of other
police organizations.[86] The Vereinigung republikanischer Polizeibeamten eventually merged with the Deutsche Staatspartei
in November, 1931, and changed its name to Polizeibeamten-
Vereinigung der Deutschen Staatspartei. Three months later it
announced its solidarity with the Eiserne Front in a common
fight against fascism.[87]

But there also existed a core of nationalistic police officials,
whose loyalty to the Prussian regime was more doubtful. It was
found in two other organizations: the Association of Security
Police Officials of Prussia (Josupeit-Verband), and the Prussian
Police Officers' Association. The former catered to the lower
ranks of the security police. It sympathized with the German
National People's Party (DNVP) and the German National
Socialist Workers' Party (NSDAP), but could scarcely rival the
Association of Prussian Police Officials in numerical impor-
tance.[88]

The Prussian Police Officers' Association, however, claimed
the allegiance of nearly 90 percent of the officer corps.[89] It is
interesting that in spite of repeated affirmations of loyalty to
the German constitution, the Officers' Association, by the ad-
mission of its own spokesmen, remained throughout the Republic under the lingering suspicion of political opposition.[90]
The Association took too much pride, perhaps, in its "traditional
Prussian sense of duty and officialdom" to harmonize with the
government's democratic aims. It sought too hard to establish

a place in Berlin's upper society comparable to that of the army officers' corps before the war.[91]

The prominent personalities in its leadership were all known for their conservative—if not reactionary—political stand. Polizei-Oberst Otto Dillenburger, who chaired the association throughout the twenties, was a partisan of the right wing within the officers' ranks, though he never openly rejected the Republic.[92] Polizei Major *a. D.* Eldor Borck, the Association's unofficial spokesman in the Prussian Diet was a member of the German National People's Party and also associated with the Josupeit-Verband. Borck publicly denounced Schrader for having stabbed the royal Schutzmannschaft in the back and conspired with Germany's enemies in the winter of 1918. He accused Police Presidents Friedensburg, Zörgiebel, and Weiss of secret collusion with the Communists.[93] In the early thirties, he supported the Nazi deputies in the Landtag in every parliamentary discussion of police affairs, and after July, 1932, was mentioned as a possible candidate for chief of the police department in the Prussian Ministry of Interior.[94]

But the Prussian Police Officers' Association was by then rapidly moving farther to the right than Borck. On January 5, 1933, it elected Polizei Major Walther Wecke as its new chairman, an official who already headed the National-Socialist Fellowship of the Berlin Security Police (NSBAG, or National-sozialistische Beamten-Arbeitsgemeinschaft Berlin, Fachgruppe Schutzpolizei) and before long was to help in the political purge of the Prussian police.[95]

It must be said to the credit of the Association of Prussian Police Officials that it refused to be moved by the political landslide in favor of National Socialism between July 20, 1932 and January 30, 1933. On the contrary, when Ernst Schrader was forced into retirement in 1932, and the Nazis in the Prussian Diet began to clamor for the dissolution of the Association "in the interest of political cleanliness and morality,"[96] the leaders

of the Schrader-Verband urged their members to remain steadfast to the principles of democracy.[97] Just before Hitler became
chancellor, the Association elected the deposed commander of
the Berlin Schupo, Polizei-Oberst Heimannsberg, as its new
chairman, in a gesture of noble defiance.

Our discussion has reached the point where we must directly take up the political education of the Weimar Republic's
police. But before we turn to that subject, there is need for a
final remark on the internal democratization within the Schutzpolizei after the First World War.

If the police was to assume a new role in the German Republic, the internal relationship between officers and men had
to be liberalized too. This was a basic conviction of the civilian
chiefs in the twenties. The difficulty lay in implementing democratic ideas within an institution as dependent on military discipline as the security police.

To authorize the organization of police associations and
grievance committees could limit the power of officers. It did
not necessarily further that solidarity within the police corps
which, according to a circular of the Ministry of Interior on
April 18, 1928, "should rest not on rigid compulsion, but on the
unanimity of will of all parts to the whole, on a voluntary integration and subordination."[98] Officers could be held to politeness
toward their men and told to instruct instead of punish whenever possible. Subordinates could be told not to use the servile
form of addressing their superiors in the third person, and not
to jump to attention when officers entered their quarters.[99] All
this alone could not produce the "love and sympathy" Severing
hoped would prevail among the ranks of the republican police.
Grzesinski was more realistic than Severing in this respect. He
proclaimed as the motto of the democratic Schupo the traditional notions of readiness to serve, intelligence, courage, and
discipline.[100]

Fortunately for the Schupo, the men of the lower ranks

did not object to discipline. Cases of insubordination were rare. The officer corps of the Berlin Schupo, though more conservative than the men, did not show the same degree of class consciousness as their counterparts in the provinces. Whenever the police was publicly criticized, the rank and file were inclined to find in the militarism of their officers a general excuse for their own part in the excesses of the police. But individual officers were not rejected by their men, except if their performance already was subject to disciplinary inquiry.[101] There was, in spite of all the strain and frustration, a fundamental solidarity in the police. The question was how far this solidarity extended beyond this body of fighting men to the citizens of Greater Berlin, the Prussian government, and the German Republic.

Political Education

The government expected its policemen to be loyal to the Republic, but it wanted this loyalty to be freely given. To the senior police administrators, democracy meant, above all, accepting political responsibility based on individual freedom and respect for the law. Orthodoxy and indoctrination did not agree with their liberal predilections.

Some of the former officers of the Schutzmannschaft responded quickly to this tolerant policy. Polizei-Oberst Stelse, Polizei-Oberst Hellriegel, and Berlin's well-known Kommandeur Heimannsberg himself, were examples of men of the royal constabulary who became steadfast supporters of the Republic, and defended it in strategic positions in Berlin until the very end. Others, who felt less sure about the regime, were allowed a generous amount of time to overcome their personal reservations. It was not until 1931 that Police Captain Fellmann, who headed the officers' section of the Schrader-Verband, called on the government to "remove those officers who, after ten years of service, still refused to endorse the Republic."[102] This was

also the time when Minister of Interior Severing finally ordered
that police rookies must in the future offer concrete evidence
of political loyalty as a prerequisite for passing the entrance
examination.[103]

For the government's approach to new recruits had been
equally liberal during the twenties. Entrants into the police
service were submitted to only a cursory examination of their
personal background. They had to produce a passable school
record and a certificate of good conduct from their hometown.[104]
Physical aptitude counted more than democratic convictions as
long as the rookies were willing to sign an oath of allegiance
to the federal and the Prussian constitution. Allegations by
critics on the right, that the police gave SPD members preferen-
tial appointments were loudly denied by the government.[105]
There may actually have been instances when these charges
were true,[106] but the point surely is that the republicans unlike
their Nazi successors officially rejected such a policy as contrary
to their political principles. When in 1921, Walther Stennes's
special task force was disbanded on suspicion of conspiracy
against the Republic, Polizei-Oberst Weber testified in court
that "the Hundertschaft z.b.V. was designed as a special elite
force for the protection of the government. We took everyone
who applied, and no one was asked his political opinions."[107]

In place of a selective system of recruitment, the police
relied on what political education it could give to the men once
they had joined the force. An obvious starting point for this
undertaking was the police schools at Brandenburg and Eiche
(near Potsdam). This possibility, however, was never effectively
exploited. Most young rookies were ill-prepared for involved
lectures on constitutional law and other aspects of the German
legal system, and took much more readily to the straightforward
teaching of their drill sergeants. Their instructors, in turn, were
more often than not officers who, themselves not proficient in
theoretical subjects, taught their classes by rote and stifled all

independence of thought. Quite a number of them had been transferred to teaching assignments because their hostility toward the Republic had disqualified them for street duty. Under the leadership of Count Poninsky, a secret adherent of the right-wing "Stahlhelm" organization, the police school in Brandenburg became the reserve of militarism and authoritarian state ideas.[108] Poninsky was retired in 1928, but the Prussian police schools continued to harbor a large number of nationalist officers whose ill-concealed disdain for democracy, Severing recognized, posed a serious problem to the Republic.[109]

Education in the principles of democracy was available more directly in the evening seminars of the vocational schools,[110] which were taught by civilian volunteers, in the lectures and discussions of the Union of Republican Police Officials,[111] and through the semiofficial literature which was laid out in common rooms at police barracks and precinct stations.[112] The policemen who took part in such events or spent time with recommended reading materials, were, of course acting on their own initiative, and their number was never very large.

The political ideas expounded by the police in the Weimar Republic were, after all, ill-suited for peasant youngsters in uniform. Their content rather resembled academic disputations, whose inconclusiveness was out of place in the military atmosphere of police barracks. There were, moreover, three different approaches to the theoretical problem of adjusting police functions to a democratic system of government.

The first approach emphasized the need for political self-reliance on the part of every individual official. Far from acting as the blind executor of superior orders, every patrolman was called on to use his political acumen (*politisches Fingerspitzengefühl*) in handling concrete situations, and to see that his actions corresponded to the overall intention of the law.[113] To acquire the necessary sophistication and self-reliance, he needed experience in political life.

The Republic therefore urged its police officials to make use of their political rights as provided under article 130, section 2, of the German constitution of 1919. The policemen were reminded that the law entitled them as German citizens to hold and express openly their political views. They were told that they could vote for and join any legitimate political association. "Energetic measures must be taken should an official be penalized for his membership in a political party or for his endorsement of a political program."[114]

But the existence of powerful opposition parties compelled the government to add to this freedom a warning not to subordinate the general welfare of the community to the interest of a particular party. A public servant, even when not on duty, must "abstain from any conduct . . . which is likely to impair the general respect, esteem, and trustworthiness of his office."[115] A decree in 1921 ordered all Prussian officials to avoid relations with political organizations "whose aims cannot with absolute certainty be described as friendly toward the constitution."[116] Still more bluntly, an agreement between the federal and the Prussian governments on April 1, 1928, stipulated that all Schupo officials were to be "absolutely unpolitical" in their performance of their duties.[117] But only the decree of June 25, 1930, specifically forbade Prussian state officials to belong to either the Communist or the Nazi party.[118]

During most of the twenties, the exact line between a policeman's political rights as a citizen and his obligations as a public servant remained unclear. There were confusing attempts to distinguish between freedom of opinion and freedom of political expression, between politics in general and party politics.[119] In the name of "promoting good comradely relations" among the staff, the men were forbidden to agitate on behalf of political parties inside police premises, while they were still assured of complete freedom to express their political views. Propaganda leaflets could not be distributed, nor political posters displayed, but every official was allowed to bring party literature inside police buildings as private reading material.[120] The result of such awkward if not inconsistent instructions was that the political tone in each police unit was often determined by the personal predilections of the officer in command.

The defects of the political interpretation of democratic police work may largely account for its frequent substitution with a legalistic approach. This approach was based on the practical experience that policemen preferred to be told where the enemy stood, and that they would just as soon know that an order was founded on legal right rather than that it was politically judicious.[121]

Yet the legal directives for the police could be as imprecise as the political rules were confusing. Every rookie was taught to respect paragraph 10, II, 17 of the Prussian General Code of 1794, but this law merely obliged the police

> to institute the necessary measures for the maintenance of public order, safety and peace, and to remove the dangers threatening the public as a whole or individual members of it.[122]

When, after long debate, a revised version of this definition was introduced in the Police Administration Law of 1931, the powers of the police were made more flexible still. Article 14 provided that

> 1. The police must take all the necessary measures permissible under the law which *in its estimation* [italics mine] conform to its prescribed duty of removing [those] dangers to the community or to individuals which threaten public security and order.
>
> 2. In addition, the police must fulfill the particular tasks that are incumbent on it by special laws.[123]

In emergency situations, when routine law enforcement

yielded to the exigencies of riot control, the legal powers of the police could thus easily be made to cover a wide range of practical applications. In the eyes of the Communists, it gave the police unlimited license to intervene against the organized masses of the working class, since "where ordinary mortals find no trace of danger, the police likes to see a gigantic public menace."[124] The Nazis, conversely, pitied the republican Schupo for its paralysis under a legal system that told it to protect public order but could not explain precisely how.

> The police [in the Weimar period] was faced with numerous paradoxical situations. . . . Like it or not, it was often reduced to the passive role of the spectator. Whenever it did decide to intervene, its action, though legally incumbent on it, was answered with the worst of calumnies.[125]

The tenuous help that in extraordinary situations the average Schupoman could derive from the legal ideas of his government may account for the fact that an official commentary to paragraph 14 of the Code of 1931 used this practical argument to recommend its usefulness:

> The stipulation that the police should act according to its own estimation of its duty-bound obligation is important only in regard to what the police must do. It is intended to protect the police authorities from excessive damage suits should it occasionally fail to apply what objectively would have been the best way of removing a public danger.[126]

The perennial street violence in the last years of the Republic often left its police chiefs no choice but to subordinate the ideal of the supremacy of the law to considerations of combat efficiency. Time and again, legal distinctions between common lawbreakers and political criminals were shown to be useless when facing the practical problem of clearing unruly crowds from a public square.[127] At the scene of political rallies, policemen on duty were hard put to respect the organizers' house right to evict hostile intruders, and yet to intervene should the latter abuse their privilege and precipitate a brawl.[128]

The difficulty of teaching democratic ways to the republican Schupo can finally be observed in the repeated attempts in the twenties to equate democracy simply with popularity. Popularity did not mean, as in the days of 1848, close affinity with the people or a constabulary recruited from the local inhabitants. It merely referred to the need for public approval and support, which the police must earn through courteous and efficient law enforcement as much as through well-designed uniforms, public concerts, charity balls, and other means of furthering public relations.[129]

The highlight in the overall campaign for public sympathy was the Great Police Exhibition of 1926. Severing thought this event important enough to postpone his resignation as Prussian Minister of Interior by several weeks in order to attend its opening session.[130] An official publication, issued shortly afterward, candidly explained that the aim of the exhibition was to give encouragement to those among the public who were beginning to see in the police more than an inconvenient authority, here only to admonish and tutor. It was supposed to demonstrate the rapprochement of police and public which had followed the defeat of the monarchy. The success of the exhibition was measured in terms of the 50,000 people who visited the fairgrounds at Kaiserdamm. Evidence of a consequent growth in the Schupo's popularity was found in the fact that in the Christmas season of 1926, toy shops in Berlin for the first time sold dolls dressed in policemen's uniforms.[131]

Popularity acquired by dint of a one-sided appeal for recognition was at best a derivation of democratic conceptions of police service. The desire of the police for public trust did not, for example, persuade it to provide its patrolmen with service

numbers worn on their uniforms.[132] And attempts to improve
the image of the police among children produced the following
draft for a school text:

> Many people dislike the very word "police." They are not good
> people. They fear the police. Such people unfortunately exist.
> You have surely heard about [such] disreputable characters:
> burglars, thieves, and murderers. Why, only recently one of them
> murdered a little girl. . . . Surely, the villain must be caught.[133]

Frightening children into desiring the protection of the
police was joined with an invitation to wish for comparable
authority when they grew up.

> The Schupoman is king of the street. . . . Everyone obeys his
> signals. I may want to become a Schupo too. . . . Have another
> look at the Schupo. See the many people he gives his orders to.[134]

A tone of wishful make-believe could be detected in the
statements of contemporary government officials who praised
the political loyalty of the uniformed police. Carl Severing and
Wilhelm Abegg were thanked prematurely in 1929 for having
"inculcated the Schutzpolizei with a spirit of absolute loyalty
toward the Republican state.[135] Exaggerated cheer went into a
report on the Schupo's salute to the constitution in 1924:

> Bright sunshine radiated over Berlin when, on August 11, the
> Berlin Schutzpolizei celebrated Constitution Day at the Schloss-
> platz. Lampposts, trees, and terraces were bedecked with red-
> black-golden flags, the latter increasingly accepted as a symbol
> of a rejuvenated German national pride and not of the German
> Empire's collapse. . . . We regret that similar events did not take
> place in the Schutzpolizei during the last few years.[136]

The police chiefs of 1924 were closing their eyes to the
political indifference in the rank and file, just as they were to
discount the importance of the Nazi element in the police in the
years to come. There were more loyalty parades, but these

could not strengthen the republican sentiments of the average patrolman. There remained the threat of disciplinary action against disloyal policemen, but could the government punish severely those who failed to learn what it could not teach?

Subversion and Security Checks in the Schutzpolizei

The Berlin Police Presidium waited for cases of subversion to be brought to its attention by the routine reports of local officers or incidental acts of denunciation. It went on the assumption that an antirepublican police official would soon be recognized by his immediate entourage. This assumption was correct, but not the expectation that disloyal officials would be promptly denounced. The Schupo's esprit de corps mitigated against subordinates informing on officers. Commanding officers, in turn, preferred to deal personally with the men who opposed the regime, provided they did not happen to share the same political views. As to denunciations coming from the public— many times anonymous or from a suspicious source—they were readily disbelieved at the Presidium unless the preliminary investigation produced strong corroborative evidence.[137]

The political police (Department IA) did not possess a special office to fight subversion in the armed police until January, 1932. But Regierungs-Assessor Dr. Schnitzler, who was then put in charge of the new "Dezernat 4," could not be expected with his team of eight men to do more than keep track of the latest Communist leaflets turned in by obedient policemen. The IA still lacked the means for a systematic surveillance of the police staff, or a large-scale hunt for defectors. As in the past twelve years, it had to apply a haphazard method of investigating each case when and where it turned up.[138]

While the political investigators were understaffed, the disciplinary courts of the Presidium were generally lenient. More often than not, policemen with unwelcome political views were simply transferred to a different post where they were less likely to give offense. A study of about twenty political cases involving Schupo officials between 1920 and 1932, suggests that disloyal policemen were discharged from the force only under the following circumstances:

1. If the charge involved a clear breach of service regulations, and the accused could not claim leniency on account of his professional record.

2. If there was irrefutable evidence against the accused, or if he admitted to the charges against him.

3. If the accused had openly defied superior authority or his case had attracted public attention.

4. If no police union came to his rescue.

In some instances, the police seemed inclined to squash disciplinary cases in the hope of concealing the extent of political disaffection within its ranks.

The threat of subversion in the Schutzpolizei came mainly from three directions: from the Communists, from the reactionary monarchists, and from the Nazis. Their representatives inside the police differed greatly in strength, though the severity with which they were prosecuted did not apply in proportion. There were also policemen who had no political principles at all and could be expected to abandon the Republic in a moment of crisis. But this last kind of subversion eluded the sanctions of the disciplinary courts altogether.

THE COMMUNISTS

Of the three antirepublican forces, the Communists were the ones most anxious to undermine the security police through subversion. Party agents sought to recruit "contact men" in the police at restaurants and sports fields, through common hobbies and mutual acquaintances. The purpose of such contacts was espionage: the Party leaders wanted information on the identity of undercover agents of IA and the current mood inside the riot brigades, on changes in police procedures and the location of defense installations. Since they did not expect to win over any substantial number of Schupomen, they aimed at building a network of secret cells, none of them larger than four men. The members of these "Red Schupo Cells" were supposed to balance their numerical weakness with revolutionary zeal. Thus, according to plans, they were to study Communist literature even inside police buildings in spite of the risk of detection.[139]

But did a network of "Red Schupo Cells" ever come into existence? It seems that the convocation in 1931 of a "First Reich Conference of Red Schupo Cells" was merely meant to create the illusion of disaffection inside the Prussian police for the encouragement of Communist fighting cadres. The manifesto published by *Die Rote Fahne* in 1932: "Policemen's May Day Appeal: Join the KPD!" carried twenty-nine signatures, of which only one belonged to a Berlin policeman. This policeman was Fritz Hüller, who had retired from the force twelve years before.[140] The files of the Berlin Police Presidium concerning Communist subversion, which today are kept at the Federal Archive in Koblenz, contain the names of seven Berlin policemen who were reported for alleged connections with the Communist party between 1924 and 1933. Of these seven denunciations, only two were not immediately dismissed by the investigators as quite unfounded.

It therefore seems that the Communist threat inside the police existed largely on the strength of Communist propaganda, rumors, and personal speculation. Retired Police Major Eldor Borck, in a speech on June 30, 1925, for example, "guessed" that 10 percent of the police sympathized with the KPD, but offered no evidence for his claim.[141] Police Major Eduard Kolbe affirmed in an interview in 1962 that there were Schupomen in the early twenties who belonged to the Communist party but could not cite one of them by name. Outnumbered and scorned as they were, he explained, they had made themselves unobtrusive.[142] Schupo Commander Kaupisch reported to IA in 1925, that "I very much doubt that patrolmen have been seen fraternizing with Communist demonstrators in the street. If there were KPD adherents in the police, they would surely have hidden their sympathies."[143] And Kriminal-Kommissar Wilhelm Bonatz of Department IA in 1926 questioned the existence of the "Fraternity of Proletarian Police Officials," also known as the "Communist Schupo Faction." This organization was supposed to have contributed 170 marks to the International Workers' Rescue Fund that year. But given the limited pocket money of Schupomen, Bonatz argued, this sum must have been raised by at least 300 donors. Was it likely that none of these three hundred men had betrayed his activities to the political police?[144]

The virtual absence of a Communist element in the Berlin police cannot be credited to the efficiency of its security measures. A simpler explanation is that the provincial upbringing of the average Schupoman made him unreceptive to the arguments of the Communist agitators whom he met in Berlin. On the contrary, his predilection for national-conservative notions of order and discipline were strengthened by his daily confrontation with the militant elements in Berlin's working-class districts. From the street battles with Communists throughout the twenties, the Schupo developed a tradition of ruthless hostility toward anything associated with Marxism, communism, the proletariat, or just the fifth estate.[145] This tradition was indirectly nourished by the official combat instruction in the Schupo. Technical manuals on the proper use of firearms for riot control made derogatory remarks about the Red Front, whose ranks were said to contain "the most worthless, criminal elements in society," and "rabble of the meanest sort, interested only in selfish gain."[146]

THE REACTIONARIES

The democratization of the Schutzpolizei was never endangered by the Communists, but by reactionaries in the officer

corps and—from the late twenties on—by Nazi supporters
among the local rank and file.

The reactionary officers cannot be described as conspirators. They seldom bothered to conceal their political attitude
and were neither planning to sabotage the police machine nor
to use it for a direct assault on the government. What they did
was to embarrass the Republic with their disdain for its leaders,
its flag, and its principles. They discredited the regime's efforts
to teach its policemen democracy by ostentatious nonparticipa-
tion. Their behavior rendered doubtful the government's claim
that it disposed of a reliable security police for the protection
of the capital.

It was scarcely necessary to keep the reactionaries under
secret surveillance. But it was important to treat them with circumspection. They could not lightly be removed from the force
without arousing the entire officer corps. Threatened with disciplinary action, they were liable to turn secretive and to join
the extreme right wing. Treated with tolerance, however, some
of them repaid the Republic with an unexpected show of loyalty
in 1932 and 1933.

The Stennes affair was probably the most serious example
of political disaffection by a reactionary officer in the course of
the twenties. And yet it was a perfectly typical case insofar as
it involved: (1) opposition to the Republic without a clear
alternative goal; (2) open defiance of superior authority con-
doned by the senior officers of the security police; (3) disciplinary steps taken by a reluctant government under the pressure
of public opinion; (4) the conversion of the officer, after being
disciplined, into a fanatic Nazi leader.

The "Hundertschaft z.b.V." (zur besonderen Verwen-
dung) was an elite company of the armed police. Its headquarters were at the Schlosskaserne in Charlottenburg, its mission to
support the political police in protecting the government district in major emergencies. But two public trials in November

and December, 1921, brought to light some disturbing facts about this unit and its commander, Police Captain Walther Stennes.

The first trial concerned an unexplained act of brutality committed by men of this Hundertschaft against a harmless pedestrian. On the night of February 3, 1921, one of its men, Police Sergeant Schutte, had forcefully detained a passerby in Lohmeyer Strasse, manhandled him, threatened to shoot him, and finally had taken him inside the barracks. There Schutte and a number of his comrades had beaten the man unconscious. On November 16, 1921, the policemen involved stood trial on a charge of abusing their authority and were sentenced to penalties ranging from 100 marks to three months in prison.

The second trial, one week later, concerned the murder of Police Sergeant Johannes Buchholz during the preceding summer. Buchholz had worked in the accounting office at the Schlosskaserne. Shortly before his death, Walther Stennes had accused him of embezzling 173,385 marks of the company's funds. Since the captain was unable to prove the charge, Buchholz had returned to duty after only a brief period of suspension. But, so rumor had it, he was now prepared, in revenge, to make public certain internal secrets of the Hundertschaft. He allegedly had stories to tell of clandestine payments to private political agents, of hidden arms inside the Schlosskaserne, and of a secret society, the "Bund der Ringmannen," which enforced absolute solidarity within the company by means of "honor courts" in the dead of night. On June 15, 1921, someone went into his office and shot Buchholz dead.

The murder of POWM Buchholz was not the main point at the subsequent trial. The most prominent witnesses, such as Regierungsrat Mosle of the Police Presidium, Schupo Commander Kaupisch, and Geheimrat von Priesdorff, formerly commander of the Sicherheitspolizei and until recently inspector of the Schutzpolizei, were anxious first and foremost to establish a political bill of health for the entire Hundertschaft.[147] They insisted that it had proven itself as an "outstanding fighting force" and "thoroughly loyal to the republican government." But their testimony carried little conviction. Priesdorff described PHWM Meyer, the chief defendant at the trial, as a "glowing patriot" in spite of being a "mercenary type." Kaupisch explained that the confidential agents of the Hundertschaft had merely spied on potential conspirators against the Republic whose continued employment Police President Richter at any rate had already forbidden.[148]

The commander of the Hundertschaft, Walther Stennes, by then suspended, was also put on the witness stand. A former free corps leader in Westphalia and an ardent nationalist, he was known to have defiantly flown the old imperial colors from the Schlosskaserne on public holidays. He had once boasted that he commanded the allegiance of the Hundertschaft to the point that "When I am no longer their leader, the men will turn into criminals." During the Kapp putsch in the preceding year he had sided with the rebels. The government had not taken him to account at that time, but now this braggadocio who "disposed of armored cars, flame-throwers, machine guns and light artillery" in the heart of Berlin began to cause public concern. A search party of Schupos and IA men, which the government dispatched to seize the secret store of arms at the Schlosskaserne was kept at bay with machine guns until Commander Kaupisch personally arrived and ordered the men to surrender.

"This act of defiance is the clearest proof that the Hundertschaft z.b.V. is a menace and not a protection for the Republic," wrote the *Berliner Tageblatt* on December 3, 1921. While the two police sergeants who were accused of murdering Johannes Buchholz were acquitted for lack of evidence, the Police Presidium did not reinstate Stennes in his command. He resigned from the police on February 28, 1922. Shortly thereafter, Severing disbanded the Hundertschaft z.b.V. (its place was taken by

Polizei-Abteilung Zentrum) using the assault on a pedestrian in Lohmeyer Strasse as his pretext.[149]

(The Stennes affair had a curious aftermath. Stennes first tried a job in industry and then the Reichswehr, finally he joined the S.A. By 1927, he was in charge of combat training for Hitler's party soldiers throughout northern Germany. He led a short-lived mutiny of the Berlin S.A. in the late summer of 1930, which resulted in his expulsion from the NSDAP in April, 1931. Immediately afterward, Goebbels's *Angriff* denounced Stennes as a spy for the secret police. His only evidence, it seems, were letters that the retired police captain had written to two secret supporters of the Nazi movement inside the Reichswehr and the Schutzpolizei: his correspondent in the police was PWM Gildisch, whose case is mentioned below. These letters had fallen into the hands of the political police during a raid at Nazi headquarters on February 12, 1931. Stennes sued the *Angriff* for libel and easily won his case, since Goebbels had obviously called him a police spy merely to discredit the discovered documents.)[150]

The Stennes affair was followed by other incidents liable to undermine the Schupo's reputation as a defender of the Republic. There was Police Major Alfred von Majewski, commander of police inspection Charlottenburg in 1927 and 1928, who infuriated the liberal press with his obvious indifference toward Nazi outrages on the Kurfürstendamm. "We don't care what [Majewski's] political views are," wrote the *Vossische Zeitung* on May 13, 1927, "but if he will not resolutely perform his duty when radical elements of the right are involved, he should be moved to a less responsible job." Majewski was transferred, after a year's delay and more public protests, but only to a teaching post at the Higher Police School at Eiche near Potsdam, which in the Schupo amounted to a handsome promotion. But then the Presidium may have tried to manage him on account of his prominent role in the Prussian Police Officers' Association.[151]

It was even more tolerant toward Police Colonel Otto Dillenburger. Dillenburger was in command of police region East in 1928, and therefore responsible for the breakdown in police discipline in the spring of that year which resulted in a number of serious clashes with Communist demonstrators. In one of these street encounters on June 2, 1928, Deputy Police President Weiss was assaulted by a policeman in Frankfurter Allee. Following a lengthy investigation, the Police Presidium decided to remove Dillenburger from the service. Dillenburger appealed to the Prussian Police Officers' Association and won his reinstatement, albeit to a post in Oberhausen. After that victory, the colonel resigned from the force, ran for election as first chairman of the officers' union, and from this vantage ground, began a protracted feud with Minister of Interior Severing. He notably gave his support to like-minded officers in the Schutzpolizei, such as Police Major Levit.[152]

Quite apart from his political views, Levit was not a capable officer. But he attracted public attention when in 1931 he ordered the arrest of a group of civilians for loudly cheering the Republic and the Prussian Prime Minister Otto Braun in the vicinity of the government district. What Levit later defended as the strict enforcement of the Bannmeile laws, was generally viewed as an intentional slight to the government's dignity. There followed an interpellation in the Prussian Diet. Levit was suspended from the police. But Dillenburger interceded on his behalf in an open letter to Severing in which he charged that the minister was victimizing police officers in the interest of his party. Dillenburger and the Prussian Police Officers' Association won this round too. Levit's punishment was changed to transferral to a new post in Gleiwitz.[153]

It is easy to criticize the Ministry of Interior and the Police Presidium for their readiness to compromise with the conservative officers. Concessions gave the appearance of weakness and did not prevent Majewski, Dillenburger, and Levit from applying for membership in the Nazi party at the first opportunity after January 30, 1933. On the other hand, the policy of the government may well have prevented serious unrest inside the police officers' corps and a coalition of discontented officers with that radical minority in the lower ranks who secretly helped the Nazi movement well before Hitler's seizure of power.

THE NAZIS

The strength of the Nazi supporters in the Berlin Schupo can approximately be put at between 200 and 300 men. At the Berlin Document Center, there are forty-eight reports written by local S.A. leaders of various Berlin districts in December, 1934, giving the names of all locally known Schupomen who in the Weimar Republic had sympathized with and supported the Hitler movement.[154] There are, in addition, the letters of Berlin policemen who in 1933 requested promotion or other forms of compensation for their past services to the National Socialist cause. The total number of Nazis identified by name in these documents is 216 men.[155]

This figure cannot be regarded as accurate. Careful checking is difficult because the S.A. leaders sometimes misspelled a policeman's name or identified him by the wrong police unit. Some of the informers, eager to claim many converts to the cause, may also have inculpated patrolmen whose Nazi sympathies were no more than lukewarm before 1933. On the other hand, there is no telling whether some S.A. lists have not subsequently been lost, and whether more names were not withheld by inadvertance, negligence, or because of personal rancor. Most policemen who were interviewed for this study thought that there were at least as many Nazi policemen as there were policemen who were purged in 1933, yet the official purge list for the Berlin Schupo ran to 445 men.[156]

A conservative estimate of the Nazi inroads inside the security police seems nevertheless advisable since the 216 names on file include many policemen whose behavior can scarcely be construed as sabotage of the republican government. PH Koblin of police station 13 was listed as a sympathizer because "though he expressed himself with circumspection, no one was left in doubt about his inner disposition." POWM Otto Sievert of police station 32 was given credit merely for "observing a perfectly neutral attitude toward S.A. men, and in several instances meeting them halfway." POWM Nippold, who later headed the Nazi organization of Schupo officials (NSBAG) in Berlin, was praised for having greeted S.A. men in the streets of his precinct "although he risked being recognized."[157]

There were policemen whose right-wing sympathies made them neglect their duties when Nazi lawbreakers were involved. POWM Otto Stascheit of police station 127 failed to take part in an attack with truncheons against Nazi demonstrators who were angrily objecting to the American film version of *All Quiet on the Western Front* (1930).[158] PH Andrees ignored several occasions when he could legally have arrested Nazi pickets during the strike of public transportation workers in 1932.[159]

A practical service that Nazi policemen often rendered local S.A. units was the discreet tip-off on impending police operations. In addition, there were police captains who ordered S.A. prisoners released instead of sending them on to headquarters at Alexanderplatz and then turned in false reports. Others sent their men to clear an area of Communist street gangs well knowing that Nazi terrorists would soon take their place, and they pacified riotous political rallies by evicting only the opponents of Hitler.

The Nazi supporters in the police were also those who circulated the *Völkischer Beobachter* inside police stations. Occasionally one of them would pass out Nazi leaflets on the beat, or stick propaganda posters on house walls at night. One sergeant in Neukölln gave food to unemployed storm troopers, and two officials of police station 8 took shelterless Nazis into their homes after their S.A. dormitory was closed down by the political police.[160]

But Schupomen who went that far in aiding the Nazis were

rare. POWM Matzke of police station 214, who gave combat training to the storm troopers of Berlin-Britz, was such an exception,[161] and so were PL Kurt Lange and POWM Hans Schulz-Briesen, who in 1932 wanted to betray the location of defense installations inside police barracks to the Nazi headquarters in Berlin.[162] These men, however, were not necessarily dedicated National Socialists. They belonged to that group of misfits, grumblers, and political adventurers whom Dr. Johannes Stumm judged the natural prey of Nazi subversion in the Weimar police. An example was Police Master Albert Becker, who had been with the royal constabulary since 1905, and after the war had found himself overtaxed by the exigencies of modern police work.[163] Another was PWM Kurt Gildisch, a young East Prussian, who joined the Berlin Schupo in 1925, and whose record at police-inspection Mitte was marred by "his terrible carelessness and his liking for drink." Becker was removed from the police in 1929 and Gildisch in 1931 because of their support of the Nazi party. Gildisch spent the next few months as a Nazi thug terrorizing political opponents in the street, then he joined the S.S. (Schutz-Staffel).[164]

POWM Otto Linthe of police station 87 was the only National Socialist in the files of the Berlin Document Center about whose sincere dedication there can be no doubt. He openly joined the Nazi party in December, 1925—when such membership was still permitted to policemen—and was fired in 1926 when the Presidium learned that he was leading an S.A. troop at Alexanderplatz during his off-duty hours.[165]

The existence of Nazi cells inside the Schupo during the last five years of the Weimar Republic cannot be denied. But their number was not very large in relation to the size of the force, and many Nazi supporters did not go beyond a token show of agreement with the aims and principles of National Socialism. To the average policeman, his Nazi colleagues seemed harmless enough. Did it really matter if a few sergeants repeated the hackneyed phrases of Nazi newspapers over a glass of beer? Was the Republic endangered when some Schupomen chanted the "Horst Wessel" song on their way to the shooting range?

Here, of course, the average policeman was mistaken. The Nazis inside the Schupo did constitute a security risk because they spread mutual suspicion inside their units, provoked passionate quarrels, and drove the more timid into political unobtrusiveness.

This was particularly the case in areas of high political tension like Prenzlauer Berg and Friedrichshain. To be sure, the largest number of Nazi adherents listed in the S.A. reports of 1934 were found in the city districts where the Communist party was weak.[166] In Spandau, one of the earliest bastions of the NSDAP in Berlin, police stations 141 to 145 were dominated by Nazi sympathizers by 1933, and so were many police stations in Wilmersdorf, Schöneberg, and Steglitz. In the precinct stations of police-inspection Mitte, conversely, the Presidium took special pains to weed out right-wing extremists like PWM Gildisch and to place reliable Social Democrats. But in the working-class areas, which after 1927 were hotly contested by Nazi and Communist gangs, the political feud in the street spread to the staff of the precinct police. Here the supporters of Hitler were opposed by another minority of militant patrolmen who were alarmed by the growing hegemony of the S.A. commandos within their district and disagreed with their superior's liberal policy toward political dissenters in the police. These anti-Nazi officials often joined the Social Democratic party and the Reichsbanner Black-Red-Gold. They blackmailed Nazi supporters with threats of denunciation and insulted them in the hope of provoking them to commit breaches of service rules. In the territory of police-inspection Friedrichshain where, after 1929, the Communist housing defense corps was challenged by Horst Wessel's Troop 34 of Standarte V, and where POWM Emil Kuhfeld was killed in 1931, the precinct staff of police stations 82, 85, and 88 was divided into bitterly hostile factions. Politically irresolute captains like PH Fränkel at police station 85 were unable to maintain discipline over their men.[167]

The government knew what was happening inside its police staff but refused to take decisive action. In September, 1930, when a restaurant waiter was reported for boasting that fourteen officials of police-inspection Friedrichshain belonged to the Nazi party, the investigators of Department IA were satisfied with mere denials by the policemen in question, even though the circumstantial evidence and the gossip of their comrades indicated that the waiter's allegations were true. The IA restored the image of republican loyalty within this inspection by simply threatening the waiter with a suit for slander unless he withdrew his statement.[168]

The Schutzpolizei in Action: 1920–1932

Throughout the Weimar Republic, the foremost task of the Berlin Schutzpolizei was to protect the city from the chronic threat of political chaos in the streets. Hence at the Great Police Exhibition of 1926, equipment for riot control was prominently on display, and in communications to the press, the police stressed the excellence of its training program as a safeguard against civil war.[169]

The technical problems of containing the smoldering violence at thousands of political rallies did not in themselves cause the eventual defeat of the Schupo. Its failure by the summer of 1932 must rather be attributed to political exhaustion: the security police, with all its strength in men and equipment, did not withstand the corrosive effect of a war in which final victory was not allowed, and every engagement served to prepare the next. Obliged to apply the minimum in coercion for the maintenance of public security and order, and to respect in each rioter a misguided fellow countryman "acting from the highest motives," the police seldom held the initiative. The two extremist camps kept the police off balance by alternating between peaceful parades, scattered acts of terrorism and armed assaults; by switching from attacks on each other to attacks on neutral citizens, from mutual destruction to joint defiance of the law. If the Schupo was tolerant and allowed political crowds the freedom of the street, it was blamed for the ensuing disorders; if it intervened with clubs and guns, there were cries of provocation and militarism. Twelve years of this game left the policemen frustrated and resigned, tired of being put in the wrong, and ready to accept a fundamental reform in the political system.

Of the two chief opponents, the Communists alone treated the police as the inevitable enemy. It made no difference if its commander was Police Major Haupt or the more liberal Police Major Heimannsberg: the Schupo was *"a voluntary army of mercenaries* in the service of capitalism" which cannot be won over and must be disorganized and defeated.[170] Fortunately, so the Communists argued not without some justice,

> No police force is invincible. The police can only hold out against a disunited opponent who scatters his strength. It will never fight to the last man because it lacks an ideal. The policeman is doing a job. In the face of danger he will not make an ultimate sacrifice. A part of the leadership will also change sides if the opponent will give it a chance.[171]

Even the "special cars" of the government force were useless, the Communists said, in the hands of irresolute men. Besides, "an opponent who knows the qualities of the armored cars will not let their harmless and wasteful bang-bang [Geknalle] affect his morale." Only because the Communist cadres still lacked the military capacity for open insurrection were guerilla attacks by small groups of men the call of the moment.[172]

The Nazis, in contrast, were never preparing for open conflict with the armed police. Unlike the Communists, they lacked the massive support of a well-defined segment of the Berlin population and could not stage an uprising in one or more parts of the city.[173] Joseph Goebbel's *Instructions to the S.A.-Man* (1927), therefore, explicitly laid down that

> At the present time, all resistance against the police and the state is senseless, because you will always be weaker than they. No matter who is right, the state has the power to retaliate against you and the Party with prison sentences and heavy fines. When there is no other way, therefore, submit to superior strength and merely remember that one day the time of reckoning will be here.[174]

Insofar as the Nazis were planning armed action against the police at all, they were not thinking of guerilla war or insurrection, but of a putsch. They could be expected to move in the event of a crisis in which the government had already lost the confidence of the police and a surprise raid on all police installations in the city promised to meet no organized resistance.[175]

This explains why throughout the period under study the Nazis limited their struggle with the police to evasive tactics and propaganda. It also helps to explain their ultimate victory in the street battle for Berlin. For the Schupo's weakest point was in its political armor. It knew how to deal with an opponent who challenged it to open combat, but it could not tackle an enemy who fought with the "art of deception and the virtue of perseverance."[176]

The Communist propaganda war against the police had no prospects of success. It ranged from unlikely appeals for support ("Schupo officials! Your place is also in the ranks of the Red class front!"), and crude promises of "higher pay, the right to organize, work, bread, and freedom" in a Socialist Germany, to simple threats and shouts of defiance:

> We do not fear the thunder of the cannons,
> We do not fear the green-clad street police![177]

The National Socialists understood the mind of the patrolman much better. Nazi speakers gave the Schupomen credit for
their patriotism and discipline. They addressed them as fellow
Germans whose potential soldierly qualities, alas, were shame-
lessly exploited by unscrupulous political bosses. For every
policeman who beat a storm trooper, they claimed, there was a
good cop who was ashamed of being used as a "Zörgiebel-Cos-
sack." Led by officers who gave senseless orders and set them
against patriotic citizens, it was no wonder that policemen on
escort duty deserted their charges whenever danger drew
near.[178]

The insinuations of some Nazi writers that policemen
lacked courage in political encounters cannot be substantiated
in fact. There is no evidence that the Berlin Schupo of the twenties and early thirties ever flinched from physical combat, even
when it was vastly outnumbered.[179] Whether its qualities as a
fighting force were judiciously applied is, of course, another
question.

On the basis of newspaper accounts from 1920 to 1932, the
Schupo's fight to hold down the extremist forces in the streets
of Berlin can be seen to fall into five separate stages.[180]

STAGE ONE: POLICE HEGEMONY, 1920-1925

During the first five years of this period, the Sipo and its
successor, the Schutzpolizei, were in sovereign command of the
entire city. The Spartacist troubles of 1919 were over, there was
inflation and the Communist uprisings in Central Germany
(1921) and Hamburg (1923) produced no more than diversion-
ary incidents in the capital. Large-scale police raids in September and October, 1920, netted quantities of military weapons
illegally retained in civilian hands since the end of the war.[181]

The return of external calm in Berlin was founded on the
strength of its security police whose ranks, by 1921, already
counted 14,000 men. The police kept all political manifestations

under strictest control. Open-air rallies had to be cleared forty-eight hours in advance; permission for indoor meetings was difficult to obtain. On January 15, 1921, the second anniversary of Karl Liebknecht's and Rosa Luxemburg's murder, a large procession of Communist workmen moving from the Lustgarten to Brandenburg Gate was easily turned back with rifle shots fired by one Schupo officer and five sergeants.

From this position of strength, the government could afford to lift the ban on public demonstrations whenever it thought it desirable. The Berliners were encouraged to give vent to their outrage at the Allied peace terms in May, 1919; in January, 1923, they were allowed to show their anger at the French occupation of the Ruhr area.[182] In anticipation of the elections to the city parliament in September, 1921, Police President Richter invited representatives of political parties for a discussion of joint security measures at electoral meetings.

There was only one serious clash between the police and political crowds during the first half of the 1920's. On January 13, 1920, large numbers of workers from the northern districts of Berlin marched on the Reichstag to voice their discontent with a new law concerning factory councils. To avoid incidents, the Sicherheitspolizei kept most of its men in the periphery of the Königsplatz and only posted small guards at the gates to the Reichstag. At 4:00 P.M., the demonstrators tried to force their way into the building. Some of the Sipo guards were disarmed and manhandled. Their comrades fired warning shots and the workers started a full-scale assault. The reserve units of the Sipo then closed in on the Königsplatz, using machine guns and hand grenades. The police lost one dead and fifteen wounded; civilian casualties were estimated at twenty dead and about one hundred wounded.[183]

"January 13" left a deep imprint on the Berlin police for years to come. When Kurt Fleischer joined the force a few weeks later, he found his new comrades still cursing their officers for having ordered the counterattack so late. On returning to the barracks that night, they told him, the men who had guarded the Reichstag had wept like children over their humiliation at the hands of the rabble. Their bitterness toward the radical left was boundless.[184]

Though simple policemen in 1920 may have seen defeat in the encounter of January 13, the position of the police was actually stronger during these years than it was to be during the whole remaining period of the Republic. Police President Ernst gave public praise to the Sipo for its "unshakable calm and circumspection under very trying circumstances, as well as for its energetic intervention at the proper moment." Ten thousand marks was collected by the grateful Berliners for the families of the Sipo's casualties. Still remembering the Spartacist scare of the previous year, few inhabitants felt aroused by the use of grenades and machine guns against unarmed civilians. A strong police seemed to them the best way to prevent the recurrence of civil war.

Changing rules on the use of firearms, incidentally, can give some indication of the city's security problem from year to year. In January, 1919, when the constabulary was rearmed with pistols, its men were strictly ordered to use their guns only for the protection of their own person when under attack. This restriction was suspended on December 15, 1921, presumably so that the newly formed Schutzpolizei could use its firearms more effectively against hostile political masses. The police wanted to be at liberty to open fire without waiting for insurgents to shoot first, and not be hampered as they believed the Paris police had been hampered in the French revolutions of 1830 and 1848.[185]

STAGE TWO: THE EMERGENCE OF NEW FORMS
OF PUBLIC DISTURBANCE, 1925-1926

The second stage lasted about two years. In the course of

1925 and 1926, the threat of insurrection in Berlin's industrial districts gave way to three different types of security problems: rowdyism in the streets, unemployment, and habitual violence at political meetings. The police strove to develop suitable responses to each of them, with varying degrees of success.

On Sunday, August 9, 1925, the Kurfürstendamm experienced its first outbreak of terrorism. Weekend strollers were insulted and jostled by small bands of nationalist hoodlums wearing swastika armbands. One pedestrian who wore a republican badge on his coat was so hard pressed that, in fear of his life, he drew a pistol and killed one of his assailants. The disturbances continued intermittently for another three days until strong police patrols were finally sent into the area.

The troublemakers at the Kurfürstendamm were not insurgents whom police troops could round up and put down with arms. They mingled with pedestrians in the shopping district and disappeared at the approach of police reinforcements. Perhaps it was not apparent that these young rowdies were introducing Berlin to a novel form of revolutionary action: sowing insecurity among the general public to undermine its confidence in the existing regime. Yet the passivity of the local police —police station 157 in Nestorstrasse took no action until the pedestrian who had shot in self-defense went there to make a report—had already created the desired effect.

Youthful hoodlums on the boulevards of Berlin's posh West were one phenomenon. Another was the appearance of the permanently unemployed. This problem the Berlin Schupo handled with greater success. Serious clashes in the summer of 1926 between police and jobless workmen served as a timely warning that conventional police methods were out of place in this situation. Unemployed workers, the police quickly learned, were not militant fighters. Long-service men from the precinct force could deal with them better than riot police patrolling with carbines. The Schupo's adroit managing of those who were out of work paid off in subsequent years when in the world economic crisis looting broke out sporadically and the Nazis and Communists agitated among the men outside the employment agencies. The KPD organized hunger marches with chants of "Down with police dictatorship!" (March 20, 1931), but there were no serious encounters between the police and the unemployed. To the dismay of the Communists, off-duty patrolmen collected money for public relief and fed undernourished children in the police canteens. "The policemen know what hardship our hungry people are suffering," said Minister Severing at the funeral of Police Captain Anlauf on August 18, 1931. "They have often donated part of their meagre income to help feed the unemployed. They deserve some thanks."[186]

Most important, 1925 and 1926 brought the beginning of regular violence between the adherents of the KPD, the NSDAP, and—at that time also—the Stahlhelm and the Socialist Reichsbanner Black-Red-Gold. In the late evenings when excited groups were returning home from various political meetings, the opponents flew at each other with flagpoles and bicycle chains, brass knuckles and knives. Bodily assault and manslaughter among political enemies became a daily item in Berlin's police reports.

The police at first responded with a decree banning the possession of any weapons, including sticks, by participants of political rallies (February 16, 1926).[187] They also made truncheon charges into each melee, trying to bring in the ringleaders. But this procedure could not be applied indefinitely. At the Wilhelmplatz in Charlottenburg, on January 27, 1926, the riot policemen jumped from their trucks several times to clear menacing crowds from the square, but as they had moved on, the masses closed in again. Violence was not averted that night.

The Schupo next introduced escorts for participants at political rallies, but that was a thankless job too. Police escorts would be attacked by their own protégés if they tried to prevent them from picking fights with political dissenters. At the Police Presidium, there were discussions about separate routes and different points of assembly so that hostile parties would find no opportunity for physical encounters.

The balance of these two years (1925, 1926) brought new problems and the need for new countermeasures. But the police leaders were still confident enough of success to invite the International Police Congress to meet in Berlin. The Communists, in the meantime, had lost their earlier militancy toward the police. The large RFB rally at Whitsuntide, 1926, was peaceful. Three months later, at a pacifist rally in the Lustgarten, the chief of the German Communist party, Ernst Thälmann, personally shielded Deputy Police President Friedensburg against the more unruly among his followers.

STAGE THREE: RADICALIZATION,
MARCH, 1927 TO APRIL, 1929

The third stage began ominously with a short but extremely violent battle between Nazis and Communists at the railway station of Lichterfelde-Ost. This affray cut short the preceding period of reforms and of a steady improvement in the public image of the Berlin police. Caught off balance by the sudden sharpening in political warfare, the Schupo responded with intermittent acts of brutal repression. The actions of the police in turn split the political factions in Berlin into two camps: one camp was ready to eschew all organized violence for the time being; the other sought ways to confuse the lawmen with elusive attacks by small groups of terrorists.

The fight at Lichterfelde-Ost on March 21, 1927, broke out when a trainload of S.A. men on their way home from Trebbin jumped on the platform and stormed a railway carriage occupied by twenty-three uniformed Communists. The local precinct police and a flying squad from Lichterfelde were in no position to intervene against the 600 to 700 screaming S.A. men.

The engagement was over by the time riot police from inspection Steglitz could appear on the scene. The Nazis, flushed with victory, formed in marching columns outside the railway station to enter the city on foot. They roamed the neighborhood of the Kaiser Wilhelm Memorial Church in Charlottenburg and assaulted Jewish-looking persons on the Kurfürstendamm. Some storm troopers boarded subway trains at Wittenbergplatz and terrorized the passengers. Throughout the evening, the police remained virtually inactive.

Albert Grzesinski, who was then Prussian Minister of Interior, immediately recognized that an incident of this gravity could quickly undo the Schutzpolizei's work of the past few years. Hunting the ringleaders of this outrage and punishing incompetent local officials was not enough to restore the image of a Berlin nearly recovered from the aftermath of revolution and civil war. The unhindered rampage of one Nazi battalion had raised fears of an uncontrollable outbreak by the entire Berlin S.A.

But Grzesinski's concern was not limited to the Nazis. He saw a trend toward more violence in the general political climate of Berlin. He ordered the Schutzpolizei to tighten its watch over the Communists as well as the Nazis. As it happened, the Communists were the first to experience the tougher policy of the Schutzpolizei.

Feeling themselves the innocent victims of Nazi brutality, the KPD wanted to organize protest marches immediately after the attack at Lichterfelde-Ost. But the police was in no mood to allow any provocative demonstrations. On March 22, 1927, it routed a Communist protest march on the Wilhelmplatz in Charlottenburg. A police officer shot one of the demonstrators in a scuffle, causing a general tumult. The Communists ran for cover amid fleeing streetcars and automobiles, while Schupo detachments heightened the panic with more shots and charges in extended lines. This time there was none of the "calm and circumspection" that the Sipo had shown on January 13, 1920.

A similar breakdown in self-control took place the following year. On May 26, 1928, policemen tried to hold up Communist marchers in Bismarckstrasse to allow cross traffic from Krumme Strasse to pass over the intersection. They spliced the procession just where the musicians were marching. The band tried to keep together, some bandplayers broke the police lines and ran into motor traffic, and the police charged. An officer fell to the ground and another officer gave the order to shoot. A woman and a child were wounded, and a Communist workman was killed.[188]

The toughness of the police was uncalled for, especially since the Communists, anxious to avoid a government ban of their party,[189] had shown much restraint. After the shooting on Bismarckstrasse, KPD functionaries even met with police officials to see whether together they could manage traffic problems in the future. The police leaders, however, saw in such cooperation proof that their new policy was bringing results. Their faith in strong methods was seemingly justified by the disciplined behavior of the crowds on May Day, 1927, and May Day, 1928, at the dreaded "Stahlhelmtag" (War Veterans' Day) of May 8, 1927, and during sympathy marches for Sacco and Vanzetti not long afterward. But then trade union affairs were not given to violence; the veterans, who for the most part came from the provinces, were intimidated by the hostility of the Berlin workers, and Berlin, unlike Paris, did not care very deeply about the two American anarchists.

The Schupo's excessive show of strength at the scene of orderly political demonstrations did not improve its prestige. The needless shooting of Communist marchers brought public questions as to whether the police was not degenerating into a simple combat force. The enormously expensive security precautions at the Stahlhelmtag and for the parliamentary elections in May, 1928, gave the impression that the police lacked self-confidence. At a political parade on February 5, 1928, for example, there were more armed police escorts than there were marchers. The 2,300 demonstrators were surrounded by 3,500 Schupos who drove back onlookers on the sidewalks with systematic baton charges at five-minute intervals.[190]

Some police officers began to see the harm of showing the Schupo's strength to excess. There were several experiments with "invisible police" techniques: at a mass rally all security units except essential traffic personnel would be held at a discreet distance and the public allowed to come and go without passing controls. This method worked very well at a protest meeting for Sacco and Vanzetti (August 25, 1927), and at a Communist rally on April 19, 1928.

Neither massive intervention nor keeping the police out of sight worked, however, against the growing wave of terrorism perpetrated by adherents of the extreme right. Following the skirmish at Lichterfelde-Ost, the police president of Berlin had banned the NSDAP in the capital (May 5, 1927). But this ban could not prevent the recurring outbreak of individual acts of terrorism against political dissenters and Jewish pedestrians in the area of the Kurfürstendamm. Nor did the police president succeed in making the police deal more effectively than before with outbreaks of hooliganism of this kind.

Between March, 1927, and April, 1929, the republican Schutzpolizei had faced its first major test and proved ill-prepared for serious disturbances. It had tried to regain lost ground by punitive measures to the detriment of its standing among the public. The government then sought to relax the tension by rescinding the shooting order of December 15, 1921. On July 14, 1928, the Ministry of Interior once more instructed Schupomen to use their guns only to defend their own lives, to protect persons in their immediate charge, or to prevent the escape of prisoners. They were forbidden to shoot at children under any circumstances. Direct fire was always to be preceeded by warning shots.

STAGE FOUR: THE WAR AGAINST THE RED FRONT,
MAY, 1929 TO MAY, 1930

The police found it difficult to adhere to this restrictive shooting order when the political violence in Berlin, from 1929 on, assumed the proportion of regular civil war. Nervous policemen were found to use warning shots too soon and with disastrous results just to clear the way for direct fire in case of a sudden attack. The KPD persistently violated a police ban on open-air demonstrations which was in force since shortly before Christmas, 1928. In April, 1929, Communist demonstrators began to resist the police with stones when it tried to disperse illegal assemblies. Then, shortly before May Day, 1929, the Communists seemed to go on the offensive. On April 30, small attacks erupted all over Berlin. Hundreds of RFB men and Young Spartacists would suddenly converge on an intersection, overrun the patrolmen on duty, and disperse before the flying squad could come to the rescue.

The Communist attitude toward the police was stiffening. But, as the agents of Department IA noted in their reports, the KPD officials were instructing their followers not to provoke the police on May Day and not to fight unless the police resorted to violence first.[191] The police could have avoided the fighting that broke out May 1, 1929, had it allowed open-air demonstrations of the Communist party to take place as in previous years. But Schupo Commander Heimannsberg had orders to enforce the ban under all circumstances. He therefore mobilized his forces for a major emergency.[192] By the evening of May 1, full-scale fighting was raging between riot police and Communist inhabitants in parts of the Scheunenviertel, and in several blocks around Kösliner Strasse in the Wedding, and

Hermannstrasse in Neukölln. Barricades went up and martial law was proclaimed in the fighting area. Police station 220 was besieged by insurgents.[193]

It was the worst civil strife since 1919, except that its outcome was never in question.[194] The insurgents could not match the riot police in numbers since most of the workmen in Berlin did not take part in the fighting. There were peaceful KPD meetings in other parts of Berlin where speakers hailed the "five thousand comrades who at this hour are battling the police in the streets of our city," at the end of which their listeners quietly went home.[195] On the second night of the fighting, the police had to break off an attack with armored cars in Hermannstrasse, because the street suddenly filled with hundreds of peaceful Neuköllners coming out of a movie house.

The Communists also lacked arms. Subsequent interrogations of suspected barricade fighters by IA indicated that the great majority of them had fought with stones and knives and other improvised weapons.[196] Of the fifty-one wounded policemen, only one suffered a bullet wound.[197] A typewritten report entitled "Some Lessons of May First," allegedly found by the police during a search of the KPD main offices on February 18, 1930, demanded better rifle drill for Communist marksmen since "not one of them had hit a policeman in the course of three days of fighting."[198] The authenticity of this document may be open to question, but not the overwhelming superiority of the Schupo in men and equipment.

The Schupo's obvious superiority was the cause of much public criticism in subsequent weeks. When the battle was over on the evening of May 3, the twenty-five dead were either insurgents or innocent bystanders.[199] The victims included noncombatants who had not left the shooting zone fast enough or had misunderstood a police order.[200] The police duly investigated each case, but invariably refused to accept responsibility on the grounds: (1) that the identity of the policeman who fired the fatal shot could not be determined; (2) that the victim had taken unnecessary risks; or (3) that the police bullet had not been fatal, and that death may have been caused by disease.

A committee of prominent citizens—including Heinrich Mann, Carl Ossietzky, and Professor Emil Gumbel—set out to examine the performance of the Schupo during the May events. In its report, it deplored the excessive violence of the police troops who, to quote Grzesinski speaking in the Prussian Diet, had fought with "exceptional enthusiasm." Not one policeman had reported sick during the whole operation, not one had refused to carry out his orders.[201] Inside the police barracks, a veritable war psychosis had reigned.

> An order to proceed to Wedding or Neukölln immediately evoked the idea: we're off to the war! Once arrived at the "battlefield," the policemen behaved accordingly.[202]

Die Polizei devoted much space in its subsequent issues to evaluate the technical performance of various police equipment, with no apparent concern for the tragedy of the recent bloodshed.[203]

The Schupo's easy victory in Wedding and Neukölln gave it the illusion of strength. After May 6, 1929, when the Rot Frontkämpfer Bund, the Rote Jugend Front, and the Rote Marine were banned throughout Prussia, the police twice invaded the central offices of the Party on the Bülowplatz, and on January 31, 1930, took seventy-six leading Communist functionaries into custody on the unlikely suspicion of planning another uprising. On March 27, 1930, the *Vossische Zeitung* reported that the KPD had received orders from Moscow to abandon its overt fight against the representatives of the bourgeois state.

The Communists abandoned their struggle against the police and turned on the followers of the Nazi party. Several serious clashes between the two enemy camps took place in September and December, 1929. The political passion on both

Before the First World War. Military parades dominated the street picture.

Before the war. Constables of the royal Schutzmannschaft.

Members of the short-lived Sipo, Unter den Linden, 1920.

Left: The Police Presidium at Alexanderplatz after the Spartacist uprising, 1919.
Right: A Sipo patrol, 1919.

Schupo Commander Magnus Heimannsberg.

The Kapp putsch, 1920.

Armored car manned by loyal policemen during the Kapp putsch.

Schupo Commander Hugo Kaupisch during an inspection tour.

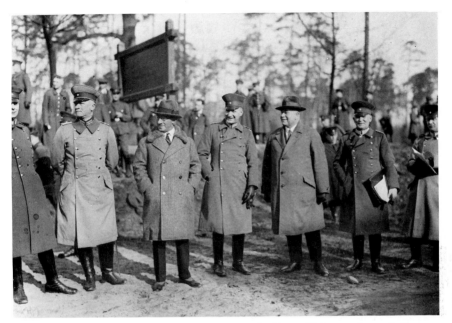

From left: Pol. Oberst Gotze, Dr. Weiss, Pol. Oberst Heimannsberg, Police President Zörgiebel, and Pol. Oberst Haupt.

Dr. Weiss and Commander Heimannsberg with police athletes.

Minister of Interior Severing opening the Second Police Exhibition, 1929.

Deputy Police President Dr. Bernhard Weiss.

Krim. Kom. Ernst Gennat. (Photograph courtesy of Frl. Grete Bomke.
Caricature courtesy of Amerika-Gedenkbibliothek, Berlin.)

Der Täterich flieht an der Spitze,
„Tennag" folgt mit großer Hitze.

Es enteilen rasend schnelle
Diese beiden von der Stelle.

Erst ganz hinten in der Fern
Nahn die beiden andern Herrn.

Above: The Schlosskaserne, Berlin-Charlottenburg.
Below: Mounted police guarding the Reichstag, 1930.

Above: Police restraining crowds on Hindenburg's birthday, October 2, 1927.
Below: Police escorting Communist May Day parade.

Police escorting Nazi parade.

Communist insurgents in Berlin-Neukölln, May, 1929.

Above: Police attacking Communists, Berlin-Neukölln, May, 1929.
Below: Schupos intercepting Communist agitation team, 1932.

Above: Armored police car at Bülowplatz, January 22, 1933.
Below: Police protecting S.A. demonstration at Bülowplatz, January 22, 1933.

Above: Outside the main Communist headquarters on Bülowplatz shortly after the murder of Anlauf and Lenck, August 9, 1931.

Below: Funeral of Horst Wessel, March 1, 1930.

Monument to Police Captains Anlauf and Lenck on Bülowplatz (Horst Wessel Platz), 1934.

sides reached a climax when S.A. leader Horst Wessel was murdered by Communists on January 17, 1930.

The police meanwhile tried to resume its role as the arbiter between the extreme right and left. It tried a new tactic of searching political assemblies for arms long before any encounter with dissenting elements could occur. But the recent battle with radical workmen had affected the political climate inside the Schutzpolizei: most of the secret Nazis in the uniformed police date from this time.[204] The Berlin S.A., which had never taken up arms against the police, became something like the Schupo's unofficial ally. The men of police station 111 in Berlin-Kreuzberg, for example, saw in the presence of Goebbels's headquarters within their territory a welcome assurance of S.A. support in case of more Communist disturbances.[205]

STAGE FIVE: THE ANTI-NAZI CAMPAIGN,
AND THE BREAKDOWN OF POLICE SECURITY,
1930 TO 1932

In the last two years of SPD rule in Berlin, the Schupo finally took up the challenge of the National Socialists. The official ban in Greater Berlin having been lifted on March 31, 1928, the Nazi party had steadily grown in strength while the police had dealt with the traditional enemy on the left. But before the anti-Nazi campaign could produce results, the Communists made the mistake of hitting the police from behind: they killed four law officers in rapid succession. The resulting uproar took the edge off the anti-Nazi campaign. The police was henceforth more inclined to let Nazis and Communists fight out their quarrels among themselves. The terror in the streets of Berlin, in turn, created a crisis of confidence in the police. It ended in the overthrow of the Social Democratic government in Prussia.

The necessity of taking steps against the Nazi movement in Berlin arose from a series of outrages that neither the public nor the police could ignore. To name but a few:

On May 16, 1930, twelve S.A. men chased a Communist news vendor at Innsbrucker Platz and trampled him to death.

On October 14, 1930, following the electoral victory of their party, Nazi hoodlums roamed the business district between the Reichstag and Potsdamer Platz, molesting pedestrians, smashing the windows of department stores, and shouting "Deutschland erwache," and "Juda verrecke!"[206]

On November 23, 1930, fifteen men from S.A.–Sturm 33 (Maikowski) carried out a gun attack against members of a workers' social club who were holding a dance party at the Eden Palast in Charlottenburg.

In December, 1930, the Nazis organized wild demonstrations against the pacifist movie *All Quiet on the Western Front*. There was a serious clash with police on December 8.

Several Nazis killed two members of the Reichsbanner in a random attack in Hufelandstrasse on New Year's Eve, 1930.

There was a lull in the Nazi attacks while the struggle between the police and the Communists briefly flared up again. But

The Nazis went on another major rampage on the Kurfürstendamm on September 12, 1931.

On January 19, 1932, about 150 Nazis attacked the allotment gardens of Felseneck which were known as a Communist stronghold. Two persons were killed.

On May 31, 1932, the anniversary of the naval battle of Skagerrak, there were riots when the Nazis tried to crash into the forbidden zone of the government district.

In view of this state of affairs, the police decided on a number of measures to curb the spread of rowdyism in Berlin. The rules on the sale of hand guns and the possession of other lethal weapons were made stiffer during 1930 and 1931. New rules on open-air rallies were drawn up to facilitate their control by the police. On June 12, 1930, Reich Minister of Interior Waentig ordered a ban on Nazi uniforms. Nazi restaurants (Sturmlokale), and S.A. dormitories were placed under tighter surveillance. Some were closed down completely, others were forbidden to open in the evenings. Even the party offices of the NSDAP in Hedemannstrasse were no longer a sanctuary. On April 3, 1932, Schupomen pursued a group of Nazi thugs right inside the building after observing them assault two Reichsbanner men in the street.

Two large-scale raids on Nazi strong points in Berlin took place in 1932. They proved that the police was capable of striking quickly and effectively if it wanted to, and that in the face of determined steps by the police, the Nazis were not ready to fight.

On March 17, 1932, the police rushed sixty S.A. bases to forestall a possible coup d'etat from the right.[207] On April 14, 1932, when Reich President Hindenburg dissolved the S.A. and S.S., the entire political police and a large part of the Schupo went immediately into action. Beginning with the home of S.A. leader Helldorf and working their way down to the local S.A. dormitories, motorized detachments of Schupomen and plainclothes detectives drew up at two hundred different places, impounded documents and party paraphernalia, sealed the doors, and placed them under guard.

But the police campaign to reduce Nazi terrorism in Berlin had also encouraged the Communists to retake the offensive. They staged the usual attacks on Nazi processions and tried to mobilize the masses of unemployed workmen against the police. And then, within a short span of time, four policemen were shot dead during clashes with Communist demonstrators.

On May 29, 1931, PHWM Paul Zänkert of police station 72

(Prenzlauer Berg) was killed at Senefelder Platz when he tried to stop a Communist assault on a group of Stahlhelm men. One month later, on June 30, 1931, POWM Emil Kuhfeld was shot down at the head of his flying squad when he tried to disperse several hundred Communists gathered in Frankfurter Allee.

Both deaths caused much commotion in the police and in the city at large. Zänkert's funeral in Hasenheide was attended by Police President Grzesinski and thousands of Berliners. Kuhfeld was given a "funeral such as no police sergeant has ever had. . . . . This was Berlin's protest against the terror in the streets."[208]

The Communists may not have intended to kill the two policemen. There is even the possibility that they were not responsible for the death of Kuhfeld at all.[209] But there can be no doubt but that the shooting of police captains Anlauf and Lenck on August 9, 1931, was murder. The local precinct police around Bülowplatz had been subjected to Communist threats for the last few weeks. The victims were shot from behind as they went on an inspection tour of the neighborhood; a third police officer who accompanied them was wounded. For three hours following the ambush, a gun battle raged around the nearby offices of the Communist party, which the police finally occupied. One hundred police detectives were assigned to hunt down the killers, and 3,000 marks was posted as reward for information leading to their apprehension.[210]

The killings of policemen stopped. But the unrest in Berlin continued to simmer. In the spring of 1932, three consecutive electoral campaigns within a span of fifty-two days required 183,000 sorties by armed Schupo officials.[211] Then, on June 14, 1932, the federal government decided to revoke the ban on Nazi uniforms.

There was an immediate resurgence of violence. In Moabit the Communists called the workers to arms and began with the building of barricades. Every available vehicle of the Berlin police was out on patrol. In the midst of threatening chaos,

Nazi deputies in the Prussian Diet accused the police president and the Schupo commander for alleged graft and incompetence.

Police President Grzesinski offered the *Vossische Zeitung* an interview on July 8, 1932. As though he sensed the imminent end of a historical era, he reviewed the last twelve years of struggle for the control of Berlin. According to him, the three-cornered fight between Communists, Nazis, and the police had been relatively subdued until the Communists had tried to eliminate the police from the fight through the individual murder of several policemen. Their stratagem failed to produce the expected result, but in the ensuing lull, the Nazi movement penetrated into formerly Communist sectors of Berlin. The political war then resumed with the Nazis this time bent on undermining the police, Grzesinski explained. By fanning the war in the streets, they wanted to prove the incompetence of the Schupo. Their motive, Grzesinski thought, was clear enough: Goebbels had never made a secret of his resentment that the police in Berlin had for so long been ruled by the SPD.

There was a note of resignation in the police president's brief account. Though he assured his interviewer that Berlin was not in a state of civil war, he admitted that the police was down to its last reserves. Even young and inexperienced rookies had now to be posted for difficult security tasks. There was no chance for order in Berlin, he concluded, as long as the warring factions would not renounce violence and murder as political arguments.

The republican police capitulated on July 20, 1932. That morning, an article entitled "In the Service of the People. A Salute to the Unknown Schupoman" appeared in the *Vossische Zeitung*, extolling the quiet courage of the riot policemen. A few hours later, the police was taken over by the commander of military district III, General Gerd von Rundstedt, and the democratic experiment of the Weimar police in Berlin had come to an end.

IV | The Detective Force

Public Opinion on Crime and the Criminal Police

In the 1920's, unlike in previous periods in the history of Berlin, the public was extraordinarily well informed in matters of crime. The immediate postwar years in particular gave the most casual observer ample opportunity to watch the evasive tricks and reckless daring of peddlers in narcotics, women, and stolen goods. At the "Kakadu," the "Esterhazy-Keller," the "Goldene Spinne," and the "Kolibri Bar," a habitué of Berlin's night life knew himself in the proximity of organized crime, but found in this less a cause for fear than a source of added titillation. Some people from the better classes even went out of their way to explore Berlin's most dangerous quarters around Schlesischer Bahnhof.[1] "The romantic appeal of Berlin's underworld was irresistible," wrote the young actor Klaus Mann about his trip to the capital in 1923, fascinated by the wickedness of its inhabitants.[2]

The daily press contributed its share to magnify the villainy of these years. The newspapers reported in detail the affair of the "Countess Colonna," a common sneak thief with social pretensions who appealed to the irreverent mood of her time;[3] of the impudent master burglars Emil and Erich Strauss;[4] and of the hotel thieves Paul and Willi Kassner, whose dexterity in climbing walls gave rise to romanticized legends and cheap magazine stories.[5] Sensational accounts of automobile traps (heavy cables strung across deserted country roads outside Berlin) led to a craze for faked holdups invented by chauffeurs and frivolous party girls to cover up minor delinquencies.[6] Even as sober a newspaper as the *Vossische Zeitung* offered its readers verbatim the exclamations heard by witnesses at the scene of a crime. Deputy Police President Weiss, who knew of the complaints of "pedantic idealists" on this score, tried to soothe their outraged feelings with assurances that crime reporting was worse in the United States, in France, and in Austria.[7]

Murder cases were more apt to shock the public into serious concern over the moral state of the nation. There was Friedrich Schumann, who in 1920 was tried for eleven murders and thirteen attempts at murder, rape, and arson.[8] The following year brought the arrest of Karl Grossmann, who admitted to killing and mutilating twenty-three women in his home in Berlin-Friedrichshain.[9] The name Fritz Haarmann evoked a mixture of horror and incredulity; and the "Schoolboy Tragedy in Steglitz" of June 27, 1927, despondency and compassion.

The Steglitz affair was a story of youthful promiscuity, parental neglect, and desperate adolescent yearning for a noble purpose in life.[10] Paul Krantz and Günther Schelling, pupils at the Oberrealschule in Berlin-Mariendorf, had decided to murder Günther's sister and her boyfriend, and subsequently to kill themselves. Günther did shoot his sister and then committed suicide, but Paul sobered in time and failed to carry out his part of the agreement. His subsequent trial on a charge of complicity in murder filled entire pages of the daily press. There were attempts to exploit the affair for political purposes: Krantz had belonged to a German-National group who had supplied him with a revolver. The German Nationalists, in turn, used his case to campaign against current projects of school reform. But "the true defendant at this trial was the moral climate of the times," wrote Pem a quarter century later. "The circumstances of the murder . . . were less important than the accusation against the changed world in which we all lived."[11]

Two observations must be made at this point. Political crimes drew hardly more attention than common crimes during the twenties. "Political crimes in these years were thought to concern only a small number of initiates," commented Dr. Johannes Stumm in an interview several decades later. Many people relegated outrages such as the assassination of Foreign Minister Rathenau or the murder of traitors within the ranks of extremist parties, to the incomprehensible world of power struggles. Common crimes, however, gave expression to the problems of the ordinary man in the street. Moreover, insofar as the public after 1918 was searching for a new set of heroes to worship or execrate, it was not particularly fastidious. A prizefighter and a film star stood as good a chance as the Communist leader Max Hölz, or the jewel thief of the Tauentzienstrasse.[12]

It must further be noted that there was comparatively little interest in knowing the individual motive of a criminal, or in learning about modern police work. Few German detective stories described elaborate plots and intricate procedures of investigation.[13] The readers of crime stories wanted accounts of daring feats, of iconoclastic breaches in traditional social norms, or macabre tales of demented sadists. If they were at all moved by a general concern for law and order, they turned to scrutinize the overall record of the criminal police.

The Kriminalpolizei, or Kripo, was known to Berliners largely through the reputation of a number of detective inspectors. The police leaders of the Weimar Republic encouraged references to their successful officials in news bulletins. They gave permission to those who wanted to publish popular books and articles on their experiences in the service.[14] This policy fell into desuetude around 1930, when the Kripo came under increasing attack, and it was finally suspended by Police President Melcher in October, 1932. But while it lasted, it did achieve its purpose of familiarizing the inhabitants of Berlin with the activities of the detective force. It went together with other efforts to enlist public interest in the work of law enforcement. The Great Police Exhibition of 1926, Kripo Fairs at the Luna-Park, and conducted tours at headquarters for Charlie Chaplin and Heinrich Mann are but a few examples that come to mind.[15]

An atmosphere of mutual trust was considered essential to speed up the investigation of unsolved cases. Beginning in August, 1919, the press was immediately informed of all capital crimes in the hope that members of the public might come forward with useful clues.[16] Rewards were posted for information leading to the arrest of fugitives from the law. Warrants for the apprehension of suspects were projected on movie screens during intermissions, and, in one gruesome instance, a shop window in Alexanderplatz displayed objects collected at the scene of a murder.[17] If we add to all these measures the work of the Kripo's consulting office for crime prevention, or the public lectures given by detectives in schools and municipal halls, we must conclude that the police, while serving the public cause, contributed substantially to the general knowledge in matters of fighting crime.[18]

Knowledge and trust, however, did not always go hand-in-hand. For example, the large-scale raids that the Kripo tried for two years after the war were too conspicuous to evade general comment. Dozens of plainclothesmen supported by large detachments of soldiers or uniformed police would suddenly surround several blocks in the city and take hundreds of suspects to headquarters for questioning. Yet their success was questionable from the beginning. These raids could not make up for the absence of regular patrols in centers of perpetual lawlessness.[19] In fact, black marketeering, illicit gambling, and plain pilfering could not be stamped out as long as the economic condition of Germany did not return to normalcy. As a method of fighting common criminality, police raids were almost completely abandoned after 1920. Subsequent dragnets were staged mainly against troublemakers of the political sort.[20]

The record of the Kripo in the twenties was the more difficult to gauge as the public tended to credit instances of success to the talent of individual inspectors and to charge failures to the whole apparatus of the Kriminalpolizei. There were raised eyebrows because the thousands of marks offered for the recovery of stolen goods did not discourage the activities of the organized gangs of burglars.[21] There were jeers of derision when the Kripo failed for months to track down a lone criminal, or when the evidence it produced in court proved insufficient to secure the conviction of defendants whose guilt was apparent to all. The high esteem enjoyed by Police Councillor Ernst Gennat, or Detective Inspectors Ludwig Werneburg and Erich Anuschat, did not diminish the readiness of the public to find fault with the overall achievement of the criminal department. While particular villains and individual police agents were measured with a sporting sense of vicarious adventure, the Kripo as an institution was judged in the light of each critic's own political predilection.[22]

The detective force of the Police Presidium in Berlin was, after all, an executive organ of the republican government. Its collective opponent was not held to be the sum of criminal elements in the city, but the general state of political and social distress following Germany's defeat in the war. Defiance of the law was associated with unemployment, revolution, and national despair. It was understood as a social phenomenon that invalidated many conventional measures of criminal responsibility.[23]

A city councillor in 1923 found in "starving children in front of bakeries and streets filled with destitute men and women" a natural explanation for the daily crop of suicides, robberies, and murders.[24] This may explain why, in times of acute hardship, crowds in the poorer quarters of northern and eastern Berlin spontaneously shielded ordinary thieves from arrest.[25] But while there were officials of the criminal police who understood the social cause of resentment against the police, few of their fellow citizens were willing to concede that the failures of the criminal police could partly be traced to lack of public support.

Needless to say, the detectives of the political police fared worse than their cousins of the Kriminalpolizei. The inclination of the public to exculpate offenders against society applied even more to the political delinquents after the war. The agents of Department IA, moreover, were naturally forced to operate with greater discretion than detectives working on common crimes and therefore could do little to further their reputation. Preventive police work to forestall attacks against the state could not benefit from publicity, Regierungsdirektor Wündisch explained in a newspaper article in 1926. The population could not be asked for help unless the police could tell it what crime had been committed, the circumstances of the crime, and the possible suspects.[26]

Of course, this rule would not apply to investigations of political crimes that were already committed. But while the names of IA investigators were not kept secret during the Weimar Republic as they were under Hitler, their achievements were not publicized as much as those of Kripo detectives. The newspapers brought terse announcements of changes in the directorship of the department, or briefly mentioned the detective inspector in charge of a given case. Thus, Kriminal-Kommissar Mühlfriedel was reported for his part in apprehending the perpetrators of a series of bomb outrages in 1929; Kriminal-Kommissar Teichmann for finding the murderers of Horst Wessel in 1930; and Kriminal-Kommissar Dr. Stumm for testifying

before a commission of inquiry of the Prussian Diet on the notorious "vehme murders" in the Black Reichswehr, in 1926.[27]
But none of these officials acquired popular stature.

The public did not readily accept the political police as a
necessary and desirable institution.[28] The functions of IA were
often thought to be as redundant and oppressive as press censorship and police control of domestic servants, vestiges of au-
tocracy which were abandoned in 1918. The security police had
ample opportunity to demonstrate its importance for the defense of the established order. The preventive work of IA, however, had no visible results while its success in bringing in
terrorists failed to give comfort to the average citizen. Schupo
officials who lost their lives in the line of duty were not popular
figures, but they gave evidence of devotion and sacrifice. IA had
no casualties known to the public at large.[29]

The political police, consequently, was the only branch of
the executive force which had to justify its work to the public. It
sometimes came close to apologizing for its existence. Leading
police officials explained that the multifarious and unpredictable
character of Germany's postwar society made policing more
necessary than under the monarchy.[30] They pleaded that while
the security problem before 1914 had merely called for a routine
surveillance of Socialist literature and events, the new situation
harbored uncounted new sources of danger in many quarters.
Yet the police leaders also took pains to assure the population
that the political police worked within the same legal limits as
its predecessor before the war. They defended the use of undercover agents and informers as indispensable, and hastily added
that most of IA's intelligence consisted of voluntary tips from
the public.[31]

When the political police was called to investigate an attack with air gun pellets against two school girls in Schönlein-
strasse (Berlin-Kreuzberg) on January 1, 1932, it found that the
shots had come from a Communist restaurant across the street.

Rumors had circulated for some time that the father of one of the victims was a secret informer for the political police. IA denied the truth of this allegation, but conceded in its report that believing a local resident to be a police spy was an understandable motive to commit a crime.[32]

The political police, finally, sought refuge in repeated assurances that it was nothing else but a regular detective force specializing in political crimes as others specialized in narcotics or homicide. Its agents, the public was told, were trained to work under the same legal rules and the same principles as other officials of the Berlin presidium.[33]

The stories of Department IA and Department IV (Kripo) were, indeed, interdependent in many ways. Their staffs were recruited from the same set of candidates; they used the same technical facilities; and they often shared in the same investigations. As the crisis of the Republic deepened toward the end of the twenties, their cooperation became more frequent. They need to be studied side by side as we search for the causes of dissension and disaffection in the intelligence staff of the Berlin police during the last years of the Weimar regime.

The Kriminalpolizei in Search of Professional Autonomy

The history of the Berlin criminal police before 1918 is irrelevant to an assessment of its quality during the Weimar Republic. Crime detection had been a specialized function within the police department since 1811, but police detectives remained subordinate to the uniformed constabulary until 1872. The criminal police was not even recognized as an independent institution in the code of criminal procedure (Strafprozessordnung), or in the constitution of law courts (Gerichtsverfassungsgesetz) of the Second Empire. In fact, it still went under the vague designation of "safety police" (Sicherheitspolizei).

The modern era of the criminal police began in January, 1919, when Oberregierungsrat Hoppe undertook the reorganization of the entire department.[34]

After the war, the Kripo had every reason to underline its separate existence from the uniformed street police, whose collapse during the days of November it had no desire to share. The criminal police, in contrast to the Schutzmannschaft, believed that it could stand aloof from the political upheaval in 1918. The armed sailors who fought skirmishes with robber bands during those winter months were not likely to assume the role of criminal investigators.[35] It was equally implausible, later, that the soldiers of the Sicherheitspolizei would replace the Kripo as an institution to combat individual crime. The detectives of the criminal police were in fact rearmed only ten days after the fall of the monarchy.[36] At their headquarters in Alexanderplatz and in the various district offices throughout Berlin, the Kripomen continued with their routine duties as if nothing had happened.[37] Not even the capture of the Police Presidium by Spartacists on January 4, 1919, caused the Kripo to interrupt its work. The men of the homicide squad, who were investigating the murder of a postman at Hotel Adlon, searched the premises with their accustomed thoroughness and ignored the sound of battle drifting in from Pariser Platz and Wilhelmstrasse.[38]

Undoubtedly, the incompetence of Erich Prinz, Eichhorn's dubious chief of detectives between November, 1918, and January, 1919, had caused much confusion inside the detective force.[39] These months of unrest brought several cases of corruption by city detectives, normally a rare occurrence in the Berlin police. There had been even more concern when Eichhorn abolished the Prussian political police, and plans were set to assign its former duties to the criminal police. High treason, subversion of friendly countries, violations of the constitution, betrayal of military secrets, insurrection and incitement to insurrection were in the future to fall under the jurisdiction of the ordinary detective force.[40] But a protest meeting of criminal policemen in Berlin on December 5, 1918, adopted a resolution demanding that ordinary detectives not be "misused" for political work, and that, to ensure the Kripo's political neutrality, its directors should come from the ranks of experienced criminalists.[41]

Both demands were immediately granted by Eichhorn, and later police presidents abided by his decision. Deputy Police President Weiss, for one, always wanted to spare the criminal police "the kind of public abuse which no political police can escape." He therefore insisted that the political police, when it was reconstituted, should not only prevent attacks against the state but also undertake the prosecution of political criminals after the deed, a task that in some other countries fell in the province of the judicial police.[42] And in 1923 the Prussian Ministry of Interior issued a decree whereby professional criminalists, in addition to administrators with legal training, could be appointed as chiefs of Department IV.[43]

In January and February, 1919, while a new political police was being formed, Kripomen were still used to hunt former Police President Emil Eichhorn and Karl Radek, the elusive agent of the Communist International.[44] After the summer of 1919, however, they were given a number of years to devote themselves mainly to the fight against common crime.

The Kripo took full advantage of this spell of freedom, so that the 1920's became a period of much fruitful experimentation and reform. Between 1919 and 1927, fingerprinting and ballistic tests were introduced, a new homicide inspectorate and a female criminal police corps were set up, and an institute for police science was founded in Charlottenburg. Most important, on June 1, 1925, the Prussian State Criminal Office (Landeskriminalamt, or LKA) was opened in Berlin, to standardize Kripo techniques in all the provinces and to serve as a clearinghouse for information on criminal activities through subordinate Criminal Police Posts (Landeskriminalpolizeistellen, or LKP's). Its chief function, of course, was to maintain liaison with similar offices in several other German states.[45]

The creation of the Prussian Criminal Police Office, an important innovation in the history of the German police, gave rise to considerable comment in professional circles. It is interesting to note, though, that these comments rarely took up the political issues involved. Instead, they stressed the need for fast communication between local detective forces in the twentieth century, and spoke of past difficulties in tracing two such killers as Sternickel and Haarmann across state boundaries between 1905 and 1924.[46] They also emphasized the obvious value of having the LKA's serve as national centers for the collection and dissemination of vital police data. The Berlin office, under the new plan, managed the central fingerprint record for the whole Reich and kept track of all cases of forgery, crimes on express trains, holdups of bank tellers, white slavery, and pornography. Munich took charge of gypsy affairs, and Dresden specialized in the search for missing persons and the identification of unknown bodies.

What commentators like Willy Gay did not explain was that the assassination of Walther Rathenau in 1922 had given the main impetus to the plan, and that its association with the Law for the Protection of the Republic had led to political complications between Berlin and the South German states.[47] Gay also disregarded the fact that the German Criminal Police Commission, which met in Karlsruhe in 1925 to work out the final details of the project, was mainly interested in expediting the prosecution of crimes against the security of the state. But, as Dr. Weiss knew only too well, professional criminalists strenuously opposed the combination of criminal and political police work, "as if a moral taint could fall on them as a result of such contact."[48] Their obduracy as well as the particularism of the state governments, made it finally necessary to limit the competence of the LKA's to common criminal affairs, although standardization and centralization were most urgently needed to suppress political terrorism.[49]

The unwillingness of the Kripo to involve itself in political affairs kept it aloof from Department IA as long as it could. The Kripo contended that political police work was irreconcilable with the objective standards of professional criminalists. A Kripo inspector held a personal mandate to conduct an investigation to the best of his ability and in accordance with clearly defined rules, so the argument went, while the official of the political police had to submit to ever-changing directives emanating from political superiors. Kripomen in the twenties, with such notable exceptions as Emil Klingelhöller and Dr. Rudolf Braschwitz, usually refused to transfer their services to the political division of the Police Presidium.[50] Detective Inspector Togotzes likened the relationship between his department and Department IA to that between two commercial rivals. No Kripoman who volunteered for political duty would be welcomed back to the fold, he said, any more than an employer would rehire a clerk who had gone over to the competitor. Though separated by only one flight of stairs in the sprawling brick building at Alexanderplatz, the staffs of Department IA and Department IV preferred to go their own way. "The people upstairs did not exist as far as we were concerned," recalled Fräulein Bomke, for many years a stenotypist for the criminal police and fiercely loyal to her former superiors.[51]

The impressive size of the ordinary detective force—some 2,360 officials in 1932, compared with about 300 officials in the political police[52]—gave it an immediate advantage over its competitor. The political police could not afford to maintain as many specialized services as the Kripo. It depended on the latter for the use of its crime laboratory and its training facilities. On the other hand, IA's numerical weakness also allowed it to demand the help of ordinary detectives in sudden emergencies, or when it simply lacked the manpower for the daily accumulation of political cases.[53]

Teams of Kripo experts helped in the preliminary investigation of extraordinary cases such as the murders of former Reich Minister of Finance Erzberger (August 26, 1921), and Foreign Minister Rathenau (June 24, 1922).[54] Lower-ranking officials of the Kripo were enlisted to sift through the many tedious complaints of alleged police brutality at political demonstrations, or to help in the painstaking hunt for the instigators of street battles between Nazis and Communists. Sometimes the enlistment of Kripo aid was justified by the uncertainty as to whether or not a crime was inspired by political motives. But on all these occasions, the Kripomen worked under the specific instruction of IA officials, free from the full professional responsibility that they would normally assume in criminal cases.

The permanent state of political tension toward the beginning of the thirties brought to an end the Kripo's cherished immunity from political duties. One hundred and forty detectives took part in a raid on the headquarters of the Communist party on February 18, 1930.[55] In January, 1932, the Kripo posted agents on the premises of Berlin University to spot political troublemakers.[56] Shortly thereafter, the whole staff of the Kripo "voluntarily" stood by to support the men of Department IA during the elections of March and April, 1932.[57]

By that time the Kripo had lost its illusion that it could permanently stand aside from the political task of its colleagues in the Berlin police—IA or, for that matter, the uniformed Schutzpolizei. For during the troubles in May, 1929, armed detectives in civilian clothes had been assigned to support the Schupo in regular street combat against barricade fighters in Kösliner Strasse.[58]

Prior to 1929, the Kripo had not often been drawn into the Schupo's security work. It enjoyed a fair independence from the street police since it maintained its own permanent posts distributed throughout the city.[59] Its staff, furthermore, had grown sufficiently large since the end of the war to undertake ambitious operations—involving hundreds of officials—without Schupo support. The Kripo, admittedly, was dependent on the Schupo for motor transportation in such an event.[60]

The Kripo cooperated with the Schupo in the routine surveillance of congested public places and in riot control. The rules called for plainclothesmen of the Kripo or IA to interrogate prisoners and witnesses during civil commotions, and to supervise all house searches.[61] There were also the regular contacts arising from the fact that precinct policemen were usually the first to arrive at the scene of a fresh crime.[62] But the detectives managed to keep the upper hand on most of these occasions, if only because the Kripo inspectors normally outranked the Schupo officer on the scene. This one-sided advantage of the civilian officials, as well as their ready assumption that detectives did a higher form of police work than patrolmen, was apt to create some resentment among their colleagues in uniform. There were Schupo officers who refused offers of positions in the criminal police on the grounds that the "clean and soldierly atmosphere" in the Schutzpolizei was better than "consorting with informers from the underworld."[63] Needless to say, the Kripo remained unruffled in its claim to intellectual and social superiority.

The Kripo of the Weimar Republic no longer as before the war drew its staff so largely from veteran patrolmen.[64] Former precinct officers who had taken general courses in detective duty and the rules of criminal procedure could be found in the "simple service" and "intermediate service" ranks after 1918, but they had few chances of promotion to detective inspector. The officials who staffed the "upper service" and the "higher service" ranks came from well-educated social circles.[65] They bypassed the subordinate ranks and applied directly for the qualifying examination as candidates for the rank of detective inspector. They all had to possess a secondary school diploma (Abitur), a good number had attended several semesters at the university, and some possessed academic degrees.[66] The few inspectors who still hailed from the royal police, and who had risen from the lower ranks without the benefit of an advanced education, found themselves out of place in the company of younger men trained for the liberal professions and whose family traditions, but for the war, would have destined them for more prestigious careers than police work. They also found themselves at a disadvantage in the competition for personal recognition and professional advancement.

Specialization was a precondition for success.[67] It required from an inspector participation in advanced courses on criminology and police science. Yet all the important courses that the police school at Eiche, or the Kripo headquarters in Berlin, introduced during the twenties were designed for the academically trained staff of the upper-service ranks. The Police Institute in Charlottenburg, which was opened on September 1, 1927, was established to keep leading officials abreast with the latest progress in criminal science "by means of courses taught on the university level."[68]

To a few officials of the Kripo, therefore, the threat to their cherished professional autonomy hardly came from the Schupo or IA as much as from the state attorney's office. Legally, the state attorney's office of the supreme court in Berlin was the supervising body in all criminal proceedings, and as such entitled to issue instructions or to intervene in other ways in the work of the criminal police. Kripomen, like all police officials, were in theory auxiliary agents (Hilfsbeamte) of the judiciary.[69] But in practice the subordination of the Kripo to the state attorney's office was de jure rather than de facto. The state attorney's office did no more than draw up the indictment at the end of a police investigation.[70] In 1927 Police Councillor Gennat noted with satisfaction that although technically speaking, the state attorney's office or the criminal court is doubtless the real authority in any criminal prosecution . . . as far as Greater Berlin is concerned, I am pleased to say, the criminal police is granted full independence in the investigation of the factual circumstances of a case.[71]

There was no reason why the judiciary and the criminal police should have seriously disagreed, except in technical details, seeing that both worked on the basis of the same legal code.[72] And yet some Kripomen nursed the suspicion that the state attorney's office aimed to subordinate the Kripo and dispose over its personnel.[73] (If that should happen, a councillor of the Berlin state attorney's office Dr. Friedensdorf mused in 1929, there might be fewer acquittals in court.)[74] The Kripo's spirit of independence was recognized by outsiders, but not always regarded as wise.

Success and Integrity in the Kriminalpolizei

The police detectives of Berlin were reputed in professional circles to be among the very best in Germany. They were especially strong in homicide cases. Of forty murders committed in Berlin between January 1, and December 31, 1928, the criminal police solved thirty-nine by the end of the year; and in twenty more cases of attempted murder, all the culprits were brought to trial.[75] Similarly, the homicide squads of Department IA were credited with apprehending nearly all the perpetrators of major political crimes.[76] Professional frustrations were found mainly among the detectives assigned to fight crimes against property, and—as far as IA men were concerned—those who tried to prevent general acts of civil disorders.[77] These two categories of crime, it will be noted, were precisely the kind of lawlessness which the public in the twenties was inclined to condone—unlike individual murders be they private or political.

At the same time, we must remember that the prestige of

the Kripo and IA was based on the achievement of individual officials rather than on good organization, equipment, or modern techniques.[78] This is not surprising, because the meticulous investigation of separate crimes had to be done by small teams of technical experts. There was, therefore, a premium on individual specialization that current experiments in criminology and police science only tended to encourage. Ambitious commissars staked out special areas of expertise, and if they were successful, put their personal stamp on the department, just as in smaller American colleges, professors influence the institutional structure. In the Kripo, this made for considerable diversity in procedure and achievement.

The criminal police was the substance of the Berlin Presidium's "Department IV."[79] It was organized in local and technical inspectorates. The local inspectorates (örtliche Inspektionen) were of subsidiary importance: officials who had lost favor at headquarters would sometimes be banished there. Only toward the end of our period were there plans to grant them greater autonomy.[80]

The technical inspectorates (Fachinspektionen) at police headquarters were the core of Berlin's Kriminalpolizei. There were altogether nine of them, each designated by a letter of the alphabet. Inspectorate A was charged with all cases of homicide and bodily assault; inspectorate B dealt with robberies; inspectorate C with thefts; inspectorate D with professional fraud, swindle, and counterfeiting; and inspectorate E was the name for the morals police. Inspectorate F specialized in violations of the commercial code and the law of bankruptcy; and inspectorate G (which was mainly staffed by women after 1927) took charge of children and female minors implicated in felonies. Lastly, there were two inspectorates performing essentially auxiliary services: inspectorate H, which organized the Kripo's regular patrolling service and undertook special hunts for wanted persons and goods; and inspectorate J, which was the service of identification (Erkennungsdienst, or E.D.). The E.D. was also the records department, where descriptions of known criminals were kept on file.

But the sphere of competence allocated to each inspectorate was not as clear-cut as this brief outline suggests. The particular talents of an official were repeatedly given their due. Kriminalrat Ernst Gennat's ability not only with homicide but also with arson cases accounts for the inclusion of the second category of crime in the competence of inspectorate A. (Gennat, after all, not only headed this inspectorate, but had organized it himself in 1926.) Kriminal-Kommissar Otto Busdorf's former experience as the steward of a landed estate induced his superiors to create for him an extra office to investigate the murder of gamekeepers and cases involving poaching.

Men of recognized ability were not only given individual duties suited to their capacities, but they could also extend their personal influence beyond their immediate offices. For the normal routine at Alexanderplatz brought the staff of the various inspectorates into frequent contact with one another. Men with different specialities were periodically assigned to temporary duty with inspectorate A, where they collaborated as one of its homicide teams. Experts in neighboring bureaus were consulted in tricky cases. Even the competition for the services of the best stenotypists led to part of the normal traffic between the nine criminal inspectorates.[81]

Under these circumstances, there was not enough bureaucratic formalism to subdue strong-minded and ambitious personalities. But in all fairness it must be said that a man's authority in the Kripo always depended, in the first place, on his proven ability as a police detective. Good results in important cases brought public citations, cash bonuses from the Ministry of Interior, and eventual promotion. Respect for professional attainments could induce the colleagues of a successful criminalist like Otto Trettin to allow him exceptional liberties in personal habits and sometimes even breaches in service rules.

But how was a man to make his mark in the competitive corridors of the Kripo establishment? There was not enough room in the elevated and higher service ranks to accommodate all the ambitious young men on the staff. As it was, the Kripo's policy of rewarding success with promotion resulted in a top-heavy department by the end of the twenties.[82]

Old professionals, some of whom had established themselves well before the Republic, could afford to concentrate entirely on solving individual cases from day to day and from year to year. Senior officials like Dr. Heinrich Kopp and Max Bünger were, after the war, no longer very active as investigators, but Dr. Erich Anuschat took a leading hand in various murder affairs between 1919 and 1928, and so did Ludwig Werneburg who not only headed inspectorate B throughout the twenties but also served as deputy chief in Ernst Gennat's inspectorate A.[83]

Gennat, the Kripo's great homicide expert, was himself the model of an empirical criminalist of the old school. Three years the senior of Anuschat and Werneburg, he had earned his commissar's rank as early as 1906. His legendary reputation as an investigator was founded on his extraordinary perseverance, his fabulous memory, and his keen psychological insight, which normally helped him to solve over 90 percent of his cases. His colleagues affectionately called him *"der volle Ernst"* on account of his corpulence and his great fondness for rich cakes and coffee. Popularity was not the least of Gennat's professional assets.[84]

A man like Gennat steadfastly held to the principle that every case deserved individual attention. He distrusted general theories on crime and crime prevention as deleterious to professional standards. He also disliked public controversy. Gennat never worked on political cases—he shunned the Helling case in Madgeburg (1926) whose issues had aroused strong emotions—he took no sides in theoretical disputes among criminologists,[85] and he never stood for election in his professional association or aspired to a post in the Ministry of Interior.

It was not easy for younger officials to emulate the professional aplomb of the "pure criminalists." Karl Draeger (born 1896, promoted to Kommissar 1921) who worked on homicides under Gennat, and Rudolf Lissigkeit (born 1896, promoted 1928) tried to clear up a common murder in Tegel in 1932 and a holdup of the Berlin Transportation Company in 1933, with professional disregard for the Papen putsch or Hitler's appointment as German chancellor. Yet Draeger, a young man caught up in the swirl of the twenties, had been involved in the land reform movement of Damaschke during his student days, and had briefly belonged to the Democratic party. By 1933 he had to make up for his political past by joining the NSDAP—which, incidentally, earned him his promotion to Kriminalrat. Lissigkeit, on the other hand, was defamed by the Nazis in 1932 for alleged past convictions and for being financially in debt.[86] Younger men, unlike old professionals, could not ignore the political challenge of their times, and when they tried, they risked being victimized.

Those who sought to prove themselves on the basis of their criminalistic work had to have suitable opportunities. Assignments to great cases like the Immertreu gang war of 1928–29, or the case of the brothers Sass in 1929–30, were of little use if they were handled by large teams of investigators. It was equally pointless to make one's mark in one or two cases and then be forgotten. Detective Inspectors Erich Lipik, Johannes Müller, and Hans Salaw may be mentioned as examples in point. Lipik and Müller solved the murder of Elisabeth Stangierski in 1927, a case that had baffled the Berlin police for two years. In January, 1931, Müller was assigned to the murder of Director Schmoller of the Mercedes Palast cinema, which had drawn much attention in the press and in criminological circles.[87] Finally, Lipik and Salaw together caught the public eye with a murder hunt in a tenement house in 1928. The *Vossische Zeitung* at that time marveled at the efficiency of their work:

> Why was the police on the right track so fast? How were the culprits found within twelve hours in spite of the lack of witnesses to the crime? Two Berlin inspectors, whose names are worth remembering, Lipik and Salaw, using refined police methods, have scored a success of which the Berlin Kripo may well be proud.[88]

Unfortunately, Müller, Lipik, and Salaw did not score again.

The temptation, then, was to seek other ways toward individual distinction. Physical bravery was one, though it did not always lead to success. Kriminal-Oberwachtmeister Albert Dettmann, "the first Berlin Kripoman to win public fame,"[89] gunned down a notorious burglar at the Café National in February, 1919, and in 1920 captured the dangerous brothers Strauss after threatening them with hand grenades. His exploits earned him popular admiration but not promotion to higher rank. Three detectives, who on November 10, 1930, entered a haunt frequented by criminals without first summoning the help of the riot police were praised for their hardiness but not for their circumspection. And Kriminal-Kommissar Busdorf, who had shown much courage in personal combat, complained that "the many occasions when I risked my hide for the Republic" were never duly appreciated in higher quarters. We shall have more to say about Busdorf.[90]

The detectives of the new generation deviated in behavior from the pattern of their seniors: they were active in the police unions, involved themselves in current politics, took an interest in criminological theories. Dr. Georg Bartsch played an important role in the Association for the Promotion of Police Science, a branch of the Schrader-Verband. Emil Klingelhöller, in 1928 a newcomer to Berlin from the police force in Essen, had published an outspoken history of the Association of Prussian Police

Officials, and was a frequent speaker at union affairs. Dr. Emil Berndorf came forward with radical plans to attack criminality at its roots,[91] and Hans Salaw published an article on the psychological prerequisites for criminal police service in 1927. The detective, according to him, needed "a practical knowledge of all spheres of life," and to "share the overall emotional reactions of the population . . . without weakening in his resolution to prosecute criminal elements relentlessly."[92] As a matter of fact, the skepticism of the empirical criminalist toward their theoretical-minded colleagues had something to do with the latter's ponderous truisms, not to mention their obstinate preoccupation with criminological fallacies.[93]

Dr. Rudolf Braschwitz and Hubert Mühlfriedel went over to the political police. Lesser men intrigued. Kriminal-Kommissare Philipp Greiner and Georg Kanthak betrayed Deputy Police President Weiss to the Nazis during a court case in October, 1932. Yet others, like Dr. Werner Kattolinsky (born 1901, detective inspector since 1930), found the simplest road to future success in clandestine Nazi activities.

The Nazi sympathizers among the Kripo's detective inspectors were not always the younger men with still a name to make for themselves.[94] But nearly all of them had personal reasons to worry about their careers, or else had been exposed to much professional frustration in their particular line of duty. Nazis could also be found in the Kripo simply because the "unpolitical" detective force was comparatively tolerant toward dissenters among its staff, except in the case of subaltern officials.[95] The National-Socialist cell in the Kripo could therefore become an important source of information for the Nazi party in Berlin, and a contact point for clandestine Party supporters in the political police, where the staff was under stricter control.[96] In 1933 its members took part in the purge of the police corps, and a number of them took jobs in the new secret police.

The personal and professional frustrations behind the polit-

ical disloyalty of certain inspectors can be studied by compar-
ing homicide duty with police work involving crimes against
property.

HOMICIDE

When Ernst Gennat formed his own inspectorate in 1926,
his aim was to end the haphazard work of the old "murder commissions."[97] In the past, homicide cases had been dealt with by
ad hoc teams put together from the available Kripo officials in
various inspectorates. The methods employed by these teams
varied, depending on who was in charge; there was little chance
to reopen an abortive investigation at some future date; and
nothing was done to exploit their accumulated experience over
the years. Gennat's new inspectorate, Kriminal-Inspektion A,
established a permanent supervisory body for all homicide investigation. It kept track of unsolved cases and compiled statistics on homicide patterns in Berlin. Above all, it gave Gennat
the chance to coordinate the work of every current investigation.

Another improvement was the provision of three homicide
teams to be held in readiness at all times: one on active duty
and two others in reserve. These teams were still largely staffed
by men from other inspectorates but now on a regular rotation
system, so that every Kripo detective knew in advance when his
turn came for emergency duty in homicide.

There were two reasons why the Kripo did not establish a
permanent staff for homicide investigations: (1) the police
chiefs believed that recurrent assignment to homicide duty was
an important part in the professional experience of every police
detective; and (2) homicide cases were regarded as being the
least related to organized criminal behavior. Most murders were
expected to arise from specific circumstances in the lives of the
persons involved. Consequently, homicide was not considered
a species of crime suitable for routine surveillance or systematic
prevention and suppression.

The second assumption was largely borne out by local experience.[98] Official as well as unofficial observers in the twenties all agreed that professional criminals in Berlin seldom resorted to violence. One of them found that but for the casualties of the political fighting, Berlin would have known a decline in physical assaults and murder during the Weimar Republic. Demented killers like Grossmann, and those responsible for the city's daily quota of assault and battery cases, rarely belonged to the habitual criminal circles. Berlin's criminal type attacked property but seldom used lethal weapons.[99]

Of the Kripo's nine technical inspectorates, inspectorate A therefore had the best reason to adhere to the principle of meticulous treatment for every individual crime however obscure its victim. Police President Grzesinski and Dr. Weiss as chief of the Berlin Kripo, personally went to the scene where an old shoemaker was murdered in January, 1926. In June of that year, high officials of the Presidium, together with Weiss and Gennat, inspected a suicide in Heerstrasse. In May, 1931, Regierungsdirektor Scholz of Department IV was joined by officials of the Ministry of Interior in the preliminary investigation of a postman's death. By then, it is true, the homicide teams had run into difficulties as a result of the daily political violence in the streets of Berlin.

Unlike in 1918 and 1919, it was difficult toward the end of the Weimar Republic to be sure of the political nature of a capital crime, even when it took place in the course of political disturbances.[100] There were no military operations in this civil war, not even attempts at organized insurrection, and political murders were not directed at well-known personalities. Small groups belonging to rival parties attacked one another at street corners and private citizens were slain in the heat of political quarrels. The diversity in the details of each incident necessitated special investigations for every case, if only to ascertain its genuine political character before it was handed on to Department IA. After the battle at the Felseneck allotment gardens in the morning hours of January 19, 1932, in which one Nazi and one Communist were killed, the Kripo helped IA comb through the entire area with searchlights for pieces of evidence and to interrogate over 200 witnesses.[101] But precisely because most of these slayings occurred in the course of spontaneous clashes and were therefore devoid of personal connections between killer and victim, conventional police inquiries were frequently hopeless. The culprits had to be caught red-handed, otherwise they stood a good chance to escape. The roster of *nasse Fische* (unsolved cases) grew incessantly.

The political police was not indifferent to the problem of the homicide teams. While it called on the Kripo's manpower for assistance, it usually accepted jurisdiction in all assumed political crimes. Mixed teams were sometimes set up for borderline cases, and when the political tension reached its peak in the spring of 1932, IA men were directed to serve in the Kripo's homicide teams until further notice.[102]

The criminal police was in any event reluctant to relinquish its role as the first authority in the investigation of capital crimes. Kripo inspectors suspected that an increasing number of persons with ordinary criminal records were drifting into the ranks of armed political gangs. While Berlin's professional crime syndicates tried to stay out of politics, individual thugs were believed to accept commissions as hired killers for political factions.[103] The geographical coincidence between the blocks of streets dominated by RFB cadres, and those controlled by habitual criminal gangs, further seemed to bear out the Kripo's contention that though not every Communist was a criminal, every criminal was a potential Communist. The Communist party was said to recruit the support of "thieves, murderers, and whores" —all outcasts of bourgeois society—and to offer them legal aid.[104] To be sure, the ranks of the S.A. were equally permeated by the rabble of Berlin's underworld.[105] The intermixture of the criminal with the political during the late twenties was at any rate significant enough for the Kripo to abide by its routine of undertaking the "first attack" (preliminary examination) in most homicide cases whatever the pressure of work.

Yet homicide duty did not produce as much professional discontent as might be expected. The transitory nature of their assignment made it relatively easy for detectives of the Kripo and the political police to shrug off their failures when lack of evidence forced them to abandon a case. They did not feel under great pressure since the daily crop of assaults were too numerous and too obscure to attract public attention to more than the general state of insecurity in Berlin. Finally, in a number of political murder cases, the police achieved astonishingly good results.

Police Master Teigeler, who joined the political police in 1928 and in 1932 was ordered to place himself at the disposal of the Kripo's homicide teams, was called out to investigate no less than four cases in the night of December 31, 1932:

> The shooting of Frau Künstler in Ackerstrasse, Berlin-Wedding, by an S.A. man on bicycle who fired his pistol at random when someone near her shouted an insult at the Nazis.

> The stabbing of Walter Wagnitz, a Hitler youth, in Utrechter Strasse, Berlin-Wedding.

> The slaying of a Communist workman by the name of Erich Hermann, in Lichtenrade.

> The death of an unidentified person on a highway outside Berlin, who shortly before had been involved in a political quarrel.

At first sight, there seemed little evidence to go on, yet the killers of Frau Künstler and Erich Hermann were caught within the next two weeks.[106]

Identifying the killers was often only the beginning of an investigation. In the murder of Hermann Kleier, on February 22, 1929, Kriminal-Kommissar Dr. Stumm and his colleague Dr.

Braschwitz were not content when they had apprehended the particular Red Frontman who had shot down the Stahlhelmer in the street. They discovered that their suspect had a record of several cases of assault and battery, and could have acted from a common criminal motive. This prolonged the investigation over several weeks and induced former Police Major Eldor Borck in the Landtag to move a vote of nonconfidence against the Prussian Minister of Interior.[107]

The most notorious murder to occur in the course of the street battle for Berlin was no doubt that of Horst Wessel. Wessel was shot in his rooms in Grosse Frankfurter Strasse on January 17, 1930. The gunmen were regular patrons of restaurant "Bär," a well-known Communist hangout in this neighborhood. There were rumors in Kripo circles and in the press that the Communist Albert Höhler, who fired the shots, and the S.A. leader Wessel were linked in a three-cornered fight over a former prostitute. But the investigators found that the motive for the crime was more complex. Höhler and his accomplices had acted to oblige Wessel's landlady, the widow of a former Party comrade. The landlady had asked for their help because she and Wessel had quarreled over the rent. The investigation of this case and the hunt for the culprits in Germany and abroad lasted several months.[108]

In the Heimbürger case—the lynching of a Communist news vendor on May 16, 1930, by twelve uniformed Nazi thugs —patient interrogations and house searches ended in the arrest of eight suspects ten days after the crime.[109]

There were few clandestine Nazis among the inspectors who handled some of the difficult homicide cases during this period. In the political police, Kriminal-Kommissare Wilhelm Meyer and Brandt of the homicide squad, and Kriminal-Direktor Fritz Scherler, the head of IA's street service, were all convinced opponents of Hitler. Kriminal-Polizeirat Reinhold Heller was noted for investigating the murder of the Hitler youth Norkus (1932) with as much objectivity as he hunted the killers of Police Captains Anlauf and Lenck (1931). Kriminal-Kommissar Walter Teichmann, the detective who solved the Horst Wessel case, was chairman of the Polizeibeamten-Vereinigung der Deutschen Staatspartei; and Kriminal-Kommissar Stumm was one of the first officials of Department IA to be demoted after the Papen putsch of 1932. One exception was Kriminal-Kommissar Harry Geisler, a Kripoman who drifted into political cases in 1932 and, while belonging to the Schrader-Verband between 1930 and 1933, secretly joined the National Socialist Fellowship (NSBAG) in 1932.[110]

In the criminal police, there were also few homicide inspectors with sympathies for the Nazis. But then the inspectorate was dominated by Gennat. His colleagues spoke of him as "democratic to the bone," even though Gennat had never shown any personal interest in politics and barely knew the meaning of National Socialism. To them he was the personification of the classical criminalist: undogmatic, incorruptible,[111] dedicated to the defense of individual rights, and suspicious of any form of regimentation. It was unthinkable to his colleagues that Gennat could have supported any other political stand but liberal democracy.[112]

If there was one person who tried to challenge Gennat's supremacy in inspectorate A, that person was Kriminal-Kommissar Otto Busdorf. Consumed with personal ambition, Busdorf tried for years to overcome his inauspicious beginnings as the son of a village baker and a hired police informer under the Empire. He had joined the Berlin Kripo in 1907—only two years after Gennat—but did not rise to Kriminal-Kommissar rank until 1925.[113]

In 1926 he was offered a chance to prove himself in the well-publicized Helling murder case in Magdeburg. Busdorf discovered the murderer in spite of the obstructionism of the examining judge and Kommissar Tenholt of the local police.

But Busdorf's hour of triumph was marred by personal jeal-
ousies and intrigues. Dr. Bernhard Weiss had to make three
trips from Berlin to mediate between the quarreling parties,
the Ministry of Interior was forced to intercede, and in the end
Busdorf had to be recalled to Berlin before he was able to close
the case.[114]

To improve his chances of promotion to Kriminalrat, this
unhappy man sought to belittle the achievements of his colleagues and subordinates through malicious rumors. He finally
turned to political intrigues. He frequented the men of Department IA, he joined the SPD in 1928, and when this produced
no results, he donated small sums to the Nazi party fund from
1931 on. Boris Grams, a Nazi spy, reported to Dr. Goebbels in
October of that year that Busdorf stood a chance of replacing
Gennat as chief of inspectorate A if only because Gennat was
losing favor in the eyes of his political bosses.[115] Democrats-
by-implication were no longer in great demand.

Of course, attempts to extend the philosophical basis of
individualism from the criminalistic to the political sphere were
rare in the circle of the old Berlin Kripo. Kriminal-Polizeirat
Dr. Hans Schneickert, perhaps the most distinguished intellectual figure of the Kripo up to his retirement in June, 1931, was
one of the few who tried. For many years head of the identification service, Schneickert was less the empirical criminalist
than the expert in police science and a theoretician. He published extensively in professional journals and lectured at the
law faculty of Berlin University.[116]

Schneickert worried about the "blind and furious passion"
engendered by political strife.[117] In 1927 he wrote an article on
the issue of capital punishment, and used this opportunity to
make one of the most eloquent statements of political faith to
be found in the technical police literature of the time. Schneickert warned that there could be no rule of law if important re-
visions of the legal code were attempted in times of political

instability. If the death penalty were abolished today, he argued, it could be reintroduced tomorrow, and then it would be reintroduced for reasons of political expediency.

> Can there be anything more heineous, more unjust, than to eliminate [political] enemies by murdering them, or by disposing of them in a formal-legal manner through the sudden reintroduction of the death penalty? When the death penalty is introduced, or reintroduced, as an accompaniment to a change in the constitution, or to protect the existing form of the state, the purpose of intimidation and self-protection is very obvious. Guaranties for the maintenance of principles of justice, and confidence in the judiciary will dwindle. . . . [The] reintroduction of the death penalty is the clear mark of a government that is either too feeble or hungry for more power.[118]

It may not be an accident that Schneickert's forceful defense of the rule of law was made in relation to the death penalty, in other words, in reference to capital crimes. In a new edition to his *Einführung in die Kriminalsoziologie und Verbrechensverhütung* in 1935, he inserted statements that were quite at variance with the views he had expressed in 1927.[119] Now he approved the sweeping police measures that the Nazis had introduced in November, 1933 and February, 1934, to wipe out Berlin's professional criminality through wholesale "preventive arrests" and banishments to concentration camps. Schneickert also spoke with disdain of the pusilanimity of the old Kripo that had only proceeded within the strictest of legal limits against every individual lawbreaker. "This kind of tolerance is obviously out of the question in today's fight against professional crime. . . ."[120]

A simple explanation for Schneickert's change in attitude would be to ascribe it to the advent of the Nazi era. But the fact that the new police measures were mainly directed against the core of Berlin's professional criminals—the thieves and burglars, pimps and swindlers—may also be of importance.[121] We cannot be sure that Schneickert had also abandoned his belief in the sanctity of individual rights in relation to crimes as singular in motive and circumstances as homicide. Is it not possible that a criminalist was more likely to discard the individualistic approach to his work only in the face of professional crime against property and organized attacks on the established social order?

PROFESSIONAL CRIMINALITY

Most of the detective inspectors who grumbled about the Republic were in charge of fighting Berlin's organized underworld. Philipp Greiner was assigned to the gambling squad, Günther Braschwitz (the older brother of Dr. Rudolf Braschwitz) specialized in burglaries; Max Bünger in safecrackers; and Ernst Engelbrecht was an expert in dealing with the local crime syndicates. He wrote an admiring article on crime fighting in Fascist Italy in 1924, and soon thereupon left the Kripo because of political differences with Dr. Weiss. Helmut Müller and Hubert Geissel were feared among the professional crooks of Berlin, and so was the Kripo's enfant terrible, Kriminal-Kommissar Otto Trettin. Dr. Werner Kattolinsky, one of the youngest inspectors, was assigned to the burglary squad dealing with robberies in residential homes, and Arthur Nebe worked several years in narcotics. Liebermann von Sonnenberg was an expert in robberies and counterfeiting; and Ulrich Possehl, in commercial fraud.[122]

It is tempting to think that the similarity in the professional experience of all these men could explain their political discontent and the preference that many of them showed for National Socialism well before 1933.

Offenses against property had risen to alarming proportions right after the war. In the three years from 1919 to 1921, the number of convictions in Berlin for simple theft was 81 percent higher than in the period from 1911 to 1913. For serious theft, the record showed an increase of 163 percent; and for receiving

stolen goods, as much as 245 percent.[123] In the railway administration and the postal service, special detective units were established to combat the spread of pilfering and embezzling.
Progress in technological devices and changes in commercial
practices created new opportunities for unscrupulous enrich-
ment by the mentally agile. Criminals were now forthcoming
from the ranks of the impoverished intellectuals and former
army officers, employees in business firms and state officials.
Individuals from the "better classes" also provided the new
genre of the "gentleman burglar" who assumed the pretensions
of English and American master criminals, avoided the traditional hangouts of the petty thieves, and moved about in lux-
urious touring cars.[124]

To the Berliners who enjoyed stories of criminal life, the
underworld clubs—"Ringvereine"—nevertheless remained the
classical milieu of professional crooks.

The term "Ringverein" strictly speaking, applied only to
the regional associations that supervised the local underworld
clubs (Vereine). There were three such associations in Berlin:
the "Grosser Ring," the "Freier Bund," and the "Freie Vereinigung." The three Ringvereine acted on behalf of a larger German syndicate, the "Mitteldeutscher Ring." They imposed rigid
statutes on the local clubs, controlled their activities, and ex-
acted money tributes for the syndicate.[125]

The local Vereine were officially registered as sports clubs,
entertainment clubs, or benevolent societies. They portrayed
what the public understood to be the Berlin underworld. In-
triguing to watch as a social enclave within the city, following
their own rituals and their own code of honor, they received
much more attention than the three actual Ringvereine. Inev-
itably, the local clubs colloquially assumed the name "Ringverein" for themselves, and their members became "Ringvereinler" or "Ringbrüder."

It is not clear exactly how many underworld clubs existed
during their heyday in the Berlin of the twenties. A police report

in 1933 suggested that eighty-five would be a conservative judgment. Estimates of the numerical strength of their membership was also subject to speculation; they ranged from as little as 1,000 to "the overwhelming majority of all criminals in Berlin." One journalist maintained that Berlin-Mitte at night was virtually in the hands of criminal gangs: doormen, bootblacks, street vendors, prostitutes, and toilet attendants were all paying members in one of the underworld clubs.

The question whether the Ringvereine should be suppressed or were better just kept under strict observation was a controversial issue for the Berlin Kripo in the Weimar Republic. The Ringvereine seemed to justify a measure of police tolerance because they exercised a mellowing influence on the professional circle of crooks. Many clubs seemed to aspire to some appearance of bourgeois respectability, going under such names as "Immertreu," "Heimatklänge," or "Hand in Hand" to suggest snug contentment and solid virtue. They were fond of their pompous yearly banquets in Berlin's better restaurants, and laid great store on proper funerals for deceased brother members.

It was an open secret, of course, that behind their innocuous facade, there were unwritten rules that restricted membership to men with criminal convictions, and severely punished any brother who informed on another to the police. The social clubs were known to serve as a place where burglars exchanged hot tips and where the dependants of jailed brothers could come for financial help and false witnesses. The Ringvereine also fought small-scale gang wars with unorganized hoodlums and terrorized innkeepers with protection rackets.

On the other hand, they strictly excluded from membership any individual guilty of manslaughter, murder, or sexual crime. The use of firearms by Ringvereinler was almost unheard of, especially against police officials. Far from resisting arrest, they often showed courtesy—sometimes even loyalty—to their favorite commissars.[126]

Orthodox criminalists of the old school supported the policy of toleration. They would rather match their wits with the same set of crooks in round after round, than to adopt wholesale methods aimed at suppressing all crime. They did not believe in the possibility of eradicating crime in any case. Speaking in more immediate terms, the conservatives warned against a sudden change in police strategy that might drive Berlin's criminal element into the political arena.[127] As experienced investigators, they appreciated stability in the behavior of the criminal world. It made police observation as well as the collection of clues in specific cases easier.

The opponents of the Ringvereine claimed that the clubs' mocking defiance of the law threatened to undermine public order. They objected to police detectives negotiating deals with confidence men in "licensed burglars' clubs." Had not some of them lost their discernment between respecting the legal rights of gangsters and abetting their crimes after the fact?[128] They resented the timidity of the criminal courts which obliged the Kripo to move with the utmost of caution in the face of insolent bandits and irresponsible journalists.[129]

Above all, they feared for the authority of the police. The Ringvereine amused the public with their display of ostentatious gregariousness, and with their sly rules that brothers must resign their membership for the night when they were out to pull a fast job. The Ringvereine used the same tactics as the two master burglars Franz and Erich Sass, whose disarming method toward the police consisted in simply denying everything and playing dumb. Everyone knew that they had robbed the Disconto Bank at Wittenbergplatz on January 28, 1929, but the police never succeeded in proving their guilt.[130] After one of their exploits, the *Vossiche Zeitung* wrote:

> It must be assumed that the brothers Sass will soon be seen at public dances again, drinking their lemonade, while secretly engaged in digging tunnels in eery graveyards, or haunting

dark cellars in Moabit. And a whole staff of police officials will feverishly try to uncover whatever the two brothers have worked out for their own amusement and for the terror of the authorities.[131]

Among the officials who fretted about the liberal police methods of the Weimar Republic were Erich Liebermann von Sonnenberg and Otto Trettin. Both enjoyed good professional reputations, the one as a specialist in counterfeiting, the other in jewel and museum thefts. But Liebermann was also known to advocate such methods of crime fighting as forced sterilization of alcoholics, epileptics, and mentally retarded. Such proposals were then under public debate, but they were not compatible with the liberal principles of the old Berlin Kripo. Liebermann was instrumental in introducing the criminal police to National Socialist methods when he took over Department IV in 1933.[132] On his retirement from that post in 1936, he thanked Kurt Daluege, the chief of the German order police, in the following words: "It has been my privilege over the last three years to lead the fight against crime using methods which I always thought proper, but which could never have been applied but for you and the National Resurrection."[133] From January 11, 1932, Liebermann was the unofficial representative of the National Socialist Fellowship of Civil Servants (NSBAG) in the Association of Higher Criminal Police Officials of Prussia.

Liebermann and Trettin often collaborated as a team, but Trettin was by far the more flamboyant of the two. His colleagues found him boisterous and overbearing, though they respected his professional success. While a master detective like Gennat worked on lower-class murders in obscure tenement houses, Trettin investigated thefts in fashionable stores on Unter den Linden and Motzstrasse. He solved a sensational holdup at Marotti and Freink's in Tauentzienstrasse under the public glare occasioned by the Great Police Exhibition of 1926. A burglary at the Hohenzollern mausoleum in Charlottenburg Castle, two robberies at the Prussian state archive, and an important art theft that inculpated one of Berlin's best-known art dealers —solutions to these crimes all belonged to his record of criminalistic achievements.[134]

Success drew Trettin close to the side of the empirical criminalists, in particular since he did not, apparently, share Liebermann's theoretical proclivities for Nazi methods of crime control. But Trettin was an immoderate man. He tried to break the Sass brothers with physical coercion, which was a serious breach of police ethics.[135] (In 1920, a detective sergeant who was suspected of beating Friedrich Schumann, the mass murderer, during interrogation, was immediately reported to the state attorney's office by his superiors.)[136] Furthermore, Trettin's honesty in money matters was several times put in doubt. The staff of the Kripo was not well paid, and Trettin's subordinates suspected him of embezzling expense money for field trips outside Berlin as well as the monetary rewards that private parties sometimes offered at the end of a successful investigation.[137] Trettin remained politically ambivalent throughout the Republic, given to noisy demonstrations of nationalist sentiments and taunts at the government, but he did not join the Nazi party until 1937.

Personal shortcomings in addition to professional disappointments may finally explain the political course of Arthur Nebe.[138] Nebe was more sophisticated than most of the other malcontents in the Kripo. Of middle-class background and well educated, he was far more successful than other colleagues in convincing the Nazis of his dedication to their political ideas and not just to the jobs they could offer. He made good use of his record as a former free corps soldier and his early admiration for the virtues of patriotism, militarism, and anti-Semitism, to prove his long ideological affinity with National Socialism.

And yet he was insincere. If he claimed, as he did in a handwritten vita in 1936, that he left the Reichswehr in 1920 because he could not suffer being subordinated to a Social Democratic Minister of Defense, his decision, next, to join the police of the Weimar Republic does not make sense. True, in 1923 he privately organized a German-National youth group in the Berlin district of Prenzlauer Berg. He also gathered together a small group of "reliable" Kripo officials to form a *völkische Gruppe* which agitated against Jews and Freemasons. Was this compatible wtih his eagerness for the approval of his colleagues in the police, most of whom wanted to stay free from political ties? Why did he seek out the friendship of the Jewish Deputy Police President Bernhard Weiss?

Perhaps Nebe's political activities were his private revenge for the slow recognition accorded to him by superiors and colleagues alike.[139] His examination for commissar's rank in 1922 had not been a brilliant performance, and he did not make a reputation for himself until 1931, when he solved the murder of a chauffeur and helped capture Franz Spernau, a dangerous bandit chief.[140] By that time, he had already established clandestine relations with the Nazi party through his wife. The legal correctness of the political police prevented it from taking disciplinary steps against him because the ban on Nazi membership for state officials did not specifically include their wives. In 1931 Nebe himself secretly joined the Party. In 1932 he was one of the chief founders of the NSBAG and served as liaison man between the Berlin police and the future Nazi police general Kurt Daluege.

Studying the Berlin detective force of the twenties requires more patience than doing the same for the uniformed street police. This group, so much smaller than the Schupo, was much more under the influence of individuals who happened to serve on its staff. Yet, character portraits of every one of the 150 officials in the elevated and higher service ranks would merely give a kaleidoscope of subjective impressions. I have therefore tried to correlate the known characteristics of the most prominent detectives with general reports on the criminal activities in Berlin, hoping to find an objective explanation for the political behavior of at least some of them.

The correlation that I have drawn between antirepublican sentiments on the one hand and professional discontent on the other (whether this discontent was derived from personal failures or from frustrations inherent in the job is not so important) could be extended from the Kripo to the political police. But our chance of reaching a correct conclusion would be smaller than it was in the first instance. Department IA was even less prone to generalizations than Department IV. While a striking number of IA officials who proved to be loyal to parliamentary democracy were successful criminalists—and the most successful kind of political police work was hunting down political killers—we cannot say that professional failures were the reason for the defection of others. Preventive police work cannot be measured in terms of arrests and convictions. There were not many defectors in IA in any case. Their motives escape the purview of the social historian.

V | The End of a Police Era

From the Papen Putsch to Hitler's Seizure of Power

In the late spring of 1932, there was increasing talk of a right-wing putsch or of drastic intervention by the federal government to forestall the total collapse of order in Berlin. The Social Democrats, the Centrists, and the Democrats had sustained heavy losses in the Prussian elections of April 24, and no effective parliamentary government could henceforth be formed. Elections for a new Reichstag were scheduled for July 31. If these also produced an intractable legislature, serious political disturbances were foreseen.

Disturbances were expected in any event, because the Reich was forcing the Prussian government into a dangerous situation. Reich Minister of Interior Freiherr von Gayl insisted that the ban on the S.A. and the S.S. be lifted in Prussia (June 14, 1932), even though their reappearance in the streets was certain to cause a resurgence of violence. As it was, the Prussian government was barely able to maintain peace and order within the major cities.[1]

In immediate terms, therefore, the crisis that broke out in the summer of 1932 concerned public security. Not surprisingly, the countermeasures planned by the Prussian Minister of Interior were also conceived in terms of police actions. On July 16, 1932, Carl Severing discussed with leaders of the Social Democratic party the possibility of calling out the police and the masses of the Eiserne Front, should federal troops try to seize control of the Prussian government. Of course, he would not expect them to put up more than a token resistance, he said, since they stood no chance in open combat against the powerful Reichswehr. He immediately dropped the subject, however, when his colleagues objected to any sacrifice of Schupomen's lives.[2]

Still, the Prussian police remained at the center of ensuing events. It was the chief target of the propaganda campaign launched by the Nazi deputies in the Prussian legislature in June. They demanded the arrest and trial of Berlin Police President Albert Grzesinski on charges of incompetence and heaped insults on his deputy Dr. Weiss.[3] In the editorial offices of *Der Angriff*, Joseph Goebbels and his staff were preparing their final assault on the hated Jewish police leader "Isidor Weiss." Goebbels wrote in his diary (July 24, 1932): "The time has come to finish him off. I have fought him for six years. Every National Socialist in Berlin sees him as the incarnation of the whole System. When he goes, the System will not survive much longer."[4]

The federal government moved on July 20. Chancellor Franz von Papen dismissed the Prussian government of Otto Braun and assumed executive powers in Prussia as Reichskommissar. He appointed Dr. Bracht as his deputy. Bracht's chief role was to assume Severing's functions as Minister of Interior. Generalleutnant von Rundstedt, the commander of military command III, imposed martial law on Greater Berlin and the province of Brandenburg, and immediately moved to take control of the capital's police. Armed soldiers appeared at the Police Presidium in Alexanderplatz to enforce the removal of Police President Grzesinski, his deputy Weiss, and Schupo Commander Heimannsberg. The latter two were placed under temporary arrest. The three men were respectively replaced by Dr. Kurt Melcher, the police president of Essen; Dr. Mosle, head of the Berlin traffic police; and Colonel Poten, the director of the police school in Eiche. To justify its intervention in the affairs of a member state, the federal government offered three basic reasons:

1. The Prussian police, in its judgment, had failed to preserve law and order.

2. The leadership of the Prussian police had been lax and uncoordinated.

3. The Prussian government had lost the confidence of the people.[5]

After the Second World War, Severing took some pains to justify his failure to call out the Schutzpolizei on July 20.[6] With the proclamation of martial law, he explained, the Prussian government had legally lost its police powers, and all law-enforcing officers had directly become subordinate to the army. This was also the opinion of Dr. Arnold Brecht, who played an important part in the Prussian government's subsequent attempts to seek legal redress. The Reich president, according to Brecht, not only was constitutionally empowered to take over the Prussian police but

The Prussian police officers, although faithful to their duties and loyally attached to Severing, knew that this was so. Therefore, in the event of an appeal to violent resistance, the Reich President would have been supported by the Army, by the "Steel Helmet" organization of former soldiers and conservatives, by the storm troops of the Nazis, and also by the civil servants, *and the police* [italics mine].[7]

Severing furthermore pleaded that the Berlin police was technically incapable of defending the Prussian government. Not only was the Schutzpolizei short of heavy arms, but its internal command structure was thrown into confusion by the sudden change in leadership. Under these circumstances, an attempt to fight would have ended in disastrous defeat. As Grzesinski put it in 1939: "To believe that the Reichswehr would not have fired upon their fellow comrades, the police, is merely wishful thinking."[8]

To the juridical and the tactical arguments, we must add the morale factor as a third. The security police had not, in these twelve years, evolved the political self-reliance that its founders had preached in the early twenties. When the legal government was in a situation of crisis, the policemen as in the past preferred to watch from the sidelines. Among the rank and file of the Schupo, there were few who felt strongly enough to fight for their political leaders anyway. But not one forgot the practical lesson of all police training: obedience to superior orders. Business continued as usual as long as none of the old police chiefs challenged the authority of the army.

Witnesses at the Police Presidium were surprised at Grzesinski's resigned attitude on July 20, when he was told to vacate his post. He twice called his department heads to his office in the course of that morning, but each time in the presence of Melcher, Mosle, and Poten, the designated new chiefs of the Berlin police. That Poten, until 1930, had commanded police region West in Berlin, and Mosle was currently serving on the Berlin staff, probably heightened the impression that the affair amounted to an internal reshuffling in personnel. Already at the first staff meeting, Grzesinski bade his subordinates farewell, and the senior department chief responded with a few polite words of regret. That very evening, Dr. Mosle quietly celebrated his promotion to deputy president with the chief of the Kripo and another colleague over a bottle of wine.[9]

The only impulses to resist came from Heimannsberg and especially Weiss. Neither of them thought of armed resistance, but Weiss at least vehemently protested the legality of the entire proceedings. Weiss and Heimannsberg were therefore arrested and charged with defying the authority of the military command. They were taken from police headquarters under guard but were released a few hours later.

Heimannsberg's detention may have been a precautionary measure by the military authorities. Rumors were flying fast that new shooting orders had been issued to the Schupo in Berlin, and that a few specially reliable riot brigades were to be used for a violent counterputsch.[10]

As a matter of fact, there were some elements in the Schupo who spontaneously thought of armed rebellion on behalf of Heimannsberg, if not on behalf of the fallen regime of Otto Braun. In an interview in 1962, Hermann Artner recounted that he and a handful of like-minded patrolmen were chafing to deal a blow at the Nazis. He told of a secret plan to alert all patrolmen who supported the SPD, to have them disarm every known Nazi in their local police stations, and then to enlist the support of their uncommitted comrades. Together with some barracked police troops under the command of republican officers—for example Polizei-Oberwachtmeister Fritz Krumbach's unit in the Maikäferkaserne—they would then have attacked all the S.A. and S.S. strong points in Greater Berlin. The plan was forwarded by the General Prussian Police Association (Betnarek-Verband) to the SPD faction of the Prussian Diet—and was never heard of again.

Spontaneous action from below was, of course, difficult in the midst of the general paralysis in the police. The absence of spirited resistance was poignantly reflected in Police-Major Walther Encke's halfhearted "conspiracy" to restore Commander Heimannsberg to power. Encke lived in the same apartment house as Heimannsberg, at Apostel-Paulus-Strasse 8, in Berlin-Schöneberg. The two men were on friendly terms. When Heimannsberg was arrested, Encke was briefly torn between personal loyalty and deference to higher authority. On the night of July 21, he cautiously sounded out a police sergeant of the Zehlendorf riot brigade on the political mood in his unit. He asked the sergeant to form a clandestine circle of Heimannsberg supporters inside his barracks and to contact the district command of the Reichsbanner Black-Red-Gold. The sergeant was Polizei-Oberwachtmeister Heinz Schumacher, who in March had denounced Polizei-Oberwachtmeister Schulz-Briesen as a Nazi spy. This time he reported Encke as a traitor to the military command.[11]

But the army need not have bothered to initiate legal steps against Police Major Encke. Anticipating trouble the next day, Encke wrote a full explanation of his behavior to the military command. In his letter he hotly denied having harbored any thoughts of insubordination. "Surely," he wrote, "I cannot be blamed for having been much upset on the evening of July 20." He condemned all attempts at using Schupo units for an illegal reinstatement of Heimannsberg as no less than "criminal," and assured the army of his submission on his word "as a police officer and a former officer of the Imperial Field Army."[12]

Who was Heimannsberg? Police Colonel Magnus Heimannsberg was not one of the great police reformers of the twenties. When the republican Schutzpolizei was organized, he was an instructor at a training center in Münster. Later, he served as Oberst-Leutnant in the security police of Potsdam. Heimannsberg was not appointed commander of the Berlin Schupo until 1927. But during the next five years, he led the armed police of Berlin through the most difficult years of the interwar period, at a time when the republican government depended increasingly on the protection of its security force in the street.[13]

He was enormously popular with the common patrolmen. They knew that he had begun his career at the bottom rung of the ladder, and had risen by dint of personal capacity alone. As Schupo commander he was always solicitous of his subordinates' welfare. "A man of unusual fascination and extraordinary strength of character," he was hailed as the prototype of a future breed of "people's police officers."[14]

For Heimannsberg never assumed the conservative stance of the police officers' corps; he never shared its social pretensions. Nor did he, like so many of his colleagues, evade political commitment when such commitment seemed to him necessary and good. As the situation of the Republic grew critical at the turn of the decade, he became one of its outspoken champions, so much so that the Nazis complained of discrimination against S.A. men during public disturbances.[15] While Heimannsberg lacked Dr. Weiss's eloquence as an intellectual protagonist of democratic police principles, he had the courage to espouse a militant republicanism at a time when many fellow officers were privately making ready for the Third Reich.

Dr. Bernhard Weiss was the other major casualty that the Berlin police sustained in the Papen putsch. He was one of the longest, and in his own way, the most faithful servant of the Berlin police during the Weimar Republic. But Weiss was also conscious of being a somewhat singular case among the police leaders of his period: a state servant of the old Prussian school given to German-National sympathies in the company of Social Democrats and trade unionists; a Jew in an entourage where Jews were rarely seen and not particularly welcome. We may assume that Dr. Weiss had no doubt but that he too owed his high office to nothing but his professional abilities.

He was a trained lawyer, whose promising career in the judiciary had been interrupted by the First World War. Returned from the front decorated with the Iron Cross (first class), the thirty-eight-year-old former judge in a lower court entered the services of the Berlin police. From deputy chief of the Kripo, he went on to rebuild the political police in 1920. An ill-calculated raid on the offices of the Soviet trade mission in May, 1924, caused his transfer back to Department IV, this time as its chief. In this capacity, Weiss helped to build the system of LKA's in 1925, and to modernize the entire detective force. In 1927 he was promoted to Regierungsdirektor and deputy police president, a position that he maintained until his forced retirement from office on July 20, 1932.

As chief of the criminal police and later as deputy police president, Dr. Weiss proved to be not only highly competent and industrious, but also remarkably versatile. He tried to know all his immediate subordinates at the Presidium and took part in many of their organized activities. Detectives found him always ready to accompany them on field trips; Schupomen to watch their operations during political demonstrations. He spoke at countless public events, edited the *Kriminalistische Monatshefte*, and wrote articles designed to improve the popular image of the police.

His *Polizei und Politik* (1928) was not a profound book and fell short in historical accuracy. It was nevertheless remarkable for its pugnacious defense of political intelligence work in a democratic state. President Kleiber of the Stuttgart police praised it as an excellent plaidoyer, though he regretted "a few quite unnecessary and not very kind asides at the expense of third parties."[16]

Dr. Weiss was indeed not given to kindliness toward those who threatened the authority and integrity of his police. This applied in particular to faultfinders among his fellow state servants. Critics outside the government were a different matter. Newspaper attacks on the police received polite and sober rebuttals. Two political authors who in 1928 assailed the police over the Jakubowski murder case were forgiven their polemical sallies. "Every objective person must see that the authors were moved not by malevolence but by the passion in their hearts," Weiss wrote.[17] But a provincial judge who dared to question

the efficiency of the Berlin Kripo in 1932 received a scathing
dressing down:

> I hear that Hildsberg is 60 years old, and has served as the crim-
> inal judge of a provincial town in Saxony for nearly 30 years. He
> has chosen the least competent of the local detectives as his
> closest collaborator . . . and never has ventured out before as an
> author or lecturer.[18]

His sarcasm gave him the reputation of ruthlessness.[19] But
he was, in fact, not the hard-bitten cop that he sometimes pre-
tended to be. He cared a good deal for the opinion of his subordinates in the police and was dismayed at his failure to win
their spontaneous affection. At headquarters, he obligated his
assistants with his unfailing courtesy and his generous gifts, but
could not prevent them from calling him "Isidor" behind his
back.[20] The Kripo staff recognized his achievements as a lawyer
and administrator, but would not accept him as a fellow criminalist. "He meddled in things that were too dangerous for him
to handle," remarked one old-timer of the Kripo years later.[21]
As to the officers and men of the Schupo, they thought him a
good politician and correct superior but resented his inspection
tours and his officious suggestions for technical improvements.
The tiny deputy president with his old-fashioned glasses cut an
odd figure in front of the martial array of the Schupo at official
parades. He was not really trusted with the command of so
formidable a fighting machine.

The Nazis' malicious campaign of ridicule against "Isidor"
Weiss was cleverly conceived insofar as it tried to present Weiss
as a pompous official who failed to inspire his subordinates with
respect for his leadership.[22]

When Heimannsberg was removed from his command in
1932, his enemies feared that his men might revolt. When Weiss
was relieved of his post, none of his subordinates thought of
fighting for him. His collaborators in the office gave him an

ovation, but sixteen Kripo officials, among them four detective inspectors, chose this time to denounce him for alleged improprieties in office.[23]

Things settled down to a deceptive quiet soon after the Papen putsch. Martial law in Berlin was lifted on July 26. The ban on all Schupo leaves, which the military had ordered during the emergency, was cancelled ten days later.[24] The legal charges against Dr. Weiss and Commander Heimannsberg were quietly withdrawn in October.[25] Town gossip had it that Weiss would soon open a private law practice.[26] In the Prussian Diet, the Nazi deputy Kurt Daluege tried to push through an indictment of Heimannsberg for alleged nepotism and graft during his term in office, but merely to undercut his claims to a retirement pension.[27] And Police President Grzesinski went on a speech-making tour to defend his policy of nonviolence during the recent crisis. On January 19, 1933, he attended a social event arranged by the newspapermen's automobile club in Berlin. High-ranking police officials were present—among them Deputy Police President Mosle, Deputy Schupo Commander Gentz, and Regierungsdirektor Scholz of the Kripo—and Grzesinski was given a hearty welcome.[28]

But there was an unmistakable change in political climate inside the police, even though the main body of the executive staff had survived almost intact. In the political police, Regierungsdirektor Goehrke, who had led the department since January, 1931, returned to his former position in Department II (aliens police).[29] Dr. Stumm, who had played a prominent role in fighting right-wing extremists for nearly ten years was banished to the local criminal police inspection of Berlin-Friedrichshain. Many of his fellow workers were reassigned to combat the left-wing opponents of the new Prussian regime.[30] These now included the SPD and the Reichsbanner Black-Red-Gold. For the first time since 1918 the activities of Social Democrats came under regular police surveillance and a new set of confidence men had to be organized for this task.[31] Finally, a special office was opened to stop Communist subversion in the army and the security police.[32] Yet to bring about this change in political course, a discreet reshuffling of personnel was all that was needed. Most IA men were eager to carry out the new directives and anxiously watched the signs of the time.[33]

Not even their colleagues in Department IV were entirely exempt from the effects of the change in regime. Though there was no reshuffling in personnel, it did matter that the National Socialist Fellowship of Civil Servants (NSBAG) now could openly recruit for its political cause, and that Liebermann and Nebe were taking the lead. The empirical criminalists of the old school had to yield to the crime-fighting strategists as Police President Melcher ordered an all-out campaign against Berlin's vice-ridden night life, and announced that the Kripo would in the future work more as a large team: the names of successful investigators were no longer to be emphasized in press reports.[34]

The security police had lost Heimannsberg. A few other officers who had been attacked as zealous republicans in the Nazi press were also suspended. They included Police Major Karl Heinrich, for many years commander of police-inspection Mitte and since recently commander of police inspection Schöneberg.[35] At the same time all disciplinary proceedings against Schupomen with Nazi affiliations were dropped. Nazi sympathizers were at last free to show their colors; a decree of July 29, 1932, lifted the ban on membership in the Nazi party for officials in the Prussian state service.[36] Policemen openly went to Nazi rallies even though Reichskommissar Bracht still asked them not to attend in uniform.[37] Those who were sent there on duty as security guards listened attentively to the speakers. The Association of Security Police Officials of Prussia (Josupeit-Verband) experienced a sudden increase in membership.[38]

To be sure, the policemen on the beat still interceded

against Nazis when they caught Brownshirts or S.S. men in flagrant violation of the law. But more often than not they managed to look the other way.[39] Storm troopers who arrogated policelike functions to themselves by searching pedestrians and tearing down SPD and KPD posters were not molested.[40] Following a shooting affray between Nazis and Communists in Gesundbrunnen on September 6, 1932, the Nazi prisoners were released at the police station while the Communists were taken to headquarters.[41] Finally, on January 22, 1933, the Schupo helped the Berlin S.A. impose its hegemony on the Bülowplatz. Fourteen thousand heavily armed police sealed off the last bastion of Communist power in the heart of Berlin and occupied the building of the Communist party so that the Nazis could hold a memorial march for Horst Wessel. That evening, Count Helldorf credited the success of the undertaking to "the predominantly national socialist disposition of the police."[42] His claim was exaggerated, but the public could hardly be blamed for believing him.

The pressure to move to the right came not only from the new police leaders, who actually tried to maintain the facade of political objectivity but also from outside sources, for example, the investigating committee on police abuses of the Prussian Diet, which was dominated by Kurt Daluege.[43] This committee summoned an entire flying squad of the Schupo to appear before it and answer for alleged acts of brutality toward S.A. men during an operation two months before.[44] A week later, it took up the events on the previous Skaggerak Day (May 31, 1932) during which police had battled Nazi intruders inside the Bannmeile.[45] These investigations were obviously calculated to intimidate the uniformed rank and file.

Under these circumstances, the sergeants on the beat eschewed all independent action and relied on superior orders more than ever before. The officer corps, however, elected a Nazi, Walther Wecke, as chairman of both the police officers' union and the police officers' civil service committee (Beamtenausschuss). Walther Wecke already headed the Schupo section of the NSBAG. With the officers turning to support Hitler, the rank and file could be trusted to serve as a fighting instrument against communism. Reichskommissar Bracht issued them new shooting orders on July 26, 1932:

> A [police] official is failing in his duties if he does not use his weapon quickly and effectively enough. An official who lives up to his duties . . . [however] . . . can be sure of my protection.[46]

This, in essence, was the order that Hermann Göring was to give to the police on February 25, 1933, to launch his general war against the enemies of the Third Reich.

But the war was no longer centered on Berlin. In the summer of 1932, the casualties of political clashes were more numerous in Altona or Greifswald than they were here.[47] The process of nazification in the police of Thuringia or Mecklenburg superceded that in the capital.[48] As Berlin was succumbing to the Nazi movement, there were signs the city was losing the leading role it had played in the history of the German Reich since 1871. Soon the exodus of intellectuals and artists would begin. Adolf Stein exulted on October 6, 1932: "The Kurfürstendamm trembles with fear and anger. Might as well pack up and leave. Please yourselves! No one is keeping you."[49]

When Hitler assumed power as chancellor on January 30, 1933, there was no state of siege, no fear of insurrection and civil war, no mobilization of the police to protect the new government or to plot the return of the old. In the evening, Police Sergeant Josef Zauritz was killed in Wallstrasse, Berlin-Charlottenburg, when S.A. storm troop 33 clashed for a last time with its Communist residents shortly after the great torchlight parade. Zauritz was posthumously made into a martyr of the National movement, together with S.A. leader Hans Maikowski who died in the same incident. But Zauritz had met his death as other unsung Schupomen had before him, a sergeant off-duty, killed by a chance bullet in a political fight in which he wanted no part.[50]

The Purge, 1933

As soon as the Nazis had come to power, there was a rush of policemen professing long-standing Nazi sympathies. At the police club "Kameradschaft," men whose loyalty to the Republic had always been taken for granted surprised their colleagues with their boisterous talk of Germany's resurging fortunes. There were also mutual denunciations and brothers betrayed one another.[51] More remarkable still, the process of political adjustment (*Gleischschaltung*) in the first few months of the Third Reich was largely handled by the police staff itself. Trustworthy officers like Captain Garski and Majors Wecke and Jacoby moved to the Ministry of Interior to supervise the removal of the opponents of naziism from the force.[52] Police Major Dr. Wolfstieg of the Charlottenburg command handled all applications by Nazi Schupomen who had been disciplined under the Republic and now wanted to return to active service.[53] In the Kripo, Regierungsrat Dr. Nicolai and Kriminalrat Liebermann advised the new police chiefs on questions of personnel.

Nearly forgotten figures from the days of the Sipo and the early Schupo made their reappearance to seek favors with the new masters of the Prussian police. A police councillor Rollin of the administrative police claimed recognition for having countermanded a public servants' strike during the Kapp putsch in 1920.[54] Secret councillor Doyé, the champion of the old Sipo, offered his services as "a national-minded man with long experience in police administration," and "a man still in his very best years."[55] Hugo Kaupisch, the Schupo's first commander under the republican regime, addressed his pleas directly to Ernst Röhm, Rudolf Hess, and to Hitler. "I was never an enemy of the

NSDAP," he naïvely explained in one of his letters. "I was [merely] indifferent to the Nazi movement—Munich is far away from Berlin, and the Berlin branch [of the Nazi party] was relatively insignificant until 1926."[56] Kriminal-Kommissar Ernst Engelbrecht applied for readmission in the Kripo now that Dr. Bernhard Weiss was gone,[57] and Kurt Gildisch, the man who was fired in 1931 for singing tendentious songs in police barracks, now risen to S.S. officer, browbeat his former superior officer into rewriting his record in the Schupo's personnel files.[58]

Department IA was obviously destined to go, just as the royal political police had been untenable after the Revolution of 1918. On February 21, 1933, Reichskommissar Göring ordered that all SPD members in Department IA be transferred immediately to nonpolitical jobs.[59] Prominent officials like Regierungsdirektoren Goehrke, Scherler and Wündisch, and Police Councillor Stumm were removed from the police altogether. The rest of the IA staff were given an opportunity to serve in the new secret police: Nazi sympathizers like Police Councillors Helmut Heisig and Wilhelm Bonatz,[60] of course, but also some others whose professional ability made their cooperation desirable, provided they were now willing to serve the Third Reich—for example, Hubert Mühlfriedel and Dr. Rudolf Braschwitz.[61]

More Gestapo recruits came from the circle of Nazi supporters in Department IV: Detective Inspectors Erich Lipik, Harry Geisler, Hubert Geissel,[62] and above all, Arthur Nebe transferred to the Prinz-Albrecht Strasse. Arthur Nebe was promoted to Kriminalrat on April 1, 1933; on August 29, he further rose to Regierungs- und Kriminalrat. One month later he had made it to Oberregierungs- und Kriminalrat. He reached the height of his career in 1935, when he was returned to the ordinary detective force and made chief of the criminal police in all Prussia.

Political sympathizers who were not taken into the secret

police were rewarded with handsome promotions. Police Councillor Alfred Mundt, an old supporter of the NSDAP, took charge of the executive department of the Kripo. Philipp Greiner was entrusted with the detective division's personnel affairs and soon rose to police councillor (1934); and in July, 1933, Erich Liebermann von Sonnenberg was appointed chief of the Berlin criminal police. He replaced Regierungsdirektor Scholz who was said to have shown little aptitude for political cases. For, as a senior official at the Police Presidium explained in 1933,

> The criminal police has now been entrusted with a considerable portion of the political delinquencies. The directorship of the Kripo must therefore be in the hands of a man with a good understanding of the political situation and who can establish a relation of mutual trust and cooperation with all national organizations [i.e., the S.A., S.S., and the Stahlhelm].[63]

As it turned out, Liebermann was not entirely free from the professional attitudes of the old Berlin Kripo either. When he was made to resign his post three years later, Police President Count Helldorf wrote to Kurt Daluege that Liebermann should be regarded as a victim of circumstances, which in this case meant that he had failed to discard the personal considerations that traditionally had determined the Kripo's procedure and organization.[64] Liebermann was removed as Otto Trettin eventually was driven to suicide, since both of them had flirted with right-wing politics under the Republic on account of their frustration as criminalists, not because they were political men. The Nazis, however, preferred pure criminalists to political bedfellows who befriended them from ulterior motives. A capable man like Ludwig Werneburg was valuable to them. Though not an "old fighter," he was quickly accorded Party membership on May 1, 1933. Ernst Gennat was retained in the police service until his death on August 21, 1939, having by then risen to Regierungs- und Kriminalrat and permanent deputy chief of the criminal police in Berlin.[65] Gennat never joined the Nazi

party. Otto Busdorf did on April 1, 1933, but his strident demands for recognition as "one of the oldest supporters of naziism in the Kripo" soon earned him the Nazis' contempt. They
cynically used him in a brutal police action against Communists
and Social Democrats in Köpenick during February, 1933. After
that, they conveniently remembered his past connections with
the SPD and threw him out of the police in April, 1933, and
out of the S.A. in 1935.

The political events of 1933 did not otherwise make deep
inroads in Department IV. Needless to say, those Kripo officials
who seemed committed to the old regime were quickly suspended from active duty: they included veterans like Oberregierungsrat Heinrich Kopp, partisans of the Schrader-Verband
like Emil Klingelhöller, and, for that matter, a young candidate
for inspector rank named Wilhelm Rodenberg, who happened
to be Grzesinski's son-in-law.[66] But they numbered hardly more
than a dozen.

As in 1918 and 1919, the security police was for technical
reasons the most troublesome in adjusting to the change in regime. There were old Party comrades in the Schupo who were
not always good policemen but whose demand for reward could
not be ignored. Polizei-Meister Albert Becker, who had lost his
job in 1929, could not be reinstated because his service record
was poor. His disciplinary penalties under the Republic, however, were stricken from the record to make him eligible for a
retirement pension. Police Lieutenant Kurt Lange, who in the
previous year had betrayed defense installations of the Schupo
to the local Nazi party, was promoted in rank, but not his associate POWM Hans Schulz-Briesen, who was judged to be
"vain to a fault" and a menace to discipline. Both, it is true,
were offered money to make up for their time of imprisonment.
To give a final example, Police Captain Arved von Knobelsdorff, the head of police station 145 in Berlin-Spandau, and a
protégé of the Nazi Gauleiter Wilhelm Kube, was given a spe-

cially easy examination at the police school in Eiche, to help him win his promotion to police major. When Knobelsdorff nevertheless failed to answer the simplest questions, he was allowed to resign from the police, Party comrade or not.

The men in the Ministry of Interior were not indiscriminate in the distribution of political prizes. They knew that not everyone who had opposed the Republic was necessarily an asset for the Nazi police. Indeed, Police Major Andrae, who had spoken in defense of the Weimar regime at a meeting of the police officers' union in 1928,[67] was given a chance to prove his patriotic zeal under the new Reich, while Police Major Levit was eliminated in 1934 because of his alcoholic excesses.[68] Police Captains Boecker and Richter, and Police Colonel Jager were purged in spite of their Nazi affiliations because of their former membership in the Schrader-Verband. The same fate was meted out to Polizei-Oberstleutnant Ferdinand Kronberger who not only was a secret member of the Nazi party since 1931 (cover name Krohne) but held an influential position as commander of police inspection Charlottenburg. Kronberger also had belonged to the Schrader-Verband.[69]

Captain Walther Fränkel of police station 85 was a pathetic example of the kind of opportunist whom the Nazis feared most. He had joined the NSDAP as early as 1924. In 1928 he was punished by his republican chiefs when they found that he had made fraudulent claims on his application for police service in 1920. He thereupon joined the SPD between 1928 and 1931 to improve his chances for future promotion. To compound his difficulties in 1933, the Nazis suspected Fränkel of being a Jew. In spite of all his secret support of the Nazi movement during the last two years, Fränkel was put on the same purge list as his obstreperous republican Sergeant Hermann Artner.[70]

There were 445 men of the Berlin Schupo purged in the first months of 1933, 63 of whom were of officer's rank.[71] The list included Commander Heimannsberg, who in effect was sus-

pended since July 20, 1932, and other republicans whose political stand had drawn attention over the past ten years. Names
like Police Majors Erwin Blell and Karl Heinrich had been cited
in press reports. Police Captains Fellmann and Gallewski were
well known for their official functions in the Schrader-Verband,
and Polizei-Oberstleutnant Meyer for his activities in the Union
of Democratic Police Officials. Among the rank and file, the
brothers Fritz and Wilhelm Krumbach had made a reputation
for their militant opposition to fascism.[72]

The Schupo's behavior in 1933 was not unlike the performance of the Schutzmannschaft fourteen years earlier, after the
fall of the monarchy. There were assurances that the new government could rely on the support of the professional constabulary, and promises that the security force would now truly
become a "people's police." At the same time, the policemen
kept a watchful eye on potential rivals to their public authority.
S.A. and S.S. men were welcome to carry out emergency "police
operations" to consolidate the authority of the Nazi regime, but
they were opposed as soon as they sought to assume the role
of a permanent order police.

On February 17, 1933, the Prussian police was ordered to
cooperate closely with all units of the S.A., the S.S., and the
Stahlhelm. On February 22, 1933, came the ominous announce-
ment that

> The growing number of outrages committed by left-radicals and
> especially by Communists has created a constant and intolerable
> menace to public security, and to the life and property of the
> state-minded population. The available police forces, whose size
> cannot at this time be enlarged, have long been taxed beyond
> their capacity. Frequent calls to emergencies outside their terri-
> tory have deflected them from their appointed sphere of duty.
> Therefore, we can no longer do without the assistance of suit-
> able volunteers as auxiliary police officials.[73]

By March 4, 1933, some five thousand auxiliary policemen (Hilfspolizei, or Hipo) were enlisted for duty in Greater Berlin. They were made up of whole units of the S.A., the S.S., and the Stahlhelm, and were used for guard duty outside government buildings and the offices of the Nazi party, and for motorized patrols in the street.

As long as they were engaged in stamping out the remaining political opposition to Hitler, the Schupomen were content to be passive spectators. Willi Lemke's riot brigade escorted S.A. detachments to the village of Novawes, and stood by as their protégés broke up Communist gangs with clubs and guns and set their houses on fire. "None of us policemen was seriously hurt," he recorded in his memoirs after the Second World War. "When the S.A. men had won the upper hand, captain D. ordered us to the sidelines and we watched the rest of the fight from atop our vehicles." In the end, the Communists turned to the riot police for help. "Like it or not, we had to take them home in our trucks. There was no getting out of it. These people had placed themselves under our protection and we had to answer for their safety."[74]

And yet, according to Lemke, the men of the same police unit were prepared to revolt on June 30, 1934, when their barracks in Lichterfelde were temporarily occupied by S.S. troops, and it looked to them as if the Berlin Schupo was about to be replaced by Himmler's security guards.

The auxiliary policemen were not appreciated as helpers in the daily routine of police work. The Schupomen complained about their brutality and ignorance and felt ashamed to go on patrol with men "of whom we knew that many possessed a criminal record." Their professional interests were secured, as in 1919 and 1920, by the timely intervention of foreign powers who saw in the arming of the S.A. and S.S., and in the creation of the Hipo, a violation of the Treaty of Versailles.[75] They were secured also by the personal rivalry of Himmler and Göring, and because even the staunchest supporters of National Socialism inside the Schupo would not renounce its esprit de corps.

The outstanding Nazi among the Schupo's officer corps in 1933 was Police Major Walther Wecke. Wecke had secretly prepared political dossiers on Schupo officials as early as March, 1932, in anticipation of Hitler's accession to power. On November 1, 1932, he officially joined the NSDAP and assumed the leadership of the Schupo section in the NSBAG. Immediately following January 30, 1933, he was called to the Prussian Ministry of Interior to act as the chief liaison between the police and the Nazi party. He was also charged with the task of eliminating the opponents of naziism from the officer corps of the Schupo. By the end of February, 1933, Wecke was placed in command of a special elite force of police troops to protect the Nazi government against armed attack.[76]

The so-called "Landespolizeigruppe Wecke z.b.V.," or "Stabswache Göring," was designed for the same purpose as Walther Stennes's Hundertschaft z.b.V. in 1920-21. And, as in the case of Walther Stennes, the political regime soon found itself faced with an intractable armed force whose loyalty to itself seemed stronger than its devotion to the government. The S.A. Gauleitung for Greater Berlin, and the Nazi party organization in the Schupo denounced Wecke as a political opportunist and a friend of the Jews.[77] In June and July, 1933, six lists containing the names of about two dozen soldiers in Wecke's police army were forwarded to Kurt Daluege with the comment that "these men were not prepared to lay down their lives for the Führer."

We do not know why Wecke's unit included such dubious figures as Police Captain Hermann Seupel, Gildisch's drinking companion in 1930, or former Social Democrats like Police Captains Gallewski (before he was purged) and Reinhold Schüler. We cannot ascertain the justice of Police Captain Hans

Oelze's bitter words as he resigned from Wecke's police unit in 1934 to accept a commission in the army: "The Reichswehr is not political, your political opinions don't count. In the police you are outlawed [*verfemt*] if you happen to be a long-time Nazi."[78]

Police Major Wecke made his position quite clear when he rejected all the accusations against himself or his men as the intrigues of disgruntled and jealous elements. In a letter dated October 28, 1933, he emphasized that "the political purge inside the police has lasted long enough and is now completed. I see no reason why we should reopen our investigations because of some vague denunciations."[79] Five weeks later, after two more accusations had been received from the local Nazi headquarters, Wecke wrote to Daluege impatiently: "We now have a National-Socialist police. In my opinion, this eliminates every reason for the Party to interfere in [the] internal affairs [of the police]."[80]

The Party bosses disagreed. Gauleiter Wilhelm Kube, referring to Wecke's role in the S.A. purge of June 30, 1934, found it appropriate to remind his friends that "After all, we won our Third Reich not with the help of the police but through the efforts of all our old party comrades."[81] Politicians and professional policemen, it seems, will always disagree in their views of society: politicians worry about justifying their power, while policemen like to take their authority for granted and merely seek to justify its application.

Epilogue

No DOUBT the history of the Berlin police subsequent to 1933 also will be written one day. Contemporary historians concerned with the politics of the Nazi Reich have already provided us with studies of Germany's internal security forces under the Hitler regime.[1] For students of police history, in particular, it should prove instructive to trace the story of Berlin through the end of the Second World War to the restoration of a democratic police force in the Western sectors under Dr. Johannes Stumm, and the formation of a "People's Police" east of the Brandenburg Gate. How did they differ from each other and from the Nazi police in their respective recruitment, training, and conception of police duties? What was their mutual relationship, and what was their behavior during the crises of June 17, 1953, and August 13, 1961?

But such a work will no longer touch the heart of Berlin's historical condition during those years. After 1933, the police had lost its prominent place in the public eye. Order was restored in the streets of the capital and crime had drastically declined. On the other hand, the days of military displays were back: first the brown, black, and field-grey uniforms of the Third Reich, then the uniforms of four occupation powers.

What other theme the historian of Berlin might choose to highlight the city's fate in the last third of a century is difficult to say. The twelve years from 1933 to 1945 were years of regimentation and deprivation, ending in widespread destruction and despair. But periods of dictatorship make barren pickings for the "Kultur- und Sittengeschichtler." Since 1945, Berlin has been the object of an international tug of war. Between the blockade of 1948 and the uprising in the Stalinallee in 1953, the city even acquired a belated popularity as a symbol of Western resistance to the Communist bloc. Precisely because of the city's international significance, however, people who have written about postwar Berlin have often been hard put trying to avoid making the cold war their all absorbing theme: Berlin's fate has become dependent on half the world.[2]

Pessimistic forecasts for Berlin's future may account for the extraordinary boom in Berliniana during the 1950's and 1960's. And with unerring flair, the current wave of publications has largely centered on the 1920's as the most fruitful period in the history of modern Berlin, a time when the world seemed to swirl around the River Spree, and, as a contemporary slogan had it, from Shanghai to Buenos Aires, "Everyone must see Berlin!" Berlin then possessed the allures of a world capital, bursting with energy, torn by deep divisions, bound together by a common anxiety, and dominated by the figure of a smartly dressed traffic policeman who assured us, with a somewhat forced smile, that whatever the future may hold in store, everything would go according to regulations.

Appendix: INTERVIEWS

The following is an alphabetical list of persons who contributed their knowledge to this inquiry, together with brief resumes of the topics on which they have offered most information. The date and address indicate the time and place of the interview, the year in parenthesis shows when these persons first entered the service of the Berlin police. The titles apply to the time of the interview.

1. Polizeimeister Hermann ARTNER (1924)
   Berlin-Steglitz
   Muthesiusstrasse 35
   September 27, 1962
   Life history. Early service with riot brigade in Berlin-Friedrichshain. Relations with local precinct police. Criminality in Berlin. Political factions inside police stations in the early thirties. Communist and Nazi attitudes toward the police. Salaries and promotion. The Papen putsch, 1932, and the purge of 1933. Police Captain Fränkel. The brothers Krumbach. The murder of Emil Kuhfeld.
2. Kriminalrat Adolf BAUER (1922)
   Berlin-Zehlendorf
   Jugenheimerweg 9

November 22, 1962
Riot police duty in Abteilung Zentrum. Police unions. Monarchists among the police officers' corps. Nazi penetration in rank and file. Communist provocations. Efficiency of KPD. The personalities of Dr. Bernhard Weiss and Kripo officials Arthur Nebe, Teichmann, Helmuth Müller, and Albert Dettmann. The case of Walther Stennes.

3. Polizeiangestellte Grete BOMKE (1929)
Berlin-Steglitz
Albrechtstrasse 73a
October 17, 1962
Personal descriptions of police leaders Grzesinski, Zörgiebel, Heimannsberg, Weiss, and Goehrke. The normal routine in the Präsidialabteilung of the Police Presidium and in Department IA before 1933. Rivalry between Kripo and IA. The personalities of Trettin, Liebermann, Gennat, and Nebe. The events of July 20, 1932 in Police President Grzesinski's office.

4. Polizeiangestellte Charlotte ELSLER (1922)
Berlin-Kreuzberg
Lilienthal Strasse 12
October 28, 1962
Secretarial work for Riemann, Gennat, Liebermann, and Trettin of Department IV, 1922-1929; after 1929 work for Wündisch, Goehrke, and Stumm at Department IA.

5. Polizei-Oberrat FINGER, Head of Police School
Berlin-Spandau
Hohenzollernring 124
September 18, 1962
Police schools before and after 1933.

6. Polizei-Obermeister Kurt FLEISCHER (1920)
At his home
Berlin-Spandau
September 19, 1962
Personal career. Relations between Sipo and "blue" constabulary. Political climate in Sipo. Schrader-Verband. Kapp putsch. Murder of Anlauf and Lenck. Papen putsch. Purge of the police corps in 1933. Popularity of Deputy Schupo Commander Gentz, of police chiefs Weiss and Zörgiebel. Surveillance techniques at political rallies.

7. Inspektionsleiter F. GEDIEHN (1920)
Berlin-Dahlem

Ladenbergstrasse 24
September 26, 1962
Personal career. Political climate in police in 1920. Police training, 1922–23. Kapp putsch. Social background of rookies. Comparison between Communist and Nazi tactics toward the Schupo. The achievements of Severing, Weiss, and Heimannsberg. The murder of Anlauf and Lenck. The impotence of the police in the Weimar Republic.

8. Kriminalrat HOBERG
Kripo Headquarters
Berlin-Schöneberg
Gothaer Strasse 19
November 6, 1962
Development of criminology in the 1920's. The work of Hans Schneick-ert, Robert Heindl, Erich Liebermann.

9. Kriminal-Hauptmeister Max JACHODE (1924), and

10. Kriminal-Obermeister Herbert M. TIETZE (1923)
Kripo Headquarters
Berlin-Schöneberg
Gothaer Strasse 19
October 25, 1962
Schupo duty in Wedding and Neukölln in the early twenties. Salaries. Political sentiments in police stations. Murder of Anlauf and Lenck, and of Horst Wessel. Communist demonstrators and the police. Communists joining the Nazi party. Ringvereine. Police unions. Social background of policemen. Fritz Krumbach. July 20, 1932.

11. Polizei-Hauptwachtmeister Erich JAHN (1919)
Library of Police Headquarters
Berlin-Tempelhof
Tempelhofer Damm 1-7
October 3, 1962
Life history. Sipo service, 1920. Educational opportunities in the police. Uniforms and equipment. Advancement, salaries. Civil service openings for retired policemen. Air police guard.

12. Polizei-Major, retired, Eduard KOLBE (1920)
Berlin-Tempelhof
Thuyring 28
October 3, 1962
Youth, war service 1914-18. Sipo and Kapp putsch. Communist propaganda. Nazis in the Schupo. Police unions. Walther Stennes. Schupo

agents in mufti at political rallies. *Die Polizei.* Schupo relations with Kripo and IA. Heimannsberg, Weiss, Helldorf. Murder of Anlauf, Lenck, and Zauritz. Papen putsch. Purges in 1933.

13. Regierungs- und Kriminalrat Paul KUCKENBURG (1912)
Berlin-Wilmersdorf
Landhausstrasse 32
October 16, 1962
Theoretical principles of detective work. Advancement and promotion in the Kripo. Kripo relations with Schupo and IA. Trettin, Liebermann. Communists among police staff, criminals among Communists.

14. Generalstaatsanwalt, retired, Wilhelm KÜHNAST
At his home
October 12 and 17, 1962
The shooting of Anlauf and Lenck. The case of Kurt Gildisch. Dr. Bernhard Weiss. Kripo and IA.

15. Kriminalmeister Otto KRAUSE (1928)
Berlin-Charlottenburg
Mindener Strasse 4
November 2, 1962
Life history. Police sports movement. Police Institute for Physical Training. Riot police duty in Berlin-Mitte. The death of Anlauf and Lenck. Disturbances in the Scheunenviertel. Political discussions among riot policemen. Papen putsch. Heimannsberg, Grzesinski, Weiss. Police unions, salaries, fringe benefits.

16. Polizei-Oberkommissar Rolf KURZIDIM (1936)
Police School
Berlin-Spandau
Hohenzollernring 124
September 19, 1962
Rural background of many Berlin policemen. National reputation of Berlin force. Political neutrality of police in Weimar Republic. Weiss, Heimannsberg, Zörgiebel as police leaders.

17. Kriminaldirektor Albert LEHNHOFF (1929)
Berlin-Friedenau
Menzelstrasse 25
October 22, 1962
Reputation of Berlin Kripo in the twenties. Structure, organization, and routine training procedure of the Kripo. Relations with IA and state prosecutor's office. Murder of Horst Wessel. Ringvereine. Criminals and

politics. Schrader-Verband. Personality of Grzesinski, Weiss, Liebermann, Trettin, Nebe, Gennat, and Geissel.

18. Polizei-Hauptkommissar Willi LEMKE (1932)
    Police School
    Berlin-Spandau
    Hohenzollernring 124
    September 18, 1962
    (Interview supplemented by Lemke's draft of his autobiography.)
    Life history. Training at Police school, 1932-33. Service with riot police in Potsdam. Clashes with Nazi and Communist demonstrators. Political opinions in the rank and file. Uniforms, armament. Changes introduced in 1933.

19. Inspektor Richard LINDNER
    Polizeifortbildungsschule
    Berlin-Tempelhof
    September 7, 1962
    Administrative structure and organization of Berlin police.

20. Polizei-Oberrat Gottfried MICZEK (1924)
    Kommando der Schutzpolizei
    Berlin-Tempelhof
    Tempelhofer Damm 1
    October 24, 1962
    Personal background. Recruitment of police personnel and police training in the twenties. Political disturbances in Berlin. Professional crooks and Communists. Walther Stennes. Monarchical officers. Schupo agents in mufti at political rallies. Liaison between Schupo and IA. Attitude to police of Nazis and Communists. Murder of Horst Wessel. Shooting of Anlauf and Lenck. Security problem in Charlottenburg and Wilmersdorf. Officers' training at Eiche. Relations between Schupo and Kripo. Ernst Gennat. Purge of 1933. Nazis among police officers.

21. Polizei-Oberkommissar Richard NASS (1923)
    Police School
    Berlin-Spandau
    Hohenzollernring 124
    September 20, 1962
    Sipo and Schutzmannschaft, 1919–1920. Police training in Brandenburg. Conditions for advancement in the Berlin Schupo during the twenties.

22. Oberinspektor PARIS

23. Oberinspektor MACH
24. Oberinspektor VOLLERT
    Polizeischule für Verwaltungspolizei
    Berlin-Tempelhof
    Columbiadamm
    September 7, 1962
    Police history. Police doctrine. The legal principles governing police
    operations during political troubles.
25. Leitender Kriminaldirektor Wolfram SANGMEISTER
    Kripo Headquarters
    Berlin-Schöneberg
    Gothaer Strasse 19
    October 25, 1962
    Legal basis of Kripo operations in Germany. Relations with judiciary.
    The place of political police work in a democracy. Specialization among
    Kripo detectives.
26. Polizei-Obersekretär Bruno SCHIRMER (1921)
    Police Presidium
    Berlin-Tempelhof
    Tempelhofer Damm 1-7
    October 11, 1962
    Life history. Service with riot brigade in Prenzlauer Berg. Security
    conditions in that district. Political sympathies within the brigade. Salaries.
    Severance pay, civil service posts for retiring policemen. Adult education
    courses in the Schupo. Cooperation of Schupo and Kripo at the scene of
    a common crime and of political troubles.
27. Kriminal-Hauptkommissar SCHUCHARDT
    Kripo Headquarters
    Berlin-Schöneberg
    Gothaer Strasse 19
    September 27, 1962
    Recruitment, training, and promotion of Kripo officials during the
    Weimar Republic.
28. Polizei-Oberwachtmeister Alfred SENDZIK (1926)
    Berlin-Neukölln
    Boddinstrasse 24a
    November 14, 1967
    Personal experience in the First World War, and between 1920 and
    1925 with the Schupo of Osterode, East Prussia. Transfer to Berlin in

1926. Police school in Brandenburg. Schrader-Verband and Betnarek-Verband. Walking the beat in Tempelhof. Police equipment. The purge in 1933.

29. Police President, retired, Dr. Johannes STUMM (1921)
   Berlin-Grunewald
   Menzelstrasse 14
   September 19 and November 27, 1962
   Surveillance of subversive elements in police. Walther Stennes, Kurt Gildisch, Otto Busdorf, Arthur Nebe, Otto Trettin, Erich Liebermann. Contrast to Ernst Gennat. IA surveillance of political meetings. Relations between IA and Kripo. Police unions. Papen putsch. Purge, 1933.

30. Kriminalmeister TEIGELER (1932)
   Berlin-Mariendorf
   Dachsteinweg 6
   October 11, 1962
   Organization of LKA Berlin. Famous criminal cases: the brothers Sass, Ringvereine, the murder of Horst Wessel, Anlauf and Lenck, the fight at Kolonie Felseneck. Cooperation between Kripo and IA. IA surveillance of political meetings. Political climate inside IA. Some police personalities: Bernhard Weiss, Otto Trettin, Albert Dettmann.

31. Kriminaldirektor, retired, Werner TOGOTZES (1927)
   At Cafe Schmidt
   Berlin-Schöneberg
   Hauptstrasse 77
   October 10, 1962
   The LKA Berlin: Vogel, Gay, Hasenjäger. Comparison between Berlin and Dresden Kripo. Trettin and Gennat. Criteria for success in the old Kripo. Brothers Sass. Murder of Horst Wessel. Ringvereine. Limited usefulness of crime statistics.

32. Hauptkommissar Otto TROTT (1941)
   Police School
   Berlin-Spandau
   Hohenzollernring 124
   September 18, 1962
   Police duty in Berlin compared with elsewhere. Legal prerogatives of police officials. Routine police procedure. Political attitudes in the rank and file.

Notes

Preface

[1] Hajo Holborn, "Research Needs in Modern German History," address to the Conference Group on Central Europe, delivered at the 78th Convention of the *American Historical Association*, Philadelphia, Dec. 28, 1963.

[2] Rolf Hochhuth, *The Deputy*, trans. Richard and Clara Winston (New York: Grove Press, 1964); Arnold Brecht, *Aus nächster Nähe: Lebenserinnerungen, 1884–1927* (Stuttgart: Deutsche Verlags-Anstalt, 1966); and W. A. Allen, *The Nazi Seizure of Power, 1932–1938* (Chicago: Quadrangle Press, 1965), are examples that readily suggest themselves.

[3] Notably Werner Hegemann, *Das steinerne Berlin. Geschichte der grössten Mietskasernenstadt der Welt* (Berlin: Gustav Kiepenheuer, 1930). An abbreviated edition in paperback was published by Ullstein in 1963.

[4] For a comment on the varieties of Berlin's *"Heimatschriftstellerei,"* see Walther Kiaulehn, *Berlin: Schicksal einer Weltstadt* (Munich and Berlin: Biederstein, 1958), pp. 336–338.

[5] Hans O. Modrow, *Berlin 1900. Querschnitt durch die Entstehung einer Stadt um die Jahrhundertwende* (Berlin: Hobbing, 1930) deserves special mention in this category.

[6] These are the novels that are set in Berlin but never mention the city by name, as if to underline the broader relevance of the story that is being told: Alfred Döblin, *Pardon wird nicht gegeben* (Olten and Freiburg i.B.: Walter, 1960); Vladimir Nabokov, *König, Dame, Bube* (Berlin: Ullstein, 1930); and Erich Maria Remarque, *Drei Kameraden* (Berlin: Ullstein, 1960).

[7] For example E. Hirschberg, *Die soziale Lage der arbeitenden Klassen in Berlin* (Berlin, 1897); Hans Brennert and Erwin Stein, eds., *Probleme der neuen Stadt Berlin* (Berlin-Friedenau, 1926); Martin Wagner and A. Behne, eds., *Das neue Berlin. Groszstadtprobleme* (Berlin, 1929). See also Hans Zopf and Gerd Heinrichs, eds., *Berlin Bibliographie* (Berlin: Walter de Gruyter, 1965).

[8] Like most German cities, Berlin has no usable history published in English. John Mander, *Berlin: The Eagle and the Bear* (London, 1959) gives us only an idea of what such a book might contain. Henry Vizetelly, *Berlin under the New Empire* (London: Tinsley, 1879), 2 vols., is more substantial but out of date.

[9] Karl Scheffler was known for two important books on Berlin: *Berlin, Ein Stadtschicksal* (Berlin, 1910), and *Berlin: Wandlungen einer Stadt* (Berlin, 1931).

[10] Rolf Italiaander and Willy Haas, eds., *Berliner Cocktail* (Hamburg and Vienna: Paul Szolnay, 1959), p. 12.

Introduction

[1] Hermann Ullmann, *Flucht aus Berlin* (Jena: Eugen Diederichs, 1932), pp. 44, 71–72.

[2] Gustav Böss, *Die Not in Berlin. Tatsachen und Zahlen* (Berlin: Zentralverlag, 1923), pp. 4–5; and H. R. Knickerbocker, *Deutschland so oder so?* (Berlin: Rowohlt, 1932), pp. x–xi.

[3] S. Cracauer, *Die Angestellten. Aus dem neuesten Deutschland* (Frankfurt a.M., 1930), p. 7.

[4] Ullmann, *Flucht aus Berlin*, pp. 7–8. See also "Los von Berlin? Eine Kundgebung der Humboldt Akademie," in *Vossische Zeitung*, April 28, 1919 (M).

[5] Mario Krammer, *Berlin im Wandel der Jahrhunderte. Eine Kulturgeschichte der deutschen Hauptstadt* (Berlin: Rembrandt, 1956), p. 260; and also the defensive stand taken on this question by Friedrich C. A. Lange in *Gross-Berliner Tagebuch, 1920–1933* (Berlin-Lichtenrade: Berlinische Verlagsbuchhandlung, 1951), p. 176. Their view is not es-

sentially challenged by Barbara M. Lane in her *Architecture and Politics in Germany, 1918–1945* (Cambridge, Mass.: Harvard University Press, 1968). See pp. 103–112.

[6] Wolfgang Schadewaldt, "Lob Berlins," in Hans Rothfels, ed., *Berlin in Vergangenheit und Gegenwart* (Tübingen: Mohr, 1961), p. 83.

[7] Ilya Ehrenburg, *Memoirs: 1921–1941*, trans. Tatania Shebunina (Cleveland and New York: World Publishing, 1965), p. 10.

[8] Ernst von Salomon, *Der Fragebogen* (Hamburg: Rowohlt, 1951), p. 248.

[9] Ferdinand Friedensburg, *Die Weimarer Republik* (Berlin, 1946), pp. 19–20.

[10] Henri Béraud, *Ce que j'ai vu à Berlin* (Paris: Éditions de France, 1926), p. 48.

[11] Axel Eggebrecht, *Volk ans Gewehr. Chronik eines Berliner Hauses, 1930–34.* (Frankfurt a.m.: Europäische Verlagsanstalt, 1959), p. 89.

[12] Walther Kiaulehn, *Berlin: Schicksal einer Weltstadt* (Munich and Berlin: Biederstein, 1958), p. 172.

[13] Ernst van den Bergh, *Polizei und Volk–Seelische Zausammenhänge* (Berlin: Gersbach, 1926), p. 102. This is not meant as a reflection on the efficiency of the royal constabulary.

[14] Franz Lederer, *Berlin und Umgebung* (Berlin, 1929), pp. 15, 17; and Rumpelstilzchen [Adolf Stein], *Piept es?* (Berlin: Tägliche Rundschau, 1930), pp. 75–77. The first Schupo parade down Unter den Linden on Easter Monday, 1932, was greeted by loyal republicans as a welcome though belated attempt to reinforce the image of the existing regime. *Vossische Zeitung*, March 29, 1932 (M).

[15] Bernhard Weiss, *Polizei und Politik* (Berlin: Gersbach, 1928), pp. 9–10; also Wilhelm Hartenstein, *Der Kampfeinsatz der Schutzpolizei bei inneren Unruhen* (Berlin-Charlottenburg: Offene Worte, 1926), p. 3.

[16] Ratcliffe (Polizei-Major), "Wie urteilt das Ausland über die preussische Polizei?" in *Die Polizei*, 29. Jhg., Nr.4, Feb. 20, 1932, pp. 71–72; Rumpelstilzchen [Adolf Stein], *Berliner Allerlei* (Berlin: Tägliche Rundschau, 1922), p. 304.

[17] For example the following passages: Hans Fallada [Rudolf Ditzen], *Kleiner Mann—was nun?* (Berlin: Rowohlt, 1932), pp. 238–239; Heinz Rein, *Berlin 1932: Ein Roman aus der Zeit der grossen Arbeitslosigkeit* (Berlin: Erich Schmidt, 1946), pp. 57 ff.; and Karl A. Schenzinger, *Der Hitlerjunge Quex* (Berlin and Leipzig: "Zeitgeschichte," 1932), pp. 7–8.

[18] Carl Severing, "Die Polizei im neuen Staat," in *Almanach zum "Fest*

der Polizei" (1929), pp. 12–13. Much the same point was made by Friedensburg in his *Weimarer Republik*, pp. 243–244.

[19] To avoid confusion, we shall adhere to this designation although in September, 1931, the political police was reclassified as "Department I."

[20] Rumpelstilzchen, *Berliner Allerlei*, pp. 54–55.

[21] Eugen Ernst, Police President of Berlin (1919), was the author of *Polizeispitzeleien und Ausnahmegesetz, 1878–1910* (Berlin: Vorwärts, 1911), an attack on the old political police.

[22] Weiss, *Polizei und Politik*.

[23] This, according to Frank Arnau, was perhaps the chief reason for its failure. Frank Arnau, *Das Auge des Gesetzes. Macht und Ohnmacht der Kriminalpolizei* (Düsseldorf and Vienna: Econ, 1962), pp. 60–61.

[24] Hedda Adlon, *Hotel Adlon. Das Haus in dem die Welt zu Gast war* (Munich: Kindler, 1955), or Hans Erman, *Bei Kempinski. Aus der Chronik einer Weltstadt* (Berlin: Argon, 1956).

[25] The first dealt with modern train robbers, the second with servant girls who worked in collusion with burglars. For the latter, see "Dienstmädchen-Einbrüche," in *Vossische Zeitung*, Feb. 24, 1920 (M); and Ernst Englebrecht and Leo Heller, *Kinder der Nacht. Bilder aus dem Verbrecherleben* (Berlin: Hermann Paetel, 1925), p. 14.

[26] We shall have more to say on this matter in chap. IV.

[27] *Vossische Zeitung*, Jan. 23, 1926 (A): "Germany's cultural niveau is not on the decline if its Security Police can still produce a symphony orchestra of such high quality."

[28] Füth (Kriminal-Oberwachtmeister), "Zur Reform der Polizei," in *Die Polizei*, 16. Jhg., Nr. 10, Aug. 14, 1919, p. 233. It should, of course, be noted that the widespread use of police authority for purposes of public administration in Germany need not imply a greater interference in individual freedom than in any other modern state. See Frederick F. Blachly and Miriam E. Oatman, *The Government and Administration of Germany* (Baltimore: Johns Hopkins Press, 1928), pp. 418–419.

[29] Menzel, "Reformmöglichkeiten bei der Polizei," in *Die Polizei*, 25. Jhg., Nr. 2, Jan. 20, 1928, pp. 31–32. Menzel played a leading role in the reform of the internal administration of the Prussian police during the late twenties.

[30] Weiss, *Polizei und Politik*, p. 11. See also Emil Klingelhöller, *Der Verband Preussischer Polizeibeamten in seinem Werden und Wirken* (Berlin: Verlag Deutsche Polizeibuchhandlung, 1926), p. 24.

[31] These must be understood as approximate figures. They are used by Albert C. Grzesinski, Police President of Berlin in 1925–26 and 1930–32, in

his *Inside Germany*, trans. Alexander S. Lipschitz (New York: E. P. Dutton, 1939), pp. 117, 124.

[32] On the establishment of Greater Berlin, see Hans Schulze, *5 Jahre Gross-Berlin* (Neustrelitz, 1927).

[33] The "Landespolizeibezirk Berlin" was composed of (1) Berlin; (2) Charlottenburg; (3) Neukölln; (4) Schöneberg, Wilmersdorf, Halensee; (5) Lichtenberg, Boxhagen, Rummelsburg, Stralau. The rural police districts that were subordinated to the Regierungspräsident (governor) in Potsdam were Tegel, Reinickendorf, Pankow, Weissensee, Tempelhof, Britz, Friedenau, and Schmargendorf. Their amalgamation in 1920 is well explained in Heinrich Lindenau, "Die Polizei von Gross-Berlin," in *Vossische Zeitung*, Feb. 18, 1920 (M).

[34] Excerpts from Jerome K. Jerome's satire of Imperial Germany *Three Men on a Bummel* were quoted in Hermann Degenhardt and Max Hagemann, *Polizei und Kind* (Berlin: Gersbach, 1926), pp. 58–60.

[35] Ullmann, *Flucht aus Berlin*, p. 87.

[36] Lederer, *Berlin und Umgebung*, p. 68. For the "Flight from the City," see also Willy Mann, *Berlin zur Zeit der Weimarer Republik* (Berlin: Das Neue Berlin, 1957), p. 81; and Rumpelstilzchen, *Piept es?*, p. 320.

[37] Leo Lania, "To-day We Are Brothers," in Harlan R. Crippen, ed., *Germany: A Self-Portrait* (London and New York: Oxford University Press, 1944), pp. 185–197.

[38] Knickerbocker, *Deutschland so oder so?*, p. 20.

[39] For the exact boundaries of the Bannmeile, (1920–34), see the map on p. 12. Hitler took advantage of the special security within this zone by choosing Hotel Kaiserhof as his residence during his visits to Berlin, 1931–33. Julius K. von Engelbrechten and Hans Volz, eds., *Wir wandern durch das nationalsozialistische Berlin* (Munich: Zentralverlag der NSDAP, 1937), p. 63.

[40] Ullmann, *Flucht aus Berlin*, p. 21

[41] Also referred to as "Berlin WW," this region encompassed the small area between Uhlandstrasse, Zoo Station, and Wittenbergplatz.

[42] Ullman, *Flucht aus Berlin, passim;* and Pem [Paul Erich Marcus], *Heimweh nach dem Kurfürstendamm. Aus Berlins glanzvollsten Tagen und Nächten* (Berlin: Lothar Blanvalet, 1952). See also Max Krell, *Das alles gab es einmal* (Frankfurt a.M.: Heinrich Scheffler, 1961).

[43] Friedrich Hussong, *"Kurfürstendamm." Zur Kulturgeschichte des Zwischenreichs* (Berlin: Tägliche Rundschau, 1934), p. 38. Calvin B. Hoover, *Germany enters the Third Reich* (New York, 1933), p. 22.

[44] Von Engelbrechten and Volz, *Nationalsozialistisches Berlin,* pp. 213–214; Joseph Goebbels, *Kampf um Berlin* (Munich: F. Eher, 1940), p. 27.

[45] In 1919 the local residents donated an armor-plated car to the detective force of the Charlottenburg police. *Die Polizei,* 16. Jhg., Nr. 3, May 8, 1919, p. 66.

[46] Friedrich Sieburg, *Gott in Frankreich?* (Frankfurt a.M.: Frankfurter Societäts-Druckerei, 1929), pp. 119–120.

[47] Béraud, *Ce que j'ai vu à Berlin,* p. 19. "Berlin at night" was a favorite subject of Berlin painters during the twenties. See Lederer, *Berlin und Umgebung,* pp. 62–63.

[48] *Ibid.,* p. 99; and Lange, *Gross-Berliner Tagebuch,* p. 38.

[49] Von Engelbrechten and Volz, *Nationalsozialistisches Berlin,* pp. 74–75.

[50] Hanns Heinz Ewers, *Horst Wessel. Ein deutsches Schicksal* (Stuttgart and Berlin: J. G. Cotta, 1934), *passim.*

[51] Interview, Otto Krause.

[52] To this district belonged Münzstrasse, Dragonerstrasse (now Max-Beer-Strasse), Grenadierstrasse (now Almstädter Strasse), Linienstrasse, Rückerstrasse, and Mulackstrasse. See Philipp Paneth, *Nacht über Berlin-Alexanderplatz* (Leipzig: Heinrich Blömer, 1932), p. 31; and Ernst Engelbrecht, *In den Spuren des Verbrechertums* (Berlin-Schöneberg: Peter J. Oestergaard, 1930 [?]), p. 102.

[53] See the State vs. Walther de Laporte, Oct. 1928, in "Akten betr. Entscheidungen in förmlichen Disziplinaruntersuchungssachen," vol. 17, 1. Senat des Preussischen Oberverwaltungsgerichts; also "Raubüberfälle der Jugendlichen," in *Archiv für Kriminologie,* 89 (Berlin, 1931), 235–238.

[54] E. Liebermann von Sonnenberg and Otto Trettin, *Kriminalfälle* (Berlin: Universitas, 1934), p. 224; and Interview, Kurt Fleischer.

[55] Interview, Teigeler. Also Wolfgang Ullrich, *Verbrechensbekämpfung. Geschichte, Organisation, Rechtssprechung* (Berlin-Spandau: Hermann Luchterhand, 1961), pp. 71–72; and Klaus Neukrantz, *Barricades in Berlin* (New York: International Publishers, 1930 [?]), *passim.* Rein, *Berlin 1932,* pp. 168–169, gives a good description of Hussitenstrasse.

[56] "Verbrecherschlacht am Schlesischen Bahnhof," in *Vossische Zeitung,* Dec. 31, 1928 (A).

[57] Interview, Max E. Jachode. Also von Engelbrechten and Volz, *Nationalsozialistisches Berlin,* pp. 185–189.

[58] Ullmann, *Flucht aus Berlin,* pp. 22–23.

[59] Interview, Gottfried Miczek, who was attached to police station

156 in 1929–31. The "Little Wedding" (between Sophie-Charlotten-Strasse, Charlottenburger Ufer, Berliner Strasse, Knie [now Ernst-Reuter-Platz], Bismarckstrasse and Kaiserdamm) is described in Jan Petersen, *Our Street. A Chronicle written in the heart of Fascist Germany*, trans. Betty Rensen (London, 1938). The Communist stronghold in Moabit is the scene of Karl Aloys Schenzinger's novel *Der Hitlerjunge Quex* (Berlin and Leipzig: "Zeitgeschichte," 1932); and the red island in Friedenau is mentioned by Axel Eggebrecht in "Mut und Uebermut im Künstlerblock," in Rolf Italiaander and Willy Haas, eds., *Berliner Cocktail* (Hamburg and Vienna: Paul Szolnay, 1959), pp. 453–456.

⁶⁰ Christopher Isherwood, *The Last of Mr. Norris* (first pub. 1935), in *The Berlin Stories* (New York: J. Laughlin, 1945), p. 86.

⁶¹ Heinrich Müller, *Ueber Präventivpolizei* (Zurich, 1937), pp. 99–101.

⁶² Grzesinski, *Inside Germany*, p. 139.

⁶³ Müller, *Präventivpolizei*, p. 123; and Wilhelm Troitzsch, *Die Polizeipflicht in politisch bewegten Zeiten* (Königsberg: Gräfe & Unzer, 1933), p. 39.

⁶⁴ Erich Eyck, *A History of the Weimar Republic*, trans. H. P. Hanson and Robert G. L. Waite, II (Cambridge, Mass.: Harvard University Press, 1963), 414 ff.

⁶⁵ On this score, see Troitzsch, *Polizeipflicht, passim*, but especially p. 26.

⁶⁶ Carl Severing, *Mein Lebensweg*, II (Cologne: Greven, 1950), 82; and Karl Dietrich Bracher, Wolfgang Sauer, and Gerhard Schulz, *Die nationalsozialistische Machtergreifung* (Cologne: Westdeutscher Verlag, 1960), pp. 427–428.

CHAPTER I

The Historical Legacy of the Schutzpolizei

¹ According to a British study, the staff of the political police in Berlin in 1917, counted no more than 21 officials. The General Staff, War Office, *The German Police System as Applied to Military Security in War* (1921), p. 11.

² Kurt Melcher, *Die Geschichte der Polizei* (Berlin: Gersbach, 1926), pp. 60–61.

³ A commentary to the Police Code of June 1, 1931, states, "the basic tendency of this Code is meant to be conservative in the sense that it retains all the valuable and practical achievements of the past hundred

years which have also proven their usefulness to the new state." Erich Klausener, Christian Kerstein, and Robert Kempner, eds., *Das Polizeiverwaltungsgesetz vom 1. Juni 1931* (Berlin: C. A. Weller, 1931), p. vii.

⁴ Secretary of State Dr. Wilhelm Abegg, addressing the Prussian Police Association on Sept. 29, 1926, declared that "the much-abused old Police was not as bad as it has often been pictured. It merely conformed to the circumstances of that period." *Vossische Zeitung*, Sept. 29, 1926 (A).

⁵ Ernst van den Bergh, *Polizei und Volk—Seelische Zusammenhänge* (Berlin: Gersbach, 1926), pp. 9–10; see also Hermann Degenhardt and Max Hagemann, *Polizei und Kind* (Berlin: Gersbach, 1926), pp. 21–22.

⁶ Füth, "Zur Reform der Polizei," in *Die Polizei*, 16. Jhg., Nr. 40, Aug. 14, 1919, p. 233.

⁷ Bill Drews, *Preussisches Polizeirecht. Ein Leitfaden für Verwaltungsbeamte*, I (Berlin: Carl Heymann, 1927), p. 13.

⁸ Van den Bergh, *Polizei und Volk*, pp. 6–7.

⁹ *Ibid.*, p. 86.

¹⁰ *Ibid.*, p. 60.

¹¹ *Ibid.*, p. 16.

¹² Wilhelm Troitzsch, in his study *Die Polizeipflicht in politisch bewegten Zeiten* (Königsberg: Gräfe & Unzer, 1933) points to a similar conflict in police instructions concerning the defacement of houses with political slogans, pp. 21–27.

¹³ Wilhelm Abegg, ed., *Die Polizei in Einzeldarstellungen* (Berlin: Gersbach, 1926–28), 12 vols.

¹⁴ Van den Bergh, *Polizei und Volk*, pp. 42–88.

¹⁵ By an edict of Jan. 16, 1742, the control of police affairs in Berlin was taken from the municipality and entrusted to the General-Directorium. See also Willy Feigell, *Die Entwicklung des Königlichen Polizei-Präsidiums zu Berlin in der Zeit von 1809 bis 1909* (Berlin, 1909), p. 5.

¹⁶ Van den Bergh, *Polizei und Volk*, p. 61.

¹⁷ *Ibid.*, pp. 67–86. See also Walther Kiaulehn, *Berlin: Schicksal einer Weltstadt* (Munich and Berlin: Biederstein, 1958), p. 84.

¹⁸ Van den Bergh, *Polizei und Volk*, p. 97.

¹⁹ *Ibid.*, p. 102.

²⁰ Paul Schmidt, *Die ersten 50 Jahre der Königlichen Schutzmannschaft zu Berlin* (Berlin: Ernst Siegfried Mittler, 1898), pp. 17 ff.

²¹ *Ibid.*, pp. 17–19, 23–25, 44. This view was shared by van den Bergh in *Polizei und Volk*, p. 78, though he expressed himself with more caution.

²² Schmidt, *Königliche Schutzmannschaft*, pp. 39, 61.

²³ *Ibid.*, pp. 50–51.

CHAPTER II

The Background of Fear and Irresolution, 1918–1920

[1] For the decimation of the Berlin staff, see Directorate of Military Intelligence, The War Office, *The German Police System*, pt. I, supp. I (June, 1920), pp. 5, 9; and Das Königliche Polizeipräsidium in Berlin, *Die innere Front* (Berlin: A. Jandorf, 1917), pp. 41–42.

[2] Paul Riege, *Kleine Polizeigeschichte* (Lübeck: Verlag für polizeiliches Fachschrifttum, 1954), p. 34; and Helmuth Koschorke, ed., *Die Polizei— einmal anders!* (Munich: Zentralverlag der NSDAP, 1937), pp. 33–34. Since the end of 1917, the War Ministry urged the Supreme Command to hold frontline troops in readiness in case of internal troubles. Rudolf Coper, *Failure of a Revolution* (Cambridge: Cambridge University Press, 1955), pp. 35–36.

[3] Roland Schönfelder, *Vom Werden der deutschen Polizei* (Leipzig: Breitkopf & Härtel, 1937), p. 286.

[4] Emil Klingelhöller, *Der Verband Preussischer Polizeibeamten in seinem Werden und Wirken* (Berlin: Deutsche Polizeibuchhandlung, 1926), pp. 19–20.

[5] *Ibid.*, p. 24.

[6] That the subdued animosity of the police toward the army had lingered on into the war can be deduced from articles such as Stephan (Polizeirat), "Müssen die von den Militärbefehlshabern ausser Kraft gesetzten Polizeiverordnungen nach dem Krieg neu erlassen werden?" in *Die Polizei*, 11. Jhg., Nr. 26, March 18, 1915, p. 611.

[7] Coper, *Failure of a Revolution*, pp. 15–16; and Willy Mann, *Berlin zur Zeit der Weimarer Republik. Ein Beitrag zur Erforschung der wirtschaftlichen und politische Entwicklung der deutschen Hauptstadt* (Berlin: Das Neue Berlin, 1957), p. 18–20.

[8] *Berliner Tageblatt*, Nov. 10, 1918, as quoted in *ibid.*, p. 21. For a similar comment see Theodore Abel, *Why Hitler came to Power* (New York: Prentice-Hall, 1938), p. 16.

[9] *Die Schutzmannszeitung*, Aug. 9, 1919, as quoted in Klingelhöller, *Verband Preussischer Polizeibeamten*, pp. 65–69.

[10] *Ibid.*, pp. 69–71; and "Mehr Sicherheit in Gross-Berlin!," in *Vossische Zeitung*, April 20, 1919 (M). See also Bernhard Weiss, *Polizei und Politik* (Berlin: Gersbach, 1928), pp. 126–127; "Der frühere Vizepräsident der Berliner Polizei erzählt aus seinen Erfahrungen," in *Berliner Forum* (RIAS-Berlin, Jan., 1950), p. 7; and Schönfelder, *Vom Werden der deutschen Polizei*, pp. 286–287.

[11] This article was published in *Die Schutzmannszeitung,* Aug. 9, 1919, and quoted in Klingelhöller, *Verband Preussischer Polizeibeamten,* pp. 55–58.

[12] According to Coper, the Presidium had already surrendered by the time a workers' delegation invited the USPD to send a man to assume police powers. Coper, *Failure of a Revolution,* p. 197.

[13] Emil Eichhorn, *Meine Tätigkeit im Berliner Polizeipräsidium und mein Anteil an den Januar-Ereignissen* (Berlin: "Freiheit," 1919), p. 8.

[14] *Ibid.,* pp. 11, 50.

[15] Eichhorn declared his allegiance to the left wing of the Socialists but denied being a Bolshevik. See "Das neue Polizeipräsidium. Präsident Eichhorn über Ziele und Aufgaben seiner Behörden," in *Vossische Zeitung,* Nov. 14, 1918 (A).

[16] Erich Klausener called *Die Polizei* an unpolitical paper designed to inform police officials of all technical developments in their field. The Ministry of Interior, he said, did not commission its articles nor censor its views: "Of course, I and many of my collaborators use it to communicate our ideas to police officials of all ranks." *Die Polizei,* 30. Jhg., Nr. 1, Jan. 5, 1933, p. 1.

[17] *Ibid.,* 15. Jhg., Nr. 17, Nov. 21, 1918.

[18] Klingelhöller, *Verband Preussischer Polizeibeamten,* p. 24.

[19] *Ibid.,* p. 41.

[20] Though retaining his post as commander of the Schutzmannschaft, Police-Major Fröhlich was soon thereafter apprehended by Eichhorn's men while helping to organize an illegal students' defence corps (Studentische Soldatenwehr) to combat left-radical movements. Emil Eichhorn, *Meine Tätigkeit,* p. 41.

[21] Kriegsgeschichtliche Forschungsanstalt des Heeres, *Die Wirren in der Reichshauptstadt und im nördlichen Deutschland, 1918–1920* (Berlin: E. S. Mittler, 1940), pp. 19–20.

[22] For the full text see *Die Polizei,* 15. Jhg., Nr. 17, Nov. 21, 1918, p. 287. The *Vossische Zeitung* responded on Nov. 14, 1918 (A): "The inhabitants [of Berlin] will gladly forget the differences of the past. . . . We are happy to see that our 'Blue Policemen' have so willingly changed their attitude."

[23] Eiben *(Polizei-Inspektor),* "Die Polizei-Exekutivbeamten der neuen Zeit," in *Die Polizei,* 15. Jhg., Nr. 19, Nov. 19, 1918, pp. 329–330.

[24] *Ibid.,* 15. Jhg., Nr. 19, Dec. 19, 1918, pp. 331–332.

[25] *Ibid.,* 15. Jhg., Nr. 18, Dec. 5, 1918, pp. 297, 303.

[26] Eichhorn, *Meine Tätigkeit,* pp. 11–14. For the Sicherheitswehr, see

ibid., pp. 23 ff.; and Kriegsgeschichtliche Forschungsanstalt, *Die Wirren in der Reichshauptstadt,* p. 20.

[27] See Eichhorn's press conference as reported in *Vossische Zeitung,* Dec. 21, 1918 (A).

[28] The *Vossische Zeitung* reported an abortive mutiny of the *Sicherheitswehr* on Dec. 12, 1918 (M). See also Eichhorn, *Meine Tätigkeit,* p. 23; and *Die Polizei,* 15. Jhg., Nr. 19, Dec. 19, 1918, p. 326.

[29] Klingelhöller, *Verband Preussischer Polizeibeamten,* p. 25.

[30] *Vossische Zeitung,* Dec. 29, 1918 (M). Eichhorn actually believed that the political reform of the police could be achieved in three to four months. Eichhorn, *Meine Tätigkeit,* p. 14.

[31] *Ibid.,* p. 15; and *Vossische Zeitung,* Nov. 30, 1918 (A).

[32] The *Vossische Zeitung* on Jan. 4, 1919 (M), began to refer to Eichhorn's conduct of police affairs as "scandalous."

[33] Eichhorn, *Meine Tätigkeit,* pp. 81–82; Kriegsgeschichtliche Forschungsanstalt, *Die Wirren in der Reichshauptstadt,* p. 20. Five weeks later, some men of the former Sicherheitswehr forced their way into Eichhorn's private home to steal food and clothing. *Vossische Zeitung,* Feb. 22, 1919 (A).

[34] *Die Polizei,* 15. Jhg., Nr. 17, Nov. 21, 1918, p. 288–289.

[35] *Ibid.,* 15. Jhg., Nr. 23, Feb. 13, 1919, pp. 410–411, 417.

[36] *Ibid.,* 15. Jhg., Nr. 25, March 13, 1919, p. 464. The *Vossische Zeitung,* which also published this article on Feb. 26, 1919, surmised that its author was a senior official of the Berlin Police Presidium.

[37] *Die Polizei,* 16. Jhg., Nr. 8, July 17, 1919, p. 193. According to a legal opinion by Prof. Dr. Martin Drath, a former judge of the Federal Constitutional Court, dated October 4, 1952, Emil Eichhorn was duly invested with police powers in Berlin between November, 1918, and January, 1919, but had no proper claim to the title of police president. [Typescript available at Library of Police Headquarters, Berlin-Tempelhof].

[38] *Ibid.,* 15. Jhg., Nr. 13, Sept. 25, 1919, p. 323. See also *ibid.,* 16 Jhg., Nr. 1, April 10, 1919, p. 38; and *ibid.,* 17. Jhg., Nr. 3, April 29, 1920, p. 63.

[39] *Ibid.,* 15. Jhg., Nr. 4, May 22, 1919, pp. 91–92.

[40] Schönfelder, *Deutsche Polizei,* p. 289, gives a list of all the recruiting posts in Berlin.

[41] Thus on June 30, 1919, the police of Schöneberg publicly criticized the local home guard as too amateurish—a few days after having sought

its help to put down looters in this district. *Vossische Zeitung*, June 24–30, 1919.

[42] Eichhorn, *Meine Tätigkeit*, p. 29; and Kriegsgeschichtliche Forschungsanstalt, *Die Wirren in der Reichshauptstadt*, p. 16.

[43] In 1919 there were about 40,000 free corps troops operating throughout Germany. The number of unofficial police in Berlin was about 3,000. War Office, *The German Police System*, pp. 44–45.

[44] For a graphic description of the free corps in Berlin, consult Ernst von Salomon, *Die Geächteten* (Reinbek bei Hamburg: Rowohlt, 1962). For the fighting in March, 1919, see Mann, *Berlin zur Zeit der Weimarer Republik*, p. 50.

[45] Wilhelm Hartenstein, *Der Kampfeinsatz der Schutzpolizei bei inneren Unruhen* (Berlin-Charlottenburg: Offene Worte, 1926), pp. 27–28; and Ernst van den Bergh, *Polizei und Volk–Seelische Zusammenhänge* (Berlin: Gersbach, 1926), pp. 114–115.

[46] Lothar Danner, *Ordnungspolizei Hamburg. Betrachtungen zu ihrer Geschichte, 1918–1933* (Hamburg: Deutsche Polizei, 1958), p. 11. Danner's comments on Hamburg often reflect conditions and attitudes prevailing throughout the Prussian police.

[47] Riege, *Kleine Polizeigeschichte*, pp. 34–35, 39–40.

[48] Haaselau, "Die öffentliche Sicherheit," in *Die Polizei*, 15. Jhg., Nr. 23, Feb. 13, 1919, pp. 410–411.

[49] Eiben, Polizei-Inspektor, "Die Polizei der Demokratie," in *ibid.*, 16. Jhg., Nr. 1, April 10, 1919, pp. 9–10; and *ibid.*, 16. Jhg., Nr. 2, April 24, 1919, pp. 31–33.

[50] "Ueber die Neuorganisierung der Berliner Polizei," in *ibid.*, 16. Jhg., Nr. 6, June 19, 1919, pp. 132–133; and Ernst van den Bergh and Karl Fahr, eds., *Das preussische Schutzpolizeibeamten-Gesetz vom 16. August 1922* (2d ed.; Berlin: Kameradschaft, 1925), p. 6.

[51] Schönfelder, *Deutsche Polizei*, p. 291; War Office, *German Police System*, pp, 19–31; and "Neueinrichtungen des Gross-Berliner Sicherheitsdienstes," in *Die Polizei*, 16. Jhg., Nr. 5, June 5, 1919, pp. 113–114.

[52] *Ibid.*, p. 114.

[53] *Ibid.*, 16. Jhg., Nr. 14, Oct. 9, 1919, p. 353.

[54] Klingelhöller, *Verband Preussischer Polizeibeamten*, p. 55.

[55] *Deutsche Polizeibeamtenzeitung*, Nr. 13, Sept. 15, 1919, as quoted in Klingelhöller, *Verband Preussischer Polizeibeamten*, pp. 69–73. The Sipo on June 24, 1920, answered with a statistical compilation of its own. "Die grüne Polizei. Eine Halbjahrs-Statistik," in *Vossische Zeitung*, June 24, 1920 (M).

[56] For example *Die Polizei*, 16. Jhg., Nr. 1, April 10, 1919, p. 21. In March, 1920, a small monument was unveiled at Lichtenrade cemetery in memory of five local policemen who were killed during the Spartacist uprising the previous year. *Vossische Zeitung*, March 5, 1920 (M).

[57] Quoted in Klingelhöller, *Verband Preussischer Polizeibeamten*, p. 54. The same news item, differently worded, was carried by the *Vossische Zeitung*, July 9, 1919 (A).

[58] Report on protest meeting of the Reichsverband der Polizeibeamten Deutschlands, in *Die Polizei*, 16. Jhg., Nr. 13, Sept. 25, 1919, p. 319.

[59] *Schutzmannszeitung*, Nr. 32, Aug. 9, 1919, as quoted in Klingelhöller, *Verband Preussischer Polizeibeamten*, p. 57.

[60] Füth, "Zur Reform der Polizei," in *Die Polizei*, 16. Jhg., Nr. 10, Aug. 14, 1919, p. 236.

[61] Kurt Wolzendorf, "Die polizeiliche Bedeutung der Berliner Exekutive," in *Die Polizei*, 16. Jhg., Nr. 12, Sept. 11, 1919, pp. 289–291.

[62] *Ibid.*, 16. Jhg., Nr. 13, Sept. 25, 1919, p. 319.

[63] *Schutzmannszeitung*, Nr. 32, Aug. 9, 1919, as quoted in Klingelhöller, *Verband Preussischer Polizeibeamten*, pp. 65–69. The Berlin city parliament also voiced strong objections. See "Die Zukunft der Berliner Polizei. Erregte Aussprache in der Berliner Stadtverordneten-Versammlung," in *Vossische Zeitung*, Sept. 19, 1919 (M).

[64] Danner, *Ordnungspolizei Hamburg*, p. 9; Ferdinand Friedensburg, *Die Weimarer Republik* (Berlin, 1946), p. 245.

[65] *Die Polizei*, 16. Jhg., Nr. 16, Nov. 6, 1919, p. 411.

[66] Report on a meeting of the Verband der Gross-Berliner Schutzmannschaft, in *Vossische Zeitung*, Oct. 8, 1919 (M).

[67] "Zur Umgestaltung der Polizei in Berlin," in *Die Polizei*, 16. Jhg., Nr. 11, Aug. 28, 1919, p. 264.

[68] Schönfelder, *Deutsche Polizei*, p. 293; and Bergh and Fahr, eds., *Schutzpolizeibeamten-Gesetz 1922*, pp. 6–7.

[69] Albert C. Grzesinski, *Inside Germany*, trans. Alexander S. Lipschitz (New York: E. P. Dutton, 1939), p. 100; Mann, *Berlin zur Zeit der Weimarer Republik*, p. 56; Emil Julius Gumbel, *Zwei Jahre Mord* (4th ed.; Berlin: Neues Vaterland, 1921 [?]), pp. 39–40; and S. William Halperin, *Germany tried Democracy* (New York: W. W. Norton, 1965), p. 178.

[70] Doyé to Göring, letter dated Herischdorf i. Rsgb., Feb. 20, 1933, in the ORPO files at the Berlin Document Center; Klingelhöller, *Verband Preussischer Polizeibeamten*, pp. 74–75; and Danner, *Ordnungspolizei*

Hamburg, p. 33. Another conspirator was the former Berlin Police President Traugott von Jagow.

[71] See Walther Stennes's handwritten vita, dated July 11, 1928, in Akten des Polizei-Präsidiums zu Berlin, NS 26/Vorl. 1368, available at Bundesarchiv, Koblenz.

[72] Interviews, Kurt Fleischer, F. Gediehn. Their account is corroborated by Danner in his account of the events in Hamburg. Danner, *Ordnungspolizei Hamburg,* pp. 35–36.

[73] Interviews, Fleischer, Gediehn, and Eduard Kolbe. The *Vossische Zeitung,* which suspended publication during the Kapp putsch, printed a detailed chronicle of the events over the previous eleven days on March 24, 1920.

[74] *Ibid.;* and Interview, Fleischer.

[75] Interview, Fleischer.

[76] Interview, Gediehn.

[77] Interviews, Fleischer, Gediehn.

[78] "Das Verbrechen am deutschen Volke," in *Die Sicherheitspolizei,* March 31, 1920, as quoted in Klingelhöller, *Verband Preussischer Polizeibeamten,* pp. 75–77.

[79] *Ibid.,* pp. 79–80.

[80] *Vossische Zeitung,* March 27, 1920 (M).

[81] Walter Stennes's subsequent role in the police and the Nazi party is mentioned on pp. 85–88.

[82] Grzesinski, *Inside Germany,* pp. 88–89.

[83] Klingelhöller, *Verband Preussischer Polizeibeamten,* p. 75.

[84] See "Revanchekrieg und Sicherheitspolizei. Eine Unterredung mit Minister Severing," in *Vossische Zeitung,* July 3, 1920 (M), or later Bernhard Weiss, "Der frühere Vizepräsident der Berliner Polizei erzählt aus seinen Erfahrungen," in *Berliner Forum* (RIAS-Berlin, Jan., 1950), p. 8.

[85] "Die Auflösung der Sicherheitspolizei und Umbildung der Polizei in Preussen," in *Die Polizei,* 17. Jhg., Nr. 16, Oct. 28, 1920, p. 334.

[86] Anonymous, *Volk und Schupo* (Cologne: Gilde, 1929 [?]), pp. 9–10. See also the defense of the Sipo in Bergh and Fahr, eds., *Schutzpolizeibeamten-Gesetz 1922,* p. 6.

CHAPTER III

The Berlin Schutzpolizei, 1920–1932

[1] Karl Schröder, "Strassen- und Häuserkampf," reprint from *Die Polizei,*

Nr. 22, Nov., 1927, p. 550; and Carl Severing, *Mein Lebensweg*, II (Cologne: Greven, 1950), 121.

² Paul Riege, *Kleine Polizeigeschichte* (Lübeck: Verlag für polizeiliches Fachschrifttum, 1954), pp. 35–36.

³ The only other Kommandeur in the Prussian police was the chief of the security police in Essen, who was responsible for the safety of the surrounding industrial region. See *Vossische Zeitung*, Jan. 9, 1933 (A).

⁴ See map p. 9. The Seventh Polizeigruppe was the designation for the mounted police stationed at Friesenstrasse.

⁵ Riege, *Kleine Polizeigeschichte*, pp. 35–36; also Preussisches Staatsministerium, *Handbuch über den preussischen Staat für das Jahr 1925*, 131. Jhg., (Berlin: R. v. Deckers, 1925), p. 140.

⁶ Anonymous, *Volk und Schupo* (Cologne: Gilde, 1929 [?]), pp. 27–29.

⁷ Vorschriften für die staatliche Polizei Preussens (V.f.d.P.). *Vorschrift für die Waffenausbildung der Schutzpolizei*, Teil II (Berlin: Kameradschaft, 1932), para. I, sect. 2; and *ibid.*, *Die Körperschulung beim Vollzugsdienst* (2d ed.; Berlin: Kameradschaft, 1931), p. 10; also Schröder, "Strassen- und Häuserkampf," p. 550.

⁸ Anonymous, *Volk und Schupo*, p. 29.

⁹ Riege, *Kleine Polizeigeschichte*, p. 36. This figure applies to 1926.

¹⁰ "Die Ueberfallkommandos," in *Vossische Zeitung*, Sept. 4, 1921 (M); and "Der Fernruf nach Hilfe," in *ibid.*, Nov. 2, 1921 (A).

¹¹ Ferdinand Friedensburg, *Die Weimarer Republik* (Berlin, 1946), p. 246.

¹² Of the remaining 20 candidates, 12 more were eliminated in aptitude tests. Willi Lemke, "Memoirs," unpublished MS courtesy of the author.

¹³ See "5 Jahre Preussische Polizeischule für Leibesübungen," in *Die Polizei*, 22. Jhg., Nr. 9, Aug. 5, 1925, pp. 269–270.

¹⁴ *Ibid.*, 18. Jhg., Nr. 3, May 5, 1921, p. 66; and Anonymous, *Volk und Schupo*, p. 51.

¹⁵ H. Degenhardt and M. Hagemann, *Polizei und Kind* (Berlin: Gersbach, 1926), p. 34.

¹⁶ Interviews, Trott, Fleischer, Krause, and Lemke.

¹⁷ "Am Stammtisch," in *Die Polizei*, 22. Jhg., Nr. 3, May 5, 1925, p. 90. The Nazis, however, thought that the comradeship in the republican police sports movement erred in encouraging individual competition and contacts with pacifist workers' sports clubs. In contrast, the Communists charged that police sports were designed to brutalize the men, notably the American football played by the riot brigades. See Roland Schönfelder, ed., *15 Jahre deutsche Polizei-Sportbewegung* (Berlin: Freiheits-

verlag, 1936); and W. Duddins, "Wir und die Schutzpolizei. Freund oder Feind?" (1929) [a Communist typewritten document in Bundesarchiv, R 58/686/1].

[18] Schönfelder, *Polizei-Sportbewegung*, p. 19. See also Rumpelstilzchen [Adolf Stein], *Was sich Berlin erzählt* (Berlin: Dom, 1922), pp. 257–258, on the importance of sports to keep Germany's manhood fit for combat.

[19] Lemke, "Memoirs."

[20] Salingré, "Reform des Polizeischulwesens," in *Vossische Zeitung*, June 5, 1928 (M).

[21] Lemke, "Memoirs."

[22] *Vorschrift für die Waffenausbildung*, para. I, sect. 3.

[23] Gustav Schmitt, *Waffentechnisches Unterrichtsbuch für den Polizei-beamten* (4th ed.; Berlin: Eisenschmidt, 1925), p. 106. See also W. H. B. Smith, *Small Arms of the World* (Harrisburg, Pa.: Military Service, 1957), pp. 450 ff.

[24] Schmitt, *Waffentechnisches Unterrichtsbuch*, pp. 18–19. Crowding the police was a Communist tactic to neutralize its fire power. Ratcliffe, ed., "Denkschrift über Kampfvorbereitung und Kampfgrundsätze radikaler Organisationen" (1931) [mimeo, document available at Bundesarchiv, Koblenz].

[25] *Die Polizei*, 27. Jhg., Nr. 12, June 20, 1930, p. 295.

[26] Schönfelder, *Vom Werden der deutschen Polizei* (Leipzig: Breitkopf & Härtel, 1937), p. 293.

[27] Schmitt, *Der Einsatz der Schutzpolizei im Aufruhrgebiet* (3d ed.; Berlin: Eisenschmidt, 1929), p. 99; *ibid.*, *Strassenpanzerwagen: Die Sonderwagen der Schutzpolizei* (Berlin: Eisenschmidt, 1925), *passim;* and Interview, Otto Krause.

[28] Anonymous, *Volk und Schupo*, p. 34.

[29] Voit (Polizei-Oberstleutnant), "Einsatz der Nachrichtenmittel der Berliner Polizei am 1. Mai 1929," in *Die Polizei*, 26. Jhg., Nr. 11, June 5, 1929, pp. 257–258.

[30] On the Sipo's air squadron, see Directorate of Military Intelligence, The War Office, *The German Police System*, pt. I, June, 1920, pp. 31–32. On its prohibition by the Allies, *Vossische Zeitung*, Jan. 3, 1921 (A).

[31] Interview, Erich Jahn, who joined the police air guard in the mid-twenties.

[32] Anonymous typed report, presumably dated 1933, accusing Oberre-gierungsrat Paetsch, the director of the Police Institute of Technology and Communications in Berlin, of activities hostile to the Nazi movement. In

the ORPO files of the Berlin Document Center. A police study in 1931, in turn, warned that the Nazis were planning to use airplanes in future actions. Ratcliffe ed., "Denkschrift über Kampfvorbereitung," p. 65.

[33] "Die Preussische Landespolizei, 1933–1935. Ein Rückblick anlässlich ihrer Ueberführung in das Heer am 1. August 1935." Mimeo. text, in the file: "Polizei–Verschiedenes," at the Berlin Document Center.

[34] Ernst van den Bergh and Karl Fahr, eds., *Das preussische Schutz-polizeibeamten-Gesetz vom 16. August 1922* (2d ed.; Berlin: Kamerad-schaft, 1925), p. 8; and Albert Horst, *Der Dienstvorgesetzte als Lehrer* (Berlin, 1927), p. 22.

[35] *Vossische Zeitung*, March 26, 1920 (M); and "Revanchekrieg und Sicherheitspolizei," in *ibid.*, July 3, 1920 (M). Also Arnold Brecht, *Aus nächster Nähe. Lebenserinnerungen 1884–1927* (Stuttgart: Deutsche Verlags-Anstalt, 1966), pp. 233, 236–237.

[36] Interviews, Jachode, Tietze, Miczek. In the period from Oct. 1, 1928 to Sept. 30, 1929, of all the applications for service in the Prussian police, 32.97 percent came from rural villages, 13.43 percent from communities of less than 10,000 inhabitants, and only 6.51 percent were from the in-dustrial working class. 77.31 percent had not passed beyond grade school. *Volk und Schupo* p. 41.

[37] Interviews, Jahn, Schirmer, Krause. Also Otto Krause's vita, written 1940, in the personnel files of the Berlin Document Center.

[38] At the beginning of 1926, 750 riot policemen from rural East Prussia were transferred to the capital and given "one week in which to become Berliners." Interview, Sendzik; and "Berliner Schupo für das Rheinland. Ostpreussischer Ersatz für die Reichshauptstadt," in *Vossische Zeitung*, Jan. 1, 1926 (M). Six years later, the Communists thought that the world economic crisis might persuade young workers to join the police without changing their Socialist views, but there is no evidence that their hopes were fulfilled. Zentralkommittee der KPD, "Richtlinien für Aufbau und Tätigkeit des Spezialressorts zur Arbeit unter den bewaffneten Kräften (Am-Apparat)," *Information Nr. 2* (Feb. 1932), mimeo. docu-ment at Bundesarchiv, R 58/513.

[39] In 1929, 43,500 persons applied to the Prussian police service—10½ percent were accepted, mainly applicants from the countryside. "Polizeiar-beit in Zahlen. Der neue Wegweiser," in *Vossische Zeitung*, Jan. 23, 1930 (M).

[40] After their first year as probationers, patrolmen were liable until their twelfth year to dismissal at one month's notice.

[41] Communist observers found the morale in the security police much improved because of the restoration of previous salary scales in 1932. Zentralkommittee der KPD, "Richtlinien für . . . (Am-Apparat)."

[42] Hans Fallada, *Kleiner Mann—was nun?* (Berlin: Rowohlt, 1932), pp. 238–239.

[43] Heinz Rein, *Berlin 1932: Ein Roman aus der Zeit der grossen Arbeitslosigkeit* (Berlin: Erich Schmidt, 1946), pp. 51–52.

[44] "Mehr Sicherheit in Gross-Berlin!" in *Vossische Zeitung*, April 20, 1919 (M).

[45] Interview, Artner.

[46] *Volk und Schupo*, pp. 32–33.

[47] "Polizeiarbeit in Zahlen. Der neue Wegweiser," in *Vossische Zeitung*, Jan. 23, 1930 (M); and a reader's letter by Dr. Krüger, instructor at the Police Vocational School in Schöneberg, in *ibid.*, Oct. 25, 1931.

[48] "Vor dem neuen Polizeibeamten-Gesetz," in *ibid.*, Feb. 23, 1927 (M); and "80,000 Mark Polizeigelder veruntreut," in *ibid.*, May 6, 1927 (M).

[49] Schriftleitung der Zeitung "Fortbildung," *Ratgeber und Musterheft für Bewerbungen der Versorgungsanwärter* (5th ed.; Berlin: Gerstmann, 1929), pp. 7–8.

[50] "Vor dem neuen Polizeibeamten-Gesetz," in *Vossische Zeitung*, Feb. 23, 1927 (M).

[51] Letter from Karl Gäde to Kurt Daluege, dated Lichterfelde, Feb. 22, 1933, in the ORPO files of the Berlin Document Center.

[52] Letter from Hugo Kaupisch, Polizei Kdr. i.R. and Oberstleutnant a.D., to Ernst Röhm, dated Schierke (Harz), Jan. 29, 1933. In the ORPO files of the Berlin Document Center.

[53] Willy Mann, *Berlin zur Zeit der Weimarer Republik* (Berlin: Das Neue Berlin, 1957), p. 111; and *Die Polizei*, 26. Jhg., Nr. 1, Jan. 5, 1929, pp. 3–4.

[54] *Vossische Zeitung*, June 16, 1926 (A).

[55] "Die Wünsche der Berliner Schutzmannschaft," in *Die Polizei*, 16. Jhg., Nr. 1, April 10, 1919, p. 42.

[56] See also the character portrait of police sergeant Gubalke in Hans Fallada's novel *Wolf unter Wölfen* (Hamburg: Rowohlt, 1952), pp. 108–109.

[57] "Richtlinien für die Neuregelung des Revierdienstes," in *Anlage III zum RdErl. v. 7.7.33—II C I 41 Nr. 189/33* [mimeo. document, courtesy Miczek].

[58] W. R. Hermann, *Was ist Beamtentum?* (Berlin: Kameradschaft, 1925), p. v; and Füth, "Zur Reform der Polizei," in *Die Polizei*. 16. Jhg., Nr. 10, Aug. 14, 1919, pp. 233–236.

[59] The "civil service committees" in the police, established in 1918 and finally regulated by a decree of Jan. 15, 1929, will not be treated here because of their subsidiary importance. Until 1929 they were largely dominated by the Association of Prussian Police Officials. For information on this subject see Fritz Tejessy and Albrecht Bähmisch, eds., *Beamtenausschüsse der Schutzpolizei* (Berlin: Kameradschaft, 1929).

[60] *Die Polizei*, 15. Jhg., Nr. 20, Jan. 2, 1919, pp. 354–355.

[61] For a summary of Schrader's career, see "Ernst Schrader," in *Die Polizei*, 23. Jhg., Nr. 23, Dec. 5, 1926, p. 705.

[62] The early history of the police unions is best described in Emil Klingelhöller, *Der Verband Preussischer Polizeibeamten in seinem Werden und Wirken* (Berlin: Deutsche Polizeibuchhandlung, 1926).

[63] *Vossische Zeitung*, Oct. 2, 1926 (A). In 1928 Schrader claimed that 90 percent of the Prussian police staff belonged to his Association. See *ibid.*, Oct. 29, 1928 (A).

[64] *Vereinigung für polizeiwissenschaftliche Fortbildung*.

[65] Bernhand Weiss, "Unser Chef," in *Vossische Zeitung*, Sept. 30, 1928 (M). There also existed a Verband ehemaliger Polizeibeamten Preussens, but its membership was negligible.

[66] *Ibid.*, March 10, 1930 (A).

[67] See pp. 35–36.

[68] *Vossische Zeitung*, Feb. 27, 1919 (A).

[69] Reich President Hindenburg sent his personal regrets when he was unable to attend the Schrader-Verband's parade on Constitution Day, 1925. *Ibid.*, Aug. 12, 1925 (M).

[70] Severing, *Mein Lebensweg*, p. 295.

[71] *Vossische Zeitung*, Sept. 30, 1926 (M); and *ibid.*, Oct. 28, 1930 (A).

[72] E.g., the Schrader-Verband concerning the "Sipo" (*Vossische Zeitung*, Oct. 8, 1919); or the Schrader and Betnarek unions concerning Grzesinski's decision not to ban the "Stahlhelmtag" (*ibid.*, April 27, 1927).

[73] Klingelhöller, *Verband Preussischer Polizeibeamten*, p. 3.

[74] *Ibid.*, p. 4.

[75] "Ueber das Streikrecht der Beamten," in *Die Polizei*, 16. Jhg., Nr. 4, May 22, 1919, pp. 91–92.

[76] Reports on meetings of the Association in *Vossische Zeitung*, April 20, 1919 (M); *ibid.*, Dec. 9, 1919 (M); and *ibid.*, Oct. 23, 1928 (M).

[77] Even the *Rote Fahne* recognized the Association's "refusal to bow to the reaction" in Nr. 353, Aug. 5, 1922.

[78] Report by investigators of the political police, dated Nov. 13, 1930, in Blattsammlung der Staatsanwaltschaft bei dem Landgericht I, Berlin "Strafsache gegen Grigutsch wegen . . . ," *5 J. Nr. 725/31.*

[79] Minister of Interior Severing and Deputy Police President Weiss personally announced this fusion. *Vossische Zeitung,* May 20, 1931 (A); and *ibid.,* May 24, 1931. According to interview with Artner, however, this fusion never took effect.

[80] Interviews, Artner, Krause.

[81] "Tagung des Allgemeinen Preussischen Polizeibeamtenverbandes," in *Vossische Zeitung,* April 18, 1928 (M).

[82] *Ibid.,* May 20, 1931 (A).

[83] See the case of Kurt Lange and Hans Schulz-Briesen, in *ibid.,* March 10, 1932 (A).

[84] "Löbe bei den republikanischen Polizeibeamten," in *ibid.,* Feb. 23, 1928 (M).

[85] See the reports in *ibid.,* May 17, 1928 (M); *ibid.,* Dec. 5, 1928 (A); and *ibid.,* April 8, 1930 (M).

[86] *Ibid.,* April 1, 1931 (M).

[87] *Ibid.,* Nov. 18, 1931 (M); and *ibid.,* Feb. 11, 1932 (M).

[88] Interview, Artner.

[89] *Vossische Zeitung,* Dec. 10, 1931 (A). A few officers under Fellmann belonged to the Schrader-Verband, and another small group to the Verband der mittleren Polizeivollzugsbeamten (Murche-Verband).

[90] *Ibid.,* Jan. 30, 1931 (M).

[91] *Ibid.,* Jan. 22, 1926 (M).

[92] *Ibid.,* April 2, 1929 (A).

[93] "Polizeioffiziere und Republik," in *ibid.,* Jan. 26, 1926 (M); "Das Ergebnis der Polizeibeamtenwahlen," in *ibid.,* May 23, 1929 (A); and *ibid.,* April 7, 1932 (A). See also Borck's draft of a speech delivered in Berlin-Wilmersdorf, June 30, 1925, in the "Borck Papers" at the Bundesarchiv, Koblenz.

[94] *Vossische Zeitung,* Jan. 3, 1933 (M).

[95] See pp. 172.

[96] *Vossische Zeitung,* June 4, 1932 (M).

[97] Speech by Ministerial-Direktor Dr. Graeser, reported in *ibid.,* Jan. 23, 1933 (A).

[98] "Disziplin and Höflichkeit in der Polizei," in *ibid.*, April 18, 1928 (M).

[99] "Weniger Disziplinarverfahren: Der Neujahrserlass des Innenminister Grzesinski," in *ibid.*, Jan. 3, 1927 (A).

[100] *Ibid.*, Feb. 27, 1926 (A).

[101] For example Commanders Fröhlich and von Heinrichs in 1919. See also *ibid.*, April 7, 1920 (M); "Militarismus in der Polizei," in *ibid.*, May 22, 1929 (M); and *ibid.*, Oct. 7, 1932 (A). Things were not very different in 1967, when the police in West Berlin came under public criticism for shooting a student during a riot. "Polizeigewerkschaft sucht Ursachen," in *Berliner Morgenpost*, Sept. 28, 1967.

[102] *Vossische Zeitung*, Oct. 29, 1931 (M).

[103] Severing, *Mein Lebensweg*, p. 275.

[104] Interview, Eduard Kolbe.

[105] Rumpelstilzchen [Adolf Stein], *Was sich Berlin erzählt*, pp. 90–91.

[106] After Jan. 30, 1933, the Nazis found in the papers of State Secretary Abegg a collection of personal requests for promotion written by police officials who belonged to the SPD. Available at the ORPO files at the Berlin Document Center.

[107] *Berliner Tageblatt*, Dec. 2, 1921. On March 30, 1927, Minister of Interior Grzesinski also denied before the Prussian Diet that police applicants were asked to state their political views to their examiners. "Grzesinski über die Polizei," in *Vossische Zeitung*, April 1, 1927 (M).

[108] The newspapers brought frequent complaints on this score. E.g., "Rekrutendrill bei der Schutzpolizei," in *Die Welt am Abend*, Nr. 80, April 7, 1926; U. Salingré, "Reform des Polizeischulwesens," in *Vossische Zeitung*, June 5, 1928 (M); F. O'Mon., "Polizeioffiziere beim 'Stahlhelm,'" in *ibid.*, Jan. 29, 1930 (M); and Hans Lange, "Polizeierziehung—Polizeierfahrung," in *Die Menschenrechte*, Nr. 9/10, Berlin, Oct. 1, 1929, p. 11.

[109] Severing, *Mein Lebensweg*, p. 294.

[110] Letter by Herr Krüger in *Vossische Zeitung*, Oct. 25, 1931 (S).

[111] *Ibid.*, Feb. 23, 1928 (M).

[112] Interview, Kolbe.

[113] Kurt Wolzendorf, "Die polizeiliche Bedeutung der Berliner Exekutive," in *Die Polizei*, 16. Jhg., Nr. 12, Sept. 11, 1919, p. 290; and Degenhardt and Hagemann, *Polizei und Kind*, p. 21.

[114] *Die Polizei*, 15. Jhg., Nr. 18, Dec. 5, 1918, p. 303.

[115] Bernhard Weiss, *Polizei und Politik* (Berlin: Gersbach, 1928), p. 12.

[116] *Ibid.*, p. 13.

[117] Claus Kaestl, "Reich und Länderpolizeien in der Weimarer Republik," in *Die Polizei*, 53. Jhg., Nr. 10, Oct. 8, 1962, pp. 303–304.

[118] *(St M I Nr. 7683/MBliV. S. 59)*. See also Arnold Brecht, *Prelude to Silence. The End of the German Republic* (New York: Oxford University Press, 1944), p. 41. This does not mean that policemen who openly supported either party were not liable to disciplinary punishment prior to 1930: e.g., Linthe, p. 92. In 1931, some senior police officials were demanding that Schupo officials be altogether deprived of voting rights for the duration of their service. *Vossische Zeitung*, Dec. 16, 1931 (M).

[119] *Ibid.*, Dec. 5, 1928 (A).

[120] Weiss, *Polizei und Politik*, pp. 11–13. Also Interview, Kolbe.

[121] Interview, Krause; Ferdinand Friedensburg, *Die Weimarer Republik*, p. 244; and Karl von Oven, *Gedanken zur Polizeiführerausbildung* (4th ed.; Berlin and Lübeck: Deutscher Polizeiverlag, 1931), p. 20.

[122] This translation is taken from Raymond D. Fosdick, *European Police Systems* (New York: Century, 1916), p. 24.

[123] For the text of this law, see Erich Klausener, Christian Kerstein, and Robert Kempner, eds., *Das Polizeiverwaltungsgesetz vom 1. Juni 1931* (Berlin: C. A. Weller, 1931).

[124] *Ibid.*, p. 112.

[125] Hans Kehrl, "Die Polizei," in *Die Verwaltungs-Akademie. Ein Handbuch für den Beamten im nationalsozialistischen Staat* (Berlin: Spaeth & Linde, 1938 [?]), p. 8.

[126] Klausener et al., eds., *Polizeiverwaltungsgesetz 1931*, p. viii. The same point is made in Robert Kempner, "Schadenersatzpflicht bei politischen Zusammenstössen," in *Die Polizei*, 27. Jhg., Nr. 14, July 20, 1930, p. 333.

[127] *Vorschrift für die Waffenausbildung der Schutzpolizei*, para. I, 1 to 4.

[128] K. Schönner, "Versammlungs- und Zeitungsverbote. Voraussetzungen, Handhabung und Wirkung," in *Die Polizei*, 26. Jhg., Nr. 8, April 20, 1929, pp. 177–179.

[129] Most textbooks for the police laid great stress on the improvement of the relations between police and public, especially in the beginning of the twenties. See, for example, the Introduction to the standard work, Neese, ed., *Das Lehrbuch für die Polizeischulen*, vol. I (Berlin: Politik und Wirtschaft, 1921). Ten years later, the concern had shifted to the relation of the police and the government.

[130] Severing, *Mein Lebensweg*, pp. 83–93.

[131] H. Hirschfeld and Karl Vetter, *Tausend Bilder: Grosse Polizei-Ausstellung Berlin 1926* (Berlin: Gersbach, 1927), pp. 5–7; and Oskar Dressler, ed., *Grosse Polizei-Ausstellung Berlin—Internationaler Polizeikongress* (Vienna: "Internationale Oeffentliche Sicherheit" Verlag für polizeiliche Fachliteratur, 1927), p. 23.

[132] See *Vossische Zeitung*, March 14, April 5, and April 10, 1930; and *ibid.*, Sept. 15, 1932.

[133] Degenhardt and Hagemann, *Polizei und Kind*, p. 50.

[134] *Ibid.*, p. 51.

[135] Anonymous, *Volk und Schupo*, pp. 38–39.

[136] "Die Verfassungsfeier der Berliner Schutzpolizei," in *Die Polizei*, 21. Jhg., Nr. 10, Aug. 20, 1924, p. 239. For comments on the subdued mood on republican constitution days, see Henri Béraud, *Ce que j'ai vu à Berlin* (Paris: Éditions de France, 1926), pp. 77–78; and Rumpelstilzchen [Adolf Stein], *Piept es?* (Berlin: Tägliche Rundschau, 1930), p. 13.

[137] Interviews, Johannes Stumm, Eduard Kolbe. Ernst Schrader of the Association of Prussian Police Officials complained that the automatic suspension of patrolmen for every anonymous denunciation was undermining morale in the rank and file. *Vossische Zeitung*, Jan. 31, 1928 (A).

[138] See correspondence between Prussian Ministry of Interior and Berlin Police Presidium in Bundesarchiv, R 58/423 (especially a report by Füth concerning Dezernat 4, dated Aug. 30, 1932), and R 58/669.

[139] Zentralkommittee der KPD, "Richtlinien für . . . (Am-Apparat)."

[140] A report concerning this manifesto was drawn up by the Landeskriminalamt I (Berlin), Sept. 8, 1933. At Bundesarchiv, R 58/547.

[141] Borck's estimate for the Schupo's political sentiments were: 50 percent right-wing, 35 percent SPD, 5 percent Catholic Center, and 10 percent KPD. The typewritten draft of his speech is in the "Borck Papers" at the Bundesarchiv, Koblenz.

[142] Interview, Kolbe.

[143] Kaupisch to Dept. IA, Berlin, Feb. 25, 1925, Tgb. Nr. 715/25, in Bundesarchiv, R 58/686/1.

[144] Report by Bonatz, dated Berlin, June 1, 1926, *III. G. St. Aussend.*, in Bundesarchiv, R 58/686/1. See also Werner T. Angress, *Stillborn Revolution* (Princeton, Princeton University Press, 1964), pp. 342-344.

[145] For the particular hostility of Schupo and Red Front, see H. R. Knickerbocker, *Deutschland so oder so?* (Berlin: Rowohlt 1932), p. 28.

[146] E.g., Schützinger (Polizei-Oberst), "Neue Kampfformen der K.P.D.,"

in *Die Polizei,* 21. Jhg., Nr. 11, Sept. 5, 1924, pp. 266–268; M. Rittau, "Verhalten des 'proletarischen Kämpfers' gegenüber Polizei und Justiz im politischen Strafverfahren," in *ibid.,* 22. Jhg., Nr. 4, May 20, 1925, pp. 102–104; and Wilhelm Hartenstein, *Der Kampfeinsatz der Schutzpolizei bei inneren Unruhen* (Berlin-Charlottenburg: Offene Worte, 1926), pp. 19, 26, 28.

[147] "Major von Priesdorff was unable to free himself of his military habits however hard he tried to carry out his assignment to demilitarize the security police." Severing, *Mein Lebensweg,* pp. 314–315.

[148] The use of an independent intelligence service by the uniformed police was strictly prohibited in a Prussian cabinet decree of Jan. 6, 1921. Weiss, *Polizei und Politik,* p. 137.

[149] A brief account of this affair can be found in Emil Julius Gumbel, *Zwei Jahre Mord* (4th ed.; Berlin: Neues Vaterland, 1921 [?]), pp. 54–55. The two trials can be followed in *Berliner Tageblatt,* Nov. 4 to Dec. 3, 1921. The Stennes affair was commented on by Interviewees Stumm, Miczek, Kolbe, and Bauer. Bauer in 1922 served in Polizei-Abteilung Zentrum. Stennes's vita is available in the police files at the Bundesarchiv, NS 26/Vorl. 1368.

[150] See *Vossische Zeitung,* Feb. 12, 1931 (A); April 7, 1931 (M); May 23, 1931 (A); Jan. 16, 1932 (A); and Jan. 17, 1932 (M). Also Severing, *Mein Lebensweg,* p. 268.

[151] *Vossische Zeitung,* May 13, 1927 (A); June 6, 1928 (M); and Jan. 30, 1931 (M). See also Majewski's article in *Die Polizei,* 27. Jhg., Nr. 1, Jan. 5, 1930, pp. 1–5.

[152] "Polizeioffiziere gegen Polizeipräsidenten," in *Vossische Zeitung,* Feb. 1, 1929 (M); and *ibid.,* April 2, 1929 (A).

[153] Severing, *Mein Lebensweg,* pp. 294–295; and *Vossische Zeitung,* Dec. 10, 1931 (A); Jan. 6, 1932 (M); and Oct. 8, 1932 (M).

[154] This was in response to a circular request by the chief of the Prussian police, *Nr. 270/34 (G.–).*

[155] By this term we do not mean policemen who were registered members of the Nazi party. Of these there were only slightly over 300 in the entire Schutzpolizei of Prussia. "Namentliche Uebersicht der Alt-Pg. vor 1932 (ohne 1932) der Offiziere der Schutzpolizei und Gendarmerie," typescript available at the Berlin Document Center.

[156] This count is based on "Verzeichnis der auf Grund des Gesetzes (vom 7.4.33) zur Wiederherstellung des Berufsbeamtentums wegen politischer Unzuverlässigkeit entlassenen Polizei-Offiziere und Polizei-Wacht-

meister der preussischen Schutzpolizei," mimeo. copy available at the Berlin Document Center.

[157] See the reports by S.A. Sturm 99/6, S.A. Sturm 3/2, and S.A. Sturm 1/6, each dated Berlin, Dec. 12, 1934, in the ORPO files at the Berlin Document Center.

[158] Report by S.A. Brigade 25 to Gruppe Berlin-Brandenburg, dated Berlin-Friedenau, Dec. 17, 1934, Tgb. Nr. G. 20/34 SB., in the ORPO files at the Berlin Document Center.

[159] Report by S.A. Brigade 29, Standarte 12, dated Berlin-Pankow, Dec. 14, 1934, in the ORPO files at the Berlin Document Center.

[160] They were Police Masters Giessmann and Junghans. See report by S.A. Sturm I/6, dated Berlin, Dec. 17, 1934, in the ORPO files at the Berlin Document Center. On the S.A. dormitories in Berlin between 1931–32, see Heinrich Bennecke, *Hitler und die SA* (Munich and Vienna: Olzog, 1962), p. 175.

[161] Report dated Berlin-Neukölln, Dec. 17, 1934, Tgb. Nr. 10/34, G.D. II/1, in the ORPO files at the Berlin Document Center.

[162] See letters by Schulz-Briesen, dated Brandenburg (H.), Nov. 6, 1933, and by Lange, dated Berlin, Feb. 2, 1934, in the ORPO files at the Berlin Document Center. The *Vossische Zeitung* reported on the case on March 10, 1932 (A), and March 11, 1932 (M). The police sergeant who denounced Schulz-Briesen to the political police was Heinz Schumacher, who a few months later was to betray Police Major Encke to the military authorities. See p. 157.

[163] Letter from Daluege to the Leiter der Privatkanzlei des Führers, dated Berlin, Aug. 20, 1934, in the ORPO files of the Berlin Document Center.

[164] The Gildisch case can be followed through the documents of his trial in 1951 for the murder of Ministerialdirektor Dr. Erich Klausener on June 30, 1934. See "Strafsache gegen Gildisch, Kurt, wegen Verbrechen gegen die Menschlichkeit," *Staatsanwaltschaft bei dem Landgericht Moabit, 1 P. Ks 4/51, Band I.* More information on Gildisch's discharge from the police was obtained from Dr. Stumm, who led the investigation against him in 1930–31. See also *Vossische Zeitung,* May 23, 1931 (A).

[165] Letter from Otto Linthe to Kurt Daluege, dated Berlin, Feb. 4, 1933, plus enclosures, in the ORPO files at the Berlin Document Center.

[166] See map, p. 12.

[167] Interview, Hermann Artner, who served at police station 88 from 1928 to 1930, and at police station 85 from 1930 to 1933. For Fränkel,

see p. 169. Information on the political quarrels at police station 88 can be found in an urgent report by the NSDAP-Gauleitung Gross-Berlin to Daluege, dated Berlin, Feb. 15, 1933, plus enclosures, in the ORPO files at the Berlin Document Center.

[168] This gossip was mentioned in the document cited in n. 167. The investigation can be followed in "Strafsache gegen Grigutsch wegen . . . ?" in *Blattsammlung der Staatsanwaltschaft bei dem Landgericht I Berlin*, 5 J Nr. 725/31. The two main suspects, POWM Wilhelm Heitmann of police station 83 and PWM Berthold Wichmann of police station 86, were later cited for their services to the Nazis in a report by S.A.-Standarte 5 ("Horst Wessel"), dated Berlin, Dec. 13, 1934, in the ORPO files at the Berlin Document Center.

[169] E.g., Albert Grzesinski, "Polizei und Strassendemonstrationen," in *Vossische Zeitung*, June 15, 1926 (M); and "Bierabend des Berliner Polizeipräsidenten," in *ibid.*, Nov. 4, 1927 (A).

[170] "Rücktritt des Polizeikommandeurs Haupt," in *Die Rote Fahne*, Nr. 129, June 3, 1927; and "Krieg dem imperialistischen Krieg!" in *Oktober*, Jhg. 5, Nr. 4, Aug. 1930.

[171] Quoted from a Communist document in Ratcliffe, ed., "Denkschrift über Kampfvorbereitung," p. 53.

[172] *Ibid.*, pp. 43–44, 48.

[173] Joseph Goebbels, *Kampf um Berlin* (Munich: F. Eher, 1940), p. 70.

[174] *Vossische Zeitung*, May 6, 1927 (A); and Ratcliffe, ed., "Denkschrift über Kampfvorbereitung," p. 77.

[175] *Ibid.*, pp. 78–79.

[176] Julius K. von Engelbrechten and Hans Volz, eds. *Wir wandern durch das nationalsozialistische Berlin* (Munich: Zentralverlag der NSDAP, 1937), p. 19.

[177] "Wir fürchten nicht den Donner der Kanonen, Wir fürchten nicht die grüne Polizei!" Interview, Bauer; and Weiss, *Polizei und Politik*, pp. 13–15. A collection of Communist leaflets addressed to the Berlin Schupo can be found in the *Blattsammlung der Staatsanwaltschaft bei dem Landgericht I Berlin*, "Strafsache gegen Unbekannt," 1 pol J. 2470/32.

[178] The Nazi attitude toward the police can be found in various Party-sponsored publications, such as Wilfrid Bade, *Die S.A. erobert Berlin. Ein Tatsachen Bericht* (Munich: Knorr & Hirth, 1933), pp. 201, 211–212; Roland Schönfelder, *Vom Werden der deutschen Polizei* (Leipzig: Breitkopf & Härtel, 1937), p. 298; or Helmuth Koschorke, ed., *Die Polizei— einmal anders!* (Munich: Zentralverlag der NSDAP, 1937), pp. 35–36.

[179] That the Schupo was aware of the existence of such insinuations is reflected in an instructive story published by *Die Polizei:* A civilian, seeing police cars leaving the route of a political procession, smiles: "Aha! they've had enough and make themselves scarce!" "Not at all," answers his friend from the police, "they are merely taking a shortcut to ensure the security of the next intersection!" Ulli Amman, "Eine Fahrt durch Berlin," in *Die Polizei*, 25. Jhg., Nr. 13, July 5, 1928, pp. 435–436.

[180] The following account is based on the daily reports of the *Vossische Zeitung* during this period of twelve years. Footnotes are only used for additional comments and supplementary references.

[181] Hans Roden, *Polizei greift ein—Bilddokumente der Schutzpolizei* (Leipzig: Breitkopf & Härtel, 1934 [?]), p. 45; and Friedensburg, *Die Weimarer Republik*, pp. 126–127.

[182] See also the public appeal by the police president of Berlin in *Die Polizei*, 16. Jhg., Nr. 5, June 5, 1919; and Weiss, *Polizei und Politik*, pp. 16–17.

[183] S. W. Halperin, *Germany Tried Democracy* (New York: W. W. Norton, 1965), p. 164, records 42 dead and 105 wounded.

[184] Interview, Fleischer.

[185] Schröder, "Strassen- und Häuserkampf," pp. 490–491; and Schützinger, "Neue Kampfformen der KPD," in *Die Polizei*, 21. Jhg., Nr. 11, Sept. 5, 1924, pp. 266–268.

[186] See also Zentralkommittee der KPD, "Richtlinien für . . . (Am-Apparat)," on alleged discontent of policemen concerning forced donations.

[187] "Polizeiverordnung betreffend Waffentragen vom 16. Februar 1926," in Bernhard Weiss, ed., *Die Polizeiverordnungen für Berlin*, I (Berlin: C. A. Weller, 1931), p. 3.

[188] At the funeral of this workman, June 2, 1928, there were more disturbances in the course of which Deputy Police President Weiss was hit by a policeman.

[189] The federal government outlawed the RFB in April, 1928.

[190] For some statistics on the number of political demonstrations and police operations in 1927, see Heimannsberg, "Rückschau 1927—Vorschau 1928," in *Vossische Zeitung*, Jan. 1, 1928 (S).

[191] See the report by KBS Köhn to Abt. I, dated Berlin, April 13, 1929, A.D. II G. St., in Bundesarchiv, R 58/744.

[192] Heimannsberg to Abt. IA, dated April 28, 1929, Tgb. Nr. 1562/29, in Bundesarchiv, R 58/744.

[193] For a Communist description of these events see Mann, *Berlin zur Zeit der Weimarer Republik*, pp. 141–143; and especially Klaus Neukrantz, *Barricades in Berlin* (New York: International Publishers, 1930 [?]).

[194] *Die Rote Fahne*, May 25, 1929.

[195] Report by KA Ludwig and KA Radloff to Abt IA, concerning the meeting of the 17th district branch of the KPD in Berlin-Lichtenberg, May 1, 1929, in Bundesarchiv, R 58/331.

[196] The reports of the interrogations are at the Bundesarchiv, R 58/529.

[197] Heimannsberg, "Der 1. Mai und seine Folgeerscheinungen in Berlin," in *Die Polizei*, 26 Jhg., Nr. 10, May 20, 1929, p. 232.

[198] "Einige Erfahrungen des 1. Mai," [typescript, n. d., n. s.,] in Bundesarchiv, R 58/513.

[199] According to the political police, between May 1 and 6, 1929, 1,228 persons were taken into custody, 194 persons were wounded (48 of them policemen), and 25 civilians were killed. Abt. I, Berlin, May 8, 1929, III G. St., Betr.: Unruhen aus Anlass der Maifeier, in Bundesarchiv, R 58/513.

[200] IA reports on the dead victims can be found in Bundesarchiv, R 58/574.

[201] *Die Welt am Abend*, Nr. 112, May 16, 1929; and "Die Ergebnisse der Maiuntersuchung," in *Die Menschenrechte*, Nr. 9/10, Jhg. IV, Berlin, Oct. 1, 1929.

[202] "Die Ergebnisse der Maiuntersuchung," p. 11.

[203] E.g., Voit, "Einsatz der Nachrichtenmittel der Berliner Polizei am 1. Mai 1929," in *Die Polizei*, 26. Jhg., Nr. 11, June 5, 1929, pp. 257–258; or A. Gutknecht, "Material und Personal des Kraftfahrtechnischen Sonderdienstes der Polizeiverwaltung Berlin," in *ibid.*, 26. Jhg., Nr. 12, June 20, 1929, pp. 290–294.

[204] See also F. O'Mon., "Nationalsozialistische Zellen," in *Vossische Zeitung*, April 16, 1930 (M).

[205] Interview, Eduard Kolbe, who headed police station 111 between 1928 and 1932. Kolbe was not a member of the NSDAP either then or later.

[206] This incident is also mentioned in Severing, *Mein Lebensweg*, p. 258.

[207] By 1931, there were 108 S.A. dormitories (S.A.-Heime) in Greater Berlin. For more details on this raid see Bennecke, *Hitler und die SA*, pp. 178 ff.

[208] *Vossische Zeitung*, July 8, 1931 (M).

[209] The Communists claimed that the killer was a Nazi by the name of

Grabsch, who lived in Kadinerstrasse and committed suicide the following day. This version is supported by (Interview) Hermann Artner, who then served at police station 85. Artner delivered Kuhfeld to the first-aid station where he died. He claims that his written report was suppressed by a Kripo official at police station 85 who sympathized with the Nazis.

[210] A copy of the court verdict of the Schwurgericht I beim Landgericht Berlin against Kuntz, Klause, Broede, et al. for the murder of Police Captains Anlauf and Lenck, dated June 19, 1934, *(500) 1 pol. a. K.7.34(41.34)*, was kindly put at my disposal by Generalstaatsanwalt a.D. Wilhelm Kühnast. See also Christopher Isherwood, *The Berlin Stories* (New York: J. Laughlin, 1945), p. 272.

[211] Albert C. Grzesinski, "Die Leistung der Berliner Polizei im Wahlkampf," in *Die Polizei*, 29. Jhg., Nr. 10, May 20, 1932, pp. 221–222.

CHAPTER IV

The Detective Force

[1] "Bei der Berliner Unterwelt. Reportage vom Schlesischen Bahnhof," in *Vossische Zeitung*, Aug. 6, 1930 (M); Pem [Paul Erich Marcus], *Heimweh nach dem Kurfürstendamm: Aus Berlins glanzvollsten Tagen und Nächten* (Berlin: Lothar Blanvalet, 1952), pp. 40–41; and Erich Frey, *Ich beantrage Freispruch* (Hamburg, 1959), p. 102.

[2] Klaus Mann, "Siebzehnjährig in Berlin," in Rolf Italiaander and Willy Haas, eds., *Berliner Cocktail* (Hamburg and Vienna: Paul Szolnay, 1959), pp. 337–339.

[3] *Vossische Zeitung*, Nov. 10, 1919 (M); and *ibid.*, July 2–3, 1920. She is referred to as "Countess Caletta" in Frey, *Ich beantrage Freispruch*, pp. 120–135.

[4] Emil Strauss was known for having stolen a set of burglar's tools at the Kripo's museum of crime in 1919. *Vossische Zeitung*, Jan. 4, 1919 (M).

[5] Richter (Ministerialrat), *Der Kampf gegen Schund- und Schmutzschriften in Preussen* (Berlin: R. von Decker, 1929), p. 31; and Paul Reiwald, *Die Gesellschaft und ihre Verbrecher* (Zurich: Paul, 1948), pp. 118–119.

[6] Werneburg (Kriminal-Kommissar), "Die Autofalle," in *Kriminalistische Monatshefte*, 5. Jhg., Heft 11, Nov. 1931, pp. 254–257.

[7] Bernhard Weiss, "Kriminalsensationen," in *Vossische Zeitung*, Jan. 16, 1927 (M).

[8] *Ibid.*, April 11, 1920 (M).

[9] *Ibid.*, Aug. 22, 1921 (A). See also Frey, *Ich beantrage Freispruch*, pp. 79–81; and S. Fischer-Fabian, *Müssen Berliner so sein . . .* (Berlin: Argon, 1960), p. 34.

[10] For a detailed account, see the memoirs of Paul Krantz's defense council: Frey, *Ich beantrage Freispruch*, pp. 269–384. Interesting comments on this affair can be found in Walther Kiaulehn, *Berlin: Schicksal einer Weltstadt* (Munich and Berlin: Biederstein, 1958), pp. 262–263; Friedrich Hussong, "*Kurfürstendamm.*" *Zur Kulturgeschichte des Zwischenreichs* (Berlin: Tägliche Rundschau, 1934), pp. 76–78; Fischer-Fabian, *Müssen Berliner so sein . . .*, pp. 41–43; and Werner Mahrholz, "Politisierung der Verbrechen," in *Vossische Zeitung*, July 10, 1927 (M).

[11] Pem, *Kurfürstendamm*, pp. 102–103.

[12] Interview, Stumm; and Hussong, "*Kurfürstendamm*," p. 40.

[13] Reiwald, *Gesellschaft und ihre Verbrecher*, p. 116; and Franz von Schmidt, *Vorgeführt erscheint. Erlebte Kriminalistik* (Stuttgart: Deutsche Volksbücher, 1955), p. 23.

[14] Thus Ernst Engelbrecht and Leo Heller published *Berliner Razzien* (Berlin: Hermann Paetel, 1924) and *Kinder der Nacht. Bilder aus dem Verbrecherleben* (Berlin: Hermann Paetel, 1925). Ernst Engelbrecht himself wrote *15 Jahre Kriminalkommissar* (Berlin-Schöneberg: Peter Oestergaard, 1927) and *In den Spuren des Verbrechertums* (Berlin-Schöneberg: Peter Oestergaard, 1930). Ulrich Possehl wrote *Moderne Betrüger* (Berlin: Bali-Berger, 1928); Ernst Liebermann von Sonnenberg and Otto Trettin wrote *Kriminalfälle* (Berlin Universitas, 1934); and even Ernst Gennat wrote a popular piece "Spuk im Alltag" for the *Vossische Zeitung*, Jan. 1, 1931 (M).

[15] "Das Fest der Kriminalpolizei," in *ibid.*, July 1, 1928 (M); *ibid.*, March 12, 1931 (M); and *ibid.*, Jan. 22, 1931 (A). The Communists, of course, complained that the Kripo band only played old Prussian marches. "Marschmusik der Kripo," in *Die Rote Fahne*, Nr. 195, Aug. 20, 1927.

[16] *Vossische Zeitung*, Aug. 14, 1919 (A); and Wolfgang Ullrich, *Verbrechensbekämpfung. Geschichte, Organisation, Rechtssprechung* (Berlin-Spandau: Luchterhand, 1961), pp. 66, 70.

[17] Liebermann and Trettin, *Kriminalfälle*, pp. 158, 222–224.

[18] Ullrich, *Verbrechensbekämpfung*, pp. 70–72; "Die Berliner Kriminalberatungsstelle," in *Kriminalistische Monatshefte*, 4. Jhg., Heft 3, April,

1930, pp. 86–88; and Ingenieur Nelken, *Publikum und Verbrechen* (Berlin, 1927).

[19] *Vossische Zeitung*, Nov. 14, 1919 (A).

[20] In one of the few exceptions to this rule, several thousand Schupos and hundreds of Kripomen combed the region around Schlesischer Bahnhof in the night of January 15 to 16, 1929, to demonstrate the police's determination not to condone a recent outbreak of gang warfare in the neighborhood. *Vossische Zeitung*, Jan. 16, 1929 (M).

[21] Rumpelstilzchen [Adolf Stein], *Berliner Allerlei* (Berlin: Tägliche Rundschau, 1922), p. 81.

[22] Kleinschmidt (Kriminal-Direktor), "Wahrheit und Irrtum im kriminalpolizeilichen Ermittlungsverfahren," in *Kriminalistische Monatshefte*, 6. Jhg., Heft 10, Oct. 1932, p. 225.

[23] In 1928, Hans Possendorf's *Klettermaxe: Eine Berliner Kriminalgeschichte zw. Kurfürstendamm und Scheunenviertel* was banned because it presented "crime and knavery as something forgivable, understandable, and partly as fun . . ." See Richter, *Schund- und Schmutzschriften*, p. 31; also Ullrich, *Verbrechensbekämpfung*, pp. 71–72.

[24] Willy Mann, *Berlin zur Zeit der Weimarer Republik* (Berlin: Das Neue Berlin, 1957), p. 69.

[25] The *Vossische Zeitung* periodically had such incidents to report, thus on March 18, 1921; Oct. 23, 1928; and Jan. 12, 1932.

[26] Wündisch (Regierungsdirektor), "Die Aufdeckung der Fememorde. Hat die Polizei versagt?" in *ibid.*, March 28, 1926 (S).

[27] For the "vehme murders" see Friedrich Karl Kaul, *Justiz wird zum Verbrechen. Der Pitaval der Weimarer Republik* (Berlin: Das Neue Berlin, 1953), pp. 285–353.

[28] "Von den politischen Verbrechen," in Hans Schneickert, ed., Wilhelm Stieber, *Praktisches Lehrbuch der Kriminalpolizei* (Potsdam: A. W. Hayn, 1921), pp. 180–181.

[29] Bernhard Weiss in *Polizei und Politik* (Berlin: Gersbach, 1928), p. 57, reports of only one official of Department IA who was transferred to a different town because his life in Berlin was threatened. As a rare exception, too, the *Vossische Zeitung* reported on May 13, 1927 (M) that a Nazi agitator had urged his listeners to pick out the IA men for a beating at the next political rally to avenge the recent ban of the NSDAP.

[30] Weiss, "Polizei gegen Staatsverbrecher. Saubere Kampfmittel," in *Vossische Zeitung*, March 30, 1928 (M); and Albert Grzesinski's address

to the 10th Prussian Police Week at Düsseldorf, in *Die Polizei*, 26. Jhg., Nr. 20, Oct. 20, 1929, p. 520. See also Wachenfeld, "Politische Polizei," in *Kriminalistische Monatshefte*, 2. Jhg., 2. Heft, Feb. 1928, pp. 38–40.

[31] Weiss, *Polizei und Politik*, p. 102.

[32] "Strafsache gegen Unbekannt wegen Körperverletzung," in *Blatt-sammlung der Staatsanwaltschaft bei dem Landgericht II Berlin*, II. P. J. 180/32.

[33] Weiss, *Polizei und Politik*, p. 25; also Interview, Teigeler, Kuckenburg.

[34] Adolf Stein regretted the passing of the era of the "Herr Nachtrat" only some thirty years earlier, when criminal life was still in its infancy. Rumpelstilzchen [Adolf Stein], *Bei mir—Berlin!* (Berlin: Brunnen, 1924), p. 210. Also Kriminal-Direktor Wolfram Sangmeister's memorandum on the 150th anniversary of the Berlin criminal police, April 1, 1961 (K 10 30/1 61); and Menzel, "Die Entstehungsgeschichte der deutschen Kriminalpolizei," (1957) [MS available at Polizei Schule, Berlin-Spandau].

[35] Ullrich, *Verbrechensbekämpfung*, pp. 64–65.

[36] The Sipo worked on criminal cases too. See "Die grüne Polizei. Eine Halbjahrs-Statistik," in *Vossische Zeitung*, June 24, 1920 (M).

[37] Interviews, Kuckenburg, Togotzes.

[38] Hedda Adlon, *Hotel Adlon: Das Haus in dem die Welt zu Gast war* (Munich: Kindler, 1955), pp. 120–131; also *Vossische Zeitung*, Jan. 3–4, 1919.

[39] Erich Prinz, a painter by trade, was dismissed on Nov. 28, 1918, reinstated, and dismissed again on Jan. 2, 1919, for general incompetence and for mishandling public funds. He was convicted of fraud in May, 1920, and again in Nov., 1930.

[40] Max Weiss, ed., *Die Polizeischule. Systematische Darstellung und Erläuterung des deutschen Polizeirechts*, II (Dresden: Verlag der Polizeischule, 1920), 671–672; and Bernhard Weiss, *Polizei und Politik*, p. 133.

[41] *Die Polizei*, 15. Jhg., Nr. 21, Jan. 16, 1919, p. 377.

[42] Weiss, *Polizei und Politik*, pp. 64, 134.

[43] Amelung (Regierungsrat), "Soll der Chef der Kriminalpolizei Volljurist sein?" in *Kriminalistische Monatshefte*, 5. Jhg., Heft 10, Oct. 1931, pp. 219–221.

[44] *Vossische Zeitung*, Jan. 13, 1919 (M); and *ibid.*, Feb. 13, 1919 (M and A).

[45] Paetsch (Regierungsrat), "Die Errichtung der Landeskriminalpolizei im Rahmen des Polizeiwesens in Preussen," in *Die Polizei*, 21. Jhg., Nr.

20, Jan. 20, 1925, pp. 506–509; and Willy Gay, *Die preussische Landeskriminalpolizei. Ihre Errichtung, ihre bisherige und beabsichtigte Entwicklung, ihre Aufgaben* (Berlin: Kameradschaft, 1928), are basic contemporary sources.

[46] Ullrich, *Verbrechensbekämpfung*, p. vii.

[47] Publications since 1945 are more expansive. E.g., H.-J. Neufeldt, J. Huck, and G. Tessin, *Zur Geschichte der Ordnungspolizei, 1936–1945,* Schriften des Bundesarchivs 3, (Koblenz, 1957), p. 5.

[48] Weiss, *Polizei und Politik*, p. 25.

[49] Weiss, "Grundgedanken für die Reform der preussischen Kriminalpolizei," in *Die Polizei,* 21. Jhg., Nr. 20, Jan. 20, 1925, pp. 503–506. The LKA office in Berlin was no more than a "letterwriting service" in the twenties, except that it did make for a more lively exchange of personnel between local Kripo forces in Prussia. In 1928, Berlin Kripo agents investigated 87 murder cases in the provinces, and 55 in 1929. *Kriminalistische Monatshefte,* 4. Jhg., Heft 3, March, 1930.

[50] *Denkschrift des Bundes Deutscher Polizeibeamten e.V. über die Geheime Staatspolizei . . .* (Kassel, 1953), n.p.

[51] Interviews, Togotzes, Bomke, Stumm, Lehnhoff.

[52] These figures are cited in Albert C. Grzesinski, "Die Leistung der Berliner Polizei im Wahlkampf," in *Die Polizei,* 29. Jhg., Nr. 10, May 20, 1932, pp. 221–222.

[53] Interview, Teigeler; and Weiss, *Polizei und Politik*, pp. 136–137.

[54] *Vossische Zeitung,* Aug. 30, 1921 (M); and *ibid.,* June 24, 1922 (A).

[55] *Ibid.,* Feb. 18, 1930 (A).

[56] *Ibid.,* Jan. 23, 1932 (A).

[57] Grzesinski, "Die Leistungen der Berliner Polizei," p. 222.

[58] *Vossische Zeitung,* May 3, 1929 (A).

[59] See Zanck (Polizei-Major), *Wegweiser durch das polizeiliche Gross-Berlin* (Berlin: Gerstmann, 1922), pp. 26–27; and Preussisches Staatsministerium, *Handbuch über den Preussischen Staat für das Jahr 1925* (Berlin: R. von Decker, 1925), p. 140. Local inspectorates (Ortsinspektionen) of the Kripo were installed in all the 20 police posts (Polizeiämter) in Greater Berlin. They supervised the detectives in the police stations on the precinct level. In contrast, the street agents of IA were always dependent on communications from headquarters.

[60] This could be a considerable nuisance, since much red tape was involved. See "Die Kriminalpolizei klagt an," in *Vossische Zeitung,* Nov. 23, 1928 (M).

[61] Max Weiss, *Polizeischule*, I; 383; and Vorschriften für die staatliche Polizei Preussens (V.f.d.P.), *Vorschrift für die Waffenausbildung der Schutzpolizei*, Teil II (Berlin: Kameradschaft, 1932), para. III, Nrs. 125, 158.

[62] Interviews, Togotzes and Lehnhoff.

[63] Interviews, Kolbe, Miczek, Sangmeister.

[64] Weiss, *Polizeischule*, p. 378.

[65] For the training of Kripo inspectors, see Gay, *Preussische Landeskriminalpolizei*, pp. 17–18. There were the following service ranks: (1) Simple *(einfacher Dienst)*: Kriminal-Assistenten; (2) Medium *(mittlerer Dienst)*: Kriminal-Sekretäre and Kriminal-Bezirks-Sekretäre; (3) Elevated *(gehobener Dienst)*: Kriminal-Kommissare and Kriminal-Oberkommissare; (4) Higher *(höherer Dienst)*: Kriminal-Polizeiräte and Kriminal-Direktoren.

[66] In 1932 of the 132 Kriminal-Kommissare on the Berlin force, 22 held doctoral degrees. See *Dienstaltersliste der staatlichen höheren Kriminalbeamten Preussens und des Freistaates Danzig* (Essen, 1932), pp. 8–12.

[67] Weiss, *Polizeischule*, pp. 384–385; and von Schmidt, *Vorgeführt erscheint*, pp. 229–230.

[68] Anonymous, *Volk und Schupo* (Cologne: Gilde, 1929 [?]), pp. 53–54. The Institute also furthered advanced studies in law, psychology, and sociology, collected information on police developments abroad, and worked on an improved police code and better training methods for rookies.

[69] Weiss, *Polizeischule*, pp. 382–383.

[70] Ullrich, *Verbrechensbekämpfung*, p. 43.

[71] Ernst Gennat, "Die Bearbeitung von Mordsachen," in *Kriminalistische Monatshefte*, 1. Jhg., Heft 4, April 1, 1927, p. 81.

[72] Interviews, Kühnast, Lehnhoff.

[73] Menzel, "Reformmöglichkeiten bei der Polizei," in *Die Polizei*, 25. Jhg., Nr. 2, Jan. 20, 1928, p. 33; and Ullrich, *Verbrechensbekämpfung*, pp. 61–62.

[74] Friedensdorf, "Die Zusammenarbeit zwischen Polizei und Staatsanwaltschaft," in *Kriminalistische Monatshefte*, 3. Jhg., Heft 5, May, 1929, pp. 105–106.

[75] "Mit welchem Erfolg arbeitet die Polizei?" in *Vossische Zeitung*, Jan. 15, 1929 (M).

[76] "Gegen das politische Rowdytum," in *ibid.*, Feb. 7, 1926 (S); and "Grzesinski will durchgreifen," in *ibid.*, Feb. 2, 1931 (A).

[77] In 1928 the Berlin police solved less than half of the current cases of robbery and attempts at robbery. See *ibid.*, Jan 15, 1929 (M).

[78] The *Archiv für Kriminologie* urged detective inspectors to pay more attention to the progress of police science and hinted that their technical knowledge was 50 years out of date. See "Zum 200jährigen Geschäftsjubiläum des Verlags F. C. W. Vogel," in *Archiv für Kriminologie*, 87 (1930), 85–87. See also Heinrich Mann's judgment after several weeks of study at Kripo headquarters in *Vossische Zeitung*, Jan. 22, 1931 (A), and his "Die Kriminalpolizei," in Mann, *Essays*, II (Berlin: Aufbau, 1956), 223–231.

[79] Department IV also included the Prussian Criminal Police Office (LKA), the Prussian Criminal Police Post (LKP) for Greater Berlin, a general security service for guard duty, a prisoner escort service, the police prison, and the morgue. For the sake of clarity, the structure and nomenclature of the police in 1926 was used throughout this study. See *Geschäftseinteilung des Polizeipräsidiums Berlin* (Berlin: A. W. Hayn's Erben, 1926). The same source also reveals in detail the organization of Department IA.

[80] "Die Polizeiämter werden zusammengelegt," in *Vossische Zeitung*, Dec. 10, 1929 (A).

[81] Interviews, Bomke, Elsler; and Ullrich, *Verbrechensbekämpfung*, p. 73; and Max Weiss, *Polizeischule*, pp. 384–385.

[82] H. R. B., "Die sparsame Kriminalpolizei," in *Vossische Zeitung*, Sept. 11, 1929 (M).

[83] The following passage, dealing with the professional record of Kripo officials, is largely based on the crime reports of the *Vossische Zeitung* between 1918 and 1932. Anuschat is also mentioned in Engelbrecht and Heller, *Berliner Razzien, passim*.

[84] Ernst Gennat was described in Interviews with Lehnhoff, Bomke, and Elsler; see also von Schmidt, *Vorgeführt erscheint*, pp. 177–178, 217, 235; Frey, *Ich beantrage Freispruch*, p. 234; and *Der Spiegel*, 3. Jhg., Nr. 40, Sept. 29, 1949, pp. 22–25; and *ibid.*, Nr. 41, Oct. 6, 1949, pp. 22–27.

[85] See his remarkably cautious stand on the use of clairvoyance in crime detection. "Rechtssprechung," in *Kriminalistische Monatshefte*, 3. Jhg., Heft 2, Feb. 1929, p. 45.

[86] From Karl Draeger's handwritten vita, dated around 1938, in the S.S. files of the Berlin Document Center; and a typed "Notiz für die Presse" concerning Lissigkeit, dated 1932 and written by Kurt Daluege, in the ORPO files of the Berlin Document Center.

[87] See B. Kraft, "Zur Mordsache Schmoller," in *Archiv für Kriminologie,* 88 (Berlin, 1931), 123–125.

[88] *Vossische Zeitung,* March 14, 1928 (M).

[89] Von Schmidt, *Vorgeführt erscheint,* pp. 37–38, 176; and Frey, *Ich beantrage Freispruch,* pp. 100–101.

[90] See the court proceedings against Busdorf after the war in "Anklageschrift gegen Plönzke und andere–Köpenicker Blutwoche" *(35. P. Js 77.48/35. P Kls. 32.50),* p. 79 [mimeo. copy, available at the Archiv der Staatsanwaltschaft, Berlin-Moabit, Turmstrasse 91].

[91] Frey, *Ich beantrage Freispruch,* p. 261.

[92] Hans Salaw, "Psychologische Voraussetzungen für den Kriminaldienst," in *Kriminalistische Monatshefte,* 1. Jhg., Heft 2, Feb. 1, 1927, pp. 39–41.

[93] Note especially the long debate over the merits of criminal anthropology in the *Kriminalistische Monatshefte* between Feb. and Dec., 1927, and scattered articles on clairvoyance, such as "Die Hellseherin bei der Mordaufklärung," in *ibid.,* 2. Jhg., Heft 8, Aug., 1928, pp. 182–183; or Kriminal-Kommissar Schneider, "Hellsehen," in *ibid.,* 7. Jhg., Heft 1, Jan. 1933, pp. 20–21.

[94] The oldest member of the Nazi Fellowship of Civil Servants (NSBAG) in the Kripo was probably Kriminalpolizeirat Alfred Mundt (born 1875). There were no Communist supporters in the Kripo.

[95] See the disciplinary measures taken against detective sergeants Kurt Krischer (1927) and Hans Mulack (1931) who were serving at precinct stations, in the ORPO files of the Berlin Document Center.

[96] Dr. Rudolf Braschwitz of Department IA entered the German Democratic Party, the SPD, and the Union of Republican Police Officials to please his superiors. He joined the NSDAP at the earliest opportunity in 1933. See his handwritten vita, dated 1943, in the RUSHA files of the Berlin Document Center.

[97] Gennat, "Die Bearbeitung von Mordsachen," pp. 81–83.

[98] Of the 40 murders committed in Berlin in 1928, 32 were the result of family quarrels. See *Vossische Zeitung,* Jan. 15, 1929 (M).

[99] See Reiwald's statistics for 1882–1928 in his *Gesellschaft und ihre Verbrecher,* p. 160; and Ullrich, *Verbrechensbekämpfung,* p. 49. Though none of the Kripo officials who were interviewed in 1962 wanted to describe the general traits of crime in Berlin, they were all agreed on this point.

[100] For the criminalist's view of the political troubles immediately after

the war, see Erich Wulffen, *Verbrechen und Verbrecher* (Berlin: Hanseatischer Rechts- u. Wirtschaftsverlag, 1925), p. 439; and Wilhelm Sauer, *Kriminalsoziologie* (Berlin and Leipzig: Verlag für Staatswissenschaft und Geschichte, 1933), p. 224.

[101] *Vossische Zeitung*, Jan. 19, 1932 (A), and Jan. 20, 1932 (M).

[102] Interview, Teigeler; and Albert Grzesinski, "Die Leistung der Berliner Polizei im Wahlkampf," in *Die Polizei*, 29. Jhg., Nr. 10, May 20, 1932, p. 222.

[103] Interviews, Bauer, Lehnhoff, Togotzes, Teigeler. Hans Langemann, *Das Attentat. Eine kriminalwissenschaftliche Studie zum politischen Kapitalverbrechen* (Hamburg: Kriminalistik, 1956), p. 29.

[104] See map on p. 12; also Interviews, Teigeler, Lehnhoff; von Schmidt, *Vorgeführt erscheint*, pp. 397–398; and Engelbrecht and Heller, *Kinder der Nacht*, pp. 123–127.

[105] S.A. men detailed for police duty in Feb., 1933, had to be purged of criminal elements in April. See "Feststellung der Vorstrafen von Hilfspolizisten," *S. 1a./Hipo. 01/33* (Berlin, April 7, 1933) [mimeo. document, courtesy Miczek].

[106] Interview, Teigeler; and *Vossische Zeitung*, Jan. 4, 1933 (M); Jan. 8, 1933 (M), and Jan. 11, 1933 (M).

[107] *Ibid.*, Feb. 23, 1929 (M, A); and March 1, 1929 (A).

[108] Interviews, Togotzes, Teigeler; *Vossische Zeitung*, Jan. 17, 1930 (A) to Sept. 23, 1930 (M).

[109] *Ibid.*, May 24, 1930 (M) to July 15, 1930 (A).

[110] This is based on documents in the NSDAP files, the RUSHA files, and the ORPO files at the Berlin Document Center; as well as incidental references to these officials in *Vossische Zeitung*, between 1920 and 1933.

[111] Gennat was compassionate but firm with his friend Kriminal-Kommissar Peters in 1926, one of the few Kripo officials during the Weimar Republic to turn corrupt. See *Vossische Zeitung*, April 13 and 14, 1926.

[112] Interview, Lehnhoff; von Schmidt, *Vorgeführt erscheint*, p. 235; and *Der Spiegel*, 3. Jhg., Nr. 49, Dec. 1, 1949, p. 22.

[113] See "Anklageschrift gegen Plönzke und andere," *passim*.

[114] *Vossische Zeitung*, July 16, 1926 to Aug. 10, 1926. The Helling case is also known as the "Haas-Schröder" case, after the two chief suspects. It gave rise to fears that a German Dreyfus affair was in the offing and furnished the plot for the movie *Die Affäre Blum*.

[115] Letter from Boris Grams, dated Berlin-Wilmersdorf, Oct. 23, 1931, to Joseph Goebbels, in the ORPO files of the Berlin Document Center.

[116] Lothar Philipp, "Hans Schneickert 50 Jahre alt!" in *Kriminalistische Monatshefte*, 1. Jhg., Heft 3, March 1, 1927, pp. 49–50.

[117] Schneickert, ed., Stieber, *Lehrbuch der Kriminalpolizei*, p. 180.

[118] Hans Schneickert, "Für und wider die Todesstrafe," in *Kriminalistische Monatshefte*, 1. Jhg., Heft 3, March 1, 1927, pp. 50–52.

[119] Schneickert, *Einführung in die Kriminalsoziologie und Verbrechensverhütung* (Jena: Gustav Fischer, 1935), pp. 70–73.

[120] *Ibid.*, p. 54.

[121] Schneickert never joined the NSDAP.

[122] Information on these men was gathered at the Berlin Document Center, through references in the *Vossische Zeitung*, and in general accounts of crime in Berlin, some of them written by these officials themselves. Engelbrecht's article, "Das Verbrechertum in Italien," appeared in *Die Polizei*, 21. Jhg., Nr. 18, Dec. 20, 1924. A similar view, expressed by the commander of police inspection Tempelhof in Nov., 1922, led to disciplinary measures by the Schupo command. See Bundesarchiv, R 58/686/1.

[123] Ferdinand Friedensburg, *Die Weimarer Republik* (Berlin, 1946), p. 20.

[124] See among others Wulffen, *Verbrechen und Verbrecher*, pp. 447–452; Erich Liebermann von Sonnenberg, "Von Einbrechern und ihren Wegen," in *Archiv für Kriminologie*, 77 (Leipzig, 1925), 13–18; Robert Heindl, "Kriminalität und Krieg," in *ibid.*, 78 (Leipzig, 1926), 63–64; and Friedrich Karl Kaul, *Verdienen wird gross geschrieben. Der Pitaval der Weimarer Republik*, 2 (Berlin: Das Neue Berlin, 1954), 65–67.

[125] For Berlin's underworld clubs see notably H. R. B., "Wie ist die Berliner Unterwelt organisiert?" in *Vossische Zeitung*, Jan. 5, 1929 (M); Engelbrecht, *In den Spuren des Verbrechertums*, pp. 83–90; Ullrich, *Verbrechensbekämpfung*, p. 74; and Kurt Daluege, *Nationalsozialistischer Kampf dem Verbrechertum* (Munich: F. Eher, 1936), p. 15. A very good essay by Kuban (Kriminal-Anwärter), "Ringvereine und ihre Bekämpfung" (1956), is available in manuscript form at the Police School in Berlin-Spandau.

[126] Interview, Togotzes; and Engelbrecht, *In den Spuren des Verbrechertums*, pp. 18–19.

[127] There may have been exceptions. The "Wedding Kolonne," a well-known team of burglars, was said to support the KPD: see Rumpelstilzchen, *Berliner Allerlei*, p. 43; and von Schmidt, *Vorgeführt erscheint*, p. 398. In *Sturm 33 Hans Maikowski. Geschrieben von Kameraden des*

Toten (Berlin-Schöneberg: Oskar Berger, 1942), pp. 33–34, a Ringverein is mentioned as the ally of Communist gangs.

[128] Interviews, Teigeler, Togotzes; also Kaul, *Verdienen wird gross geschrieben*, pp. 108–110.

[129] Delius, "Wie wird das Verbrechertum erfolgreicher als bisher bekämpft?" in *Die Polizei*, 17. Jhg., Nr. 3, April 29, 1920; Albert Hellwig, "Richter und Presse," in *Archiv für Kriminologie*, 87 (Leipzig, 1930), 220–224; and Wulffen, *Verbrechen und Verbrecher*, p. 460.

[130] The Sass brothers are mentioned in nearly every book concerning crime in this period. The bank robbery at Wittenbergplatz is discussed in *Archiv für Kriminologie*, 84 (Leipzig, 1929), 152–157; and in *Kriminalistische Monatshefte*, 3. Jhg., Heft 2, Feb. 1929, pp. 34–37. Erich Kästner even used it for a brief dialogue between passengers on a streetcar in his novel *Emil und die Detektive* (Berlin-Grunewald: Williams, 1929).

[131] H. R. B., "Brüder Sass machen Spass," in *Vossische Zeitung*, April 30, 1930 (A).

[132] Interview, Lehnhoff; Liebermann is also described in von Schmidt, *Vorgeführt erscheint*, pp. 168–169; and there are documents under his name in the ORPO files of the Berlin Document Center.

[133] Letter from Liebermann to Daluege, dated Berlin, Nov. 27, 1936, in the ORPO files of the Berlin Document Center.

[134] Trettin was described in interviews with Bomke, Elsler, Lehnhoff, Togotzes, Teigeler, Kuckenburg. His cases were reported in the *Vossische Zeitung*.

[135] Sling [Paul Schlesinger], "Detektiv, Polizei, Staatsanwalt," in *ibid.*, April 25, 1928 (M); see also decree of Ministry of Interior as reported in *ibid.*, July 14, 1927 (M).

[136] *Ibid.*, July 13, 1920 (M).

[137] On the question of rewards, see Bernhard Weiss, "Kriminalbeamte und Feuersozietät," in *ibid.*, July 28, 1927 (M); a letter by Dr. Loewenthal in *ibid.*, Aug. 2, 1927 (M); H. R. B., "Die sparsame Kriminalpolizei," in *ibid.*, Sept. 11, 1929 (M); and Dr. Wartenberg, "Brandursachenermittlungen durch Versicherungsgesellschaften," in *Kriminalistische Monatshefte*, 1. Jhg., Heft 3, March 1, 1927, pp. 56–58.

[138] The following account is largely based on the NSDAP files in the Berlin Document Center. Hans Bernd Gisevius draws a sympathetic picture of Nebe in *To the Bitter End* (Boston: Houghton Mifflin, 1947), and *Wo ist Nebe?* (Zurich: Doemer, 1966), both of which, however, only refer to the period after 1933.

[139] Interviews, Stumm, Lehnhoff, Bauer, Elsler, Bomke. See also *Der Spiegel*, 3, Jhg., Nr. 42, Oct. 13, 1949, p. 29.

[140] *Vossische Zeitung*, March 24, 1931 (A); and *ibid.*, May 8, 1931 (M). In this year, one of his murder cases also drew professional attention. See B. Kraft, "Notwehr, Totschlag oder Muttermord?" in *Archiv für Kriminologie*, 89 (Berlin 1931), 33 ff.

CHAPTER V

The End of a Police Era

[1] Albert C. Grzesinski, *Inside Germany*, trans. Alexander S. Lipschitz (New York: E. P. Dutton, 1939), pp. 152 ff.; Carl Severing, *Mein Lebensweg*, II (Cologne: Greven, 1950), 340–341; and Arnold Brecht, *Prelude to Silence. The End of the Weimar Republic* (New York: Oxford University Press, 1944), p. 64.

[2] Severing, *Mein Lebensweg*, p. 347.

[3] O. H., "Attacke gegen Preussens Polizei," in *Vossische Zeitung*, June 29, 1932 (A); *ibid.*, July 6, 1932 (M); and *ibid.*, July 11, 1932 (A).

[4] Joseph Goebbels, *Vom Kaiserhof zur Reichskanzlei* (Munich: F. Eher, 1934), p. 117.

[5] *Vossische Zeitung*, July 20, 1932 (A).

[6] Severing, *Mein Lebensweg*, pp. 352–355.

[7] Brecht, *Prelude to Silence*, p. 67.

[8] Grzesinski, *Inside Germany*, p. 161; and Theodor Wolff, *Through Two Decades*, trans. E. W. Dickes (London: W. Heinemann, 1936), p. 297. For a rare voice in support of mobilizing the armed police, see Willy Brandt, *My Road to Berlin* (New York: Doubleday, 1960), pp. 51–53.

[9] Interview, Bomke; and two documents marked *Zu Z. 3494 II* in the ORPO files at the Berlin Document Center: "Niederschrift über die Vernehmung des Polizeivizepräsidenten Dr. Mosle über die Vorgänge am 20. Juli 1932 im Polizeipräsidium in Berlin"; and "Abschrift über die Vernehmung des Regierungsdirektors Scholz über die politischen Vorgänge am 20. 7. 1932 im Polizeipräsidium Berlin." Frank Arnau in *Das Auge des Gesetzes. Macht und Ohnmacht der Kriminalpolizei* (Düsseldorf and Vienna: Econ, 1962), p. 61, asserts that Grzesinski and Heimannsberg asked Severing to call out the armed police, but offers no evidence for his information.

[10] Interrogation of Dr. Mosle and Reg. Dir. Scholz in the ORPO files of the Berlin Document Center, *Zu Z. 3494 II*.

[11] See p. 92.

[12] "Strafsache gegen Encke wegen Vergehen gegen die Not V. v. 20/7. 32," in *Blattsammlung der Staatsanwaltschaft bei dem Landgericht II in Berlin. II P.J. 1388/32*. The charges against Encke were dropped on Nov. 19, 1932. See *Vossische Zeitung*, Nov. 19, 1932 (A).

[13] F. O'Mon., "Heimannsberg," in *ibid.*, Aug. 13, 1931 (M).

[14] "Reformen bei der Schupo," in *ibid.*, March 31, 1927 (M); and C. M., "Der Kommandeur," in *ibid.*, Feb. 27, 1930 (M).

[15] *Ibid.*, Sept. 15, 1932 (M); and Sept. 29, 1932 (A).

[16] *Die Polizei*, 25. Jhg., Nr. 20, Oct. 20, 1928, pp. 657–658.

[17] *Kriminalistische Monatshefte*, 2. Jhg., Heft 8, Aug. 1928, p. 191.

[18] Bernhard Weiss, "Angriffe gegen die Kriminalpolizei," in *ibid.*, 6. Jhg., Heft 4, April 1932, p. 86.

[19] Rumpelstilzchen [Adolf Stein], *Un det jloobste?* (Berlin: Brunnen, 1923), p. 197.

[20] Interview, Bomke.

[21] Interview, Lehnhoff.

[22] On July 5, 1923, *Die Rote Fahne* also printed a poem attacking "Isidor" for his un-Germanic appearance. But anti-Semitic sallies of this kind were rare in Communist propaganda. See Werner T. Angress, *Stillborn Revolution* (Princeton: Princeton University Press, 1964), p. 340. On Sept. 30, 1933, the Nazi government finally divested Bernhard Weiss of his German citizenship.

[23] *Vossische Zeitung*, Oct. 20, 1932 (M); and "Strafsache gegen Weiss, Dr., wegen § 346," in *Blattsammlung der Staatsanwaltschaft bei dem Landgericht I Berlin, 1 pol. J. 3003/32*.

[24] *Vossische Zeitung*, July 23, 1932 (M) and Aug. 3, 1932 (M).

[25] *Ibid.*, Oct. 11, 1932 (M) and Nov. 2, 1932 (M).

[26] *Ibid.*, Nov. 11, 1932 (A).

[27] See draft of a letter from Kurt Daluege to Wilhelm Kube, then leader of the NSDAP in the Prussian Diet, dated Dec. 13, 1932, Tgb. Nr. 840 Ha/G., in the ORPO files of the Berlin Document Center.

[28] *Vossische Zeitung*, July 25, 1932 (A); and Jan. 20, 1933 (M).

[29] *Ibid.*, Sept. 5, 1932 (A), and Oct. 6, 1932 (M).

[30] Goebbels, *Vom Kaiserhof zur Reichskanzlei*, p. 135.

[31] See two reports by IA, Dezernat 6, both dated Berlin, Aug. 16, 1932, at Bundesarchiv, R 58/409.

[32] See p. 81.

[33] Interview, Elsler.

[34] *Vossische Zeitung*, Oct. 5, 1932 (M); and "Präsident Melcher über seine Tätigkeit," in *ibid.*, Oct. 13, 1932 (M).

[35] *Ibid.*, Aug. 1, 1932 (A); also "Ein Kämpfer für die Freiheit: Karl Heinrich," in *Berliner Polizei*, 10. Jhg., Nr. 9, Sept. 1962, p. 1.

[36] *RdErl. d. MdI v. 29.7.1932–Pd 1045 IV u. IVa I 542.*

[37] *Vossische Zeitung*, Aug. 9, 1932 (M).

[38] Interview, Artner.

[39] Interview, Fleischer.

[40] *Vossische Zeitung*, July 25, 1932 (A).

[41] *Ibid.*, Sept. 6, 1932 (A).

[42] *Ibid.*, Jan. 23, 1933 (A). Christopher Isherwood described this event in *The Berlin Stories* (New York: J. Laughlin, 1945), pp. 309–310. In his account, the Nazi march on the Bülowplatz was a spurious triumph.

[43] See Daluege's letter to Oskar Schoenherr, dated Berlin, March 7, 1934, D. 1123, in the ORPO files of the Berlin Document Center.

[44] *Vossische Zeitung*, Sept. 8, 1932 (A).

[45] *Ibid.*, Sept. 14, 1932 (A), and Sept. 15, 1932 (A).

[46] *Ibid.*, July 26, 1932 (A).

[47] C. M., "Schluss jetzt," in *ibid.*, July 18, 1932 (A); and Brecht, *Prelude to Silence*, pp. 63–64.

[48] Letter from Oberst-Leutnant Albrecht of the Schutzpolizei in Schwerin (Mecklenburg), to Kurt Daluege, May 23, 1935, in the ORPO files of the Berlin Document Center.

[49] Rumpelstilzchen [Adolf Stein], *Mang uns mang . . . 1932/33* (Berlin, 1933), p. 38.

[50] For a detailed comment on this incident, see Jan Petersen, *Our Street. A Chronicle written in the heart of Fascist Germany*, trans. Betty Rensen (London, 1938), pp. 36 ff. The Nazi version can be found in J. K. von Engelbrechten and Hans Volz, eds., *Wir wandern durch das national-sozialistische Berlin* (Munich: Zentralverlag der NSDAP, 1937), pp. 117–120; and *Sturm 33 Hans Maikowski. Geschrieben von Kameraden des Toten* (Berlin-Schöneberg: Oskar Berger, 1942).

[51] E.g., Günther Braschwitz, who disclaimed his previous friendship with Bernhard Weiss and tried to make his inquisitors believe that they were mistaking him for his brother Rudolf. See Günther Braschwitz's letter, dated Essen, March 1, 1933, in the ORPO files of the Berlin Document Center.

[52] *Vossische Zeitung*, Feb. 2, 1933 (A); and Feb. 13, 1933 (A).

[53] S.A.–Standarte 6 to Polizei-Hauptmann Koplin, Berlin, July 14, 1933, Nr. 257/11/33, in the ORPO files of the Berlin Document Center.

[54] Letter by NSBAG, Fachgruppe Verwaltungspolizei, dated Berlin,

May 4, 1933, Nr. 2312, in the ORPO files of the Berlin Document Center.

[55] Doyé to Göring, dated Herischdorf i. Rsgb., Feb. 20, 1933, in the ORPO files of the Berlin Document Center.

[56] Letter from Hugo Kaupisch to Ernst Röhm, dated Schierke (Harz), Jan. 29, 1933, in the ORPO files of the Berlin Document Center.

[57] Letter from Kommissar z.b.V. (Kurt Daluege) to the Ortsgruppe der NSDAP, Berlin-Charlottenburg, dated Berlin, Feb. 28, 1933, Tgb. Nr. Rü 332 Dr. E/B, in the ORPO files of the Berlin Document Center.

[58] Testimonial of Otto Frey at the trial of Kurt Gildisch in 1949. See "Strafsache . . . gegen Gildisch, Kurt, wegen Verbrechen gegen die Menschlichkeit," in *Staatsanwaltschaft bei dem Landgericht Moabit*, 1 P. Ks 4/51, I; 8.

[59] Decree by Göring, Berlin, Feb. 21, 1933, I 1000/49, in the file "Polizei–Verschiedenes" at the Berlin Document Center.

[60] Autobiographical statements of Helmut Heisig and Wilhelm Bonatz, both dating from the mid-thirties, are on file at the Berlin Document Center.

[61] For Mühlfriedel, see the correspondence concerning him between Daluege and the NSDAP, Gau Gross-Berlin, on Sept. 25 and Oct. 24, 1934, in the ORPO files of the Berlin Document Center.

[62] See also Hans Bernd Gisevius, *To the Bitter End* (Boston, 1947), p. 77.

[63] Letter from Leiter der Abteilung II to Min. Dir. Schellen, dated Berlin, July 18, 1933, *Tgb. Nr. SD. 3104 N/Schg.*

[64] Letter from Police President Count Helldorf to Kurt Daluege, dated Berlin, Nov. 25, 1936, in the ORPO files of the Berlin Document Center. Liebermann died of illness in Berlin on March 11, 1941.

[65] *Berliner Lokal-Anzeiger*, Aug. 22, 1939.

[66] Letter from NSDAP-Ortsgruppe Wildenbruchplatz, Neukölln, to Kurt Daluege, Nov. 22, 1932; and a report by S.S. Gruppe Ost, Pressestelle, dated Berlin, March 2, 1933, both in the ORPO files of the Berlin Document Center.

[67] "Beamte im Stahlhelm," in *Vossische Zeitung*, Nov. 3, 1928 (M); and a typewritten list, probably drawn up on Feb. 1, 1933, giving a political evaluation of the staff at the Police School in Eiche (Potsdam), in the ORPO files of the Berlin Document Center.

[68] A report, dated Nov. 26, 1934, *Reg. Nr. D 2660*, concerning Pol. Oberst-Leutnant a.D. Levit, in the ORPO files of the Berlin Document Center.

[69] See Kronberger's article on combat tactics for the police in *Die Polizei*, 22. Jhg., Nr. 13, Oct. 5, 1925, pp. 355 ff.

[70] Fränkel was purged early in 1933. His case was subsequently debated in a letter by the S.A. Sturmbann I/5 ("Horst Wessel") dated Berlin, July 5, 1933, *Tgb. Nr. 1112/33*; a letter by the Gauleitung Gross-Berlin of the NSDAP dated Berlin, Sept. 24, 1934; in a reply to the Gauleitung by Min. Rat Hall dated Jan. 2, 1935 *(Ref. ZuD. 1810)*; and a letter from Fränkel himself to Hall, dated Jan. 6, 1935. All the documents are in the ORPO files at the Berlin Document Center.

[71] See "Verzeichnis der auf Grund des Gesetzes zur Wiederherstellung des Berufsbeamtentums wegen politischer Unzuverlässigkeit entlassenen Polizei-Offiziere und Polizei-Wachtmeister der preussischen Schutzpolizei," mimeo. list available at the Berlin Document Center.

[72] Fritz Krumbach fled abroad; his brother was arrested.

[73] Decree by the Ministry of Interior, dated Berlin, Feb. 22, 1933, *II C I 59 Nr. 40/33*.

[74] Willy Lemke, "Memoirs," unpub. MS, courtesy of the author.

[75] Dispatch from the Ministry of Foreign Affairs to the Reich Ministry of Interior, dated Berlin, May 15, 1933, II F 1370, in the file "Polizei–Verschiedenes" at the Berlin Document Center.

[76] References to Wecke can be found in the *Vossische Zeitung*, Jan. 5, 1933 (A); Jan. 31, 1933 (A); Feb. 2, 1933 (A); and Feb. 4, 1933 (A).

[77] Wecke was denounced in a handwritten note by Franz Nippold, head of the NSBAG, Fachgruppe Schupo, probably dated Berlin, May 19, 1933; and in an anonymous list of about the same time naming fifteen "unreliable" police officers. Both documents are in the ORPO files of the Berlin Document Center.

[78] Letter by Hans Oelze, Hauptmann der Landespolizei, dated Berlin, Aug. 21, 1934, in the ORPO files of the Berlin Document Center.

[79] In the ORPO files of the Berlin Document Center.

[80] Letter from Wecke to Daluege, dated Berlin, Dec. 2, 1933, in the ORPO files of the Berlin Document Center.

[81] Wilhelm Kube to Kurt Daluege, Berlin, July 6, 1934, in the ORPO files of the Berlin Document Center.

Epilogue

[1] H.-J. Neufeldt, J. Huck, and G. Tessin, *Zur Geschichte der Ordnungspolizei, 1936–1945*, Schriften des Bundesarchivs 3 (Koblenz, 1957); Hans

Buchheim, "Die höheren SS- und Polizeiführer," in *Vierteljahrshefte für Zeitgeschichte*, Heft 4, Oct. 1963, pp. 362–391; and Hans Buchheim, *SS und Polizei im NS-Staat* (Duisburg bei Bonn, 1964).

[2] A good example is Leon Uris, *Armageddon* (Garden City, N. Y.: Doubleday, 1963). There are, admittedly, some novels that succeed very well in painting the life of average Berliners after the war, notably Erich Wildberger, *Ring über Ostkreuz* (Hamburg: Rowohlt, 1953); Dieter Meichsner, *Die Studenten von Berlin* (Hamburg: Rowohlt, 1954); and Ingeborg Wendt, *Notopfer Berlin* (Hamburg: Rowohlt, 1956).

Bibliography

The following is intended as a guide to the basic literature on the history of Berlin and on Prussian police history in the Weimar Republic. Books and articles pertaining to Germany's overall political condition during this period as well as special studies with marginal pertinence to our subject have not been included even when referred to in the notes to the text.

Berlin

BIBLIOGRAPHIES

Otto-Friedrich Gandert, Berthold Schulze, Ernst Kaeber, et al., eds. *Heimatchronik Berlin*. Cologne: Archiv für Deutsche Heimatpflege, 1962. [See bibliographical list by Konrad Ketting.]

Waldemar Kuhn. *Berlin, Stadt und Land. Handbuch des Schrifttums*. Berlin: Arani-Verlag, 1952.

Hans Zopf and Gerd Heinrichs, eds. *Berlin Bibliographie*. Berlin: Walter de Gruyter & Co., 1965.

GENERAL HISTORIES

Max Arendt, Eberhard Faden, Otto-Friedrich Gandert. *Geschichte der Stadt Berlin.* Berlin, 1937.

Otto-Friedrich Gandert, Berthold Schulze, Ernst Kaeber, et al., eds. *Heimatchronik Berlin.* Cologne: Archiv für Deutsche Heimatpflege, 1962. [The "official textbook"—from the stone age to the building of the Berlin Wall, 1961.]

Werner Hegemann. *Das steinerne Berlin. Geschichte der grössten Mietskasernenstadt der Welt.* Berlin: Gustav Kiepenheuer, 1930.

Walther Kiaulehn. *Berlin: Schicksal einer Weltstadt.* Munich and Berlin: Biederstein Verlag, 1958.

Mario Krammer. *Berlin im Wandel der Jahrhunderte. Eine Kulturgeschichte der deutschen Hauptstadt.* Berlin: Rembrandt-Verlag, 1956.

John Mander. *Berlin: The Eagle and the Bear* London, 1959. [Uneven.]

Hans Rothfels, ed. *Berlin in Vergangenheit und Gegenwart.* Tübingen: Mohr, 1961.

Karl Scheffler. *Berlin: Wandlungen einer Stadt.* Berlin, 1931.

DESCRIPTIONS

Peter Gay. *Weimar Culture: The Outsider as Insider.* New York and Evanston: Harper & Row, 1968. [Emphasizes the importance of Berlin as an intellectual center in the twenties.]

Friedrich Hussong. *"Kurfürstendamm." Zur Kulturgeschichte des Zwischenreichs.* Berlin: Verlag der Täglichen Rundschau, 1934. [A polemic attack on republican Berlin by the editor of the Berliner Lokalanzeiger.]

H. R. Knickerbocker. *Deutschland so oder so?* Berlin: Rowohlt Verlag, 1932. [Original American title: *The German Crisis* (New York: Farrar & Rinehart, 1932).]

Franz Lederer. *Berlin und Umgebung.* Berlin, 1929. [A defense of Berlin.]

Willy Mann. *Berlin zur Zeit der Weimarer Republik.* Berlin: Das Neue Berlin Verlag, 1957. [An important East German contribution.]

Hermann Ullmann. *Flucht aus Berlin.* Jena: Eugen Diederichs Verlag, 1932. [Acute observations on the city and its inhabitants.]

TECHNICAL MONOGRAPHS

Gustav Böss. *Die Not in Berlin. Tatsachen und Zahlen.* Berlin: Zentralverlag, 1923. [By the Lord Mayor of Berlin.]

———. *Berlin von heute. Stadtverwaltung und Wirtschaft.* Berlin, 1929.

Hans Brennert and Erwin Stein, eds. *Probleme der neuen Stadt Berlin.* Berlin-Friedenau, 1926.

Otto Büsch. *Geschichte der Berliner Kommunalwirtschaft in der Weimarer Epoche.* Berlin: Walter de Gruyter, 1960.

G. Hellmann. *Das Klima von Berlin.* Berlin, 1910.

Ernst Kaeber. *Berlin im Weltkrieg. Fünf Jahre städtische Kriegsarbeit.* Berlin, 1921. [Kaeber was then city archivist of Berlin.]

Friedrich Leyden. *Gross-Berlin. Geographie der Weltstadt.* Breslau, 1933.

Herbert Louis. *Die geographische Gliederung von Gross-Berlin.* Stuttgart, 1936.

Hans Schulze. *5 Jahre Gross-Berlin. Ein wirtschaftshistorischer Rückblick und Beitrag zur Geschichte und Organisation der Reichshauptstadt.* Neustrelitz, 1927.

Martin Wagner and A. Behne, eds. *Das neue Berlin. Groszstadtprobleme.* Berlin, 1929.

MEMOIRS AND CONTEMPORARY REPORTS

Hedda Adlon. *Hotel Adlon. Das Haus in dem die Welt zu Gast war.* Munich: Kindler Verlag, 1955.

Henri Béraud. *Ce que j'ai vu à Berlin.* Paris: Les éditions de France, 1926.

Ilya Ehrenburg. *Memoirs: 1921–1941.* Trans. Tatania Shebunina. Cleveland and New York: World Publishing Co., 1965. [Passim.]

Joseph Hergesheimer. *Berlin.* New York: Alfred Knopf, 1932.

Max Krell. *Das alles gab es einmal.* Frankfurt a.M.: Heinrich Scheffler, 1961. [Perhaps the most informative of all reminiscences concerning Berlin personalities in literature and art.]

Friedrich C. A. Lange. *Gross-Berliner Tagebuch, 1920-1933.* Berlin-Lichtenrade: Berlinische Verlagsbuchhandlung, 1951.

Philipp Paneth. *Nacht über Berlin-Alexanderplatz. Die "lasterhafte" City von Aschinger bis Zacharias.* Leipzig: Heinrich Blömer's Verlag, 1932. [Sketches from the life of Berliners during the Great Depression.]

Pem [Paul Erich Marcus]. *Heimweh nach dem Kurfürstendamm. Aus Berlins glanzvollsten Tagen und Nächten.* Berlin: Lothar Blanvalet, 1952.

Herbert Pfeiffer. *Berlin zwanziger Jahre.* Berlin: Rembrandt-Verlag, 1961. [Artists and writers.]

Rumpelstilzchen [Adolf Stein]. *Berliner Allerlei.* Berlin: Verlag der Täglichen Rundschau, 1922.

———. *Was sich Berlin erzählt.* Berlin: Dom-Verlag, 1922.

———. *Un det jloobste?* Berlin: Brunnen Verlag, 1923.

———. *Bei mir—Berlin!* Berlin: Brunnen Verlag, 1924.

———. *Piept es?* Berlin: Verlag der Täglichen Rundschau, 1930.

———. *Mang uns mang . . . 1932/33.* Berlin, 1933. [A widely read publicist with strong national-conservative leanings.]

Ernst von Salomon, *Der Fragebogen.* Hamburg: Rowohlt, Verlag, 1951. [American title: *The Questionnaire,* trans. Constantine FitzGibbon (Garden City, N. Y.: Doubleday, 1954.)]

NOVELS:

There have been numerous novels written about the Berlin of the twenties. The selection below is a cross sample, chosen for their typicalness or their political interest and not necessarily for their literary value. A few more will be found in the section on the Nazi movement in Berlin.

Vicki Baum. *Menschen im Hotel, Ein Kolportageroman mit Hintergründen.* Berlin: Ullstein, 1929. [American title: *Grand Hotel,* trans. Basil Creighton (Garden City, N.Y.: Doubleday, 1931).]

Günther Birkenfeld. *A Room in Berlin.* Trans. Eric Sutton. London: Constable, 1940. [German original title: *Dritter Hof links.* First published 1930.]

Harlan R. Crippen, ed. *Germany: A Self-Portrait. A Collection of German Writings from 1914 to 1943.* Oxford University Press, 1944.

Marie Diers. *Freiheit und Brot! Der Roman einer Arbeiterfamilie.* Berlin: Nationaler Freiheitsverlag, 1933. [National Socialist.]

Alfred Döblin. *Berlin Alexanderplatz.* Berlin: S. Fischer, 1930. [American title: *Alexanderplatz, Berlin,* trans. Eugene Jolas (New York: The Viking Press, 1931).]

———. *Pardon wird nicht gegeben.* Olten and Freiburg i.B.: Walter-Verlag, 1960. [First published 1935.]

Axel Eggebrecht. *Volk ans Gewehr. Chronik eines Berliner Hauses, 1930–34.* Frankfurt a.M.: Europäische Verlagsanstalt, 1959.

Hans Fallada [Rudolf Ditzen]. *Kleiner Mann—was nun?* Berlin: Rowohlt Verlag, 1932. [American title: *Little Man, What Now?,* trans. Eric Sutton (New York: Simon and Schuster, 1933).]

———. *Wolf unter Wölfen.* Hamburg: Rowohlt Verlag, 1952. [First published 1937.]

Christopher Isherwood. *The Berlin Stories.* New York: J. Laughlin, 1945. [This is a reissue of *The Last of Mr. Norris* (first published 1935) and *Goodbye to Berlin* (first published 1939).]

Erich Kästner. *Emil und die Detektive.* Berlin-Grunewald: Williams, 1929.

[American title: *Emil and the Detectives,* trans. May Massee (Garden City, N.Y.: Doubleday, 1930).]

——. *Pünktchen und Anton.* Berlin-Grunewald: Williams, 1933.

——. *Fabian. Die Geschichte eines Moralisten.* Stuttgart and Berlin: Deutsche Verlags-Anstalt, 1931.

Vladmir Nabokov. *King, Queen, Knave.* trans. Dimitry Nabokov. New York: McGraw Hill, 1968. [German original title: *König, Dame, Bube.* First published 1930.]

Heinz Rein. *Berlin 1932. Ein Roman aus der Zeit der grossen Arbeitslosigkeit.* Berlin: Erich Schmidt, 1946. [Written 1935.]

Erich Maria Remarque. *Drei Kameraden.* Berlin: Ullstein Verlag, 1960. [First published 1937.]

MISCELLANEOUS

Hans Erman. *Bei Kempinski. Aus der Chronik einer Weltstadt.* Berlin: Argon Verlag, 1956.

——. *Weltgeschichte auf berlinisch.* Berlin, Frankfurt a.M.: Herrenalb, 1960. [Anecdotal.]

S. Fischer-Fabian. *Müssen Berliner so sein . . .* Berlin: Argon Verlag, 1960. [Short biographies and character sketches of well-known Berliners like Erich Frey, Kurt Tucholsky, Heinrich Zille, and Max Liebermann.]

Rolf Italiaander and Willy Haas, eds. *Berliner Cocktail.* Hamburg and Vienna: Paul Szolnay Verlag, 1959.

ILLUSTRATIONS:

For pictures of the city's appearance in the 19th and 20th centuries.

Max Arendt and Paul Torge. *Berlin einst und jetzt.* 2d ed. Berlin, 1934.

Berliner Kalender 1928. Berlin: Rembrandt-Verlag, 1928.

Mario von Bucovich. *Berlin.* Berlin: Albertus-Verlag, 1928. [Note the introduction by Alfred Döblin.]

Friedrich Heiss, ed. *Deutsche Revolution. Die Wende eines Volkes.* Berlin: Volk und Reich Verlag, 1933.

Helmut Kindler. *Berlin Brandenburger Tor.* Munich: Kindler Verlag, 1956.

THE NAZIS IN BERLIN

Wilfrid Bade. *Die S.A. erobert Berlin. Ein Tatsachen Bericht.* Munich: Verlag Knorr & Hirth, 1933.

Martin Broszat. "Die Anfänge der Berliner NSDAP, 1926/27," in *Vierteljahrshefte für Zeitgeschichte,* 8. Jhg., 1960, 1. Heft, pp. 85–91.

Julius K. von Engelbrechten. *Eine braune Armee entsteht. Die Geschichte der Berlin-Brandenburger S.A.* Munich: Zentralverlag der NSDAP, 1937.

Julius K. von Engelbrechten and Hans Volz, eds. *Wir wandern durch das nationalsozialistische Berlin. Ein Führer durch die Gedenkstätten des Kampfes um die Reichshauptstadt.* Munich: Zentralverlag der NSDAP, 1937.

Hanns Heinz Ewers. *Horst Wessel. Ein deutsches Schicksal.* Stuttgart and Berlin: J. G. Cotta'sche Buchhandlung, 1934.

Joseph Goebbels. *Das Buch Isidor. Ein Zeitbild von Lachen und Hass.* Munich: F. Eher, 1929.

——. *Das erwachende Berlin.* Munich: F. Eher, 1934. [Mainly pictures.]

——. *Vom Kaiserhof zur Reichskanzlei.* Munich: F. Eher, 1934.

——. *Der Angriff. Aufsätze aus der Kampfzeit.* 3d ed. Munich: F. Eher, 1936.

——. *Kampf um Berlin.* Munich: F. Eher, 1940.

Arnold Littmann. *Herbert Norkus und die Hitlerjungen vom Beusselkietz.* Berlin: Steuben, 1934.

Ernst Ottwalt. *Ruhe und Ordnung. Roman aus dem Leben der national-gesinnten Jugend.* Berlin: Malik, 1929.

Erwin Reitmann. *Horst Wessel. Leben und Streben.* Berlin: Steuben, 1933.

Karl Aloys Schenzinger. *Der Hitlerjunge Quex.* Berlin and Leipzig: "Zeitgeschichte" Verlag, 1932.

Sturm 33 Hans Maikowski. Geschrieben von Kameraden des Toten. Berlin-Schöneberg: Oscar Berger, 1942.

THE COMMUNISTS IN BERLIN

Willi Münzenberg. *Die dritte Front. 15 Jahre proletarische Jugendbewegung.* Berlin, 1930.

Klaus Neukrantz. *Barricades in Berlin.* New York: International Publishers, 1930 [?].

Jan Petersen. *Our Street. A Chronicle written in the Heart of Fascist Germany.* trans. Betty Rensen. London, 1938.

Charles Plisnier. *Faux passeports.* Paris: Éditions Corréa, 1937.

Police

GENERAL WORKS

Wilhelm Abegg, ed. *Die Polizei in Einzeldarstellungen.* Berlin: Gersbach

& Sohn, 1926-28. [Twelve small volumes, published under the auspices of the Prussian Ministry of Interior. Note especially vol. I: Ernst van den Bergh, "Polizei und Volk–Seelische Zusammenhänge"; vol. II: Kurt Melcher, "Die Geschichte der Polizei"; vol. III: Bernhard Weiss, "Polizei und Politik"; and vol. VIII: Hermann Degenhardt and Max Hagemann, "Polizei und Kind."]

Werner Best. *Die deutsche Polizei*. 2d ed. Darmstadt, 1940.

Frederick F. Blachly and Miriam E. Oatman. *The Government and Administration of Germany*. Baltimore: Johns Hopkins Press, 1928.

Directorate of Military Intelligence, The War Office. *The German Police System*, pt. I, supp. I. June, 1920.

The General Staff, War Office, *The German Police System as Applied to Military Security in War*. 1921.

Oskar Dressler, ed. *Grosse Polizei-Ausstellung Berlin—Internationaler Polizeikongress*. Vienna: "Internationale Oeffentliche Sicherheit" Verlag für polizeiliche Fachliteratur, 1927.

Geschäftseinteilung des Polizeipräsidiums Berlin. Berlin: A. W. Hayn's Erben, 1926. [Detailed presentation of police organization in Berlin.]

Claus Kaestl. "Reich und Länderpolizeien in der Weimarer Republik," in *Die Polizei*, 53. Jhg., Nr. 10, Oct. 8, 1962, pp. 302–305.

Fritz Laufer. *Unser Polizeiwesen*. Stuttgart, 1920.

Menzel and Höhn. *Die Reform des inneren Dienstes der staatlichen Polizei Preussens*. Magdeburg: Haenelsche Buchdruckerei, 1930.

Eberhard Pickart. "Preussische Beamtenpolitik, 1918–1933," in *Vierteljahrshefte für Zeitgeschichte*, 6. Jhg., 1958, 2. Heft, pp. 119–137.

Die Polizei. Zeitschrift für Polizeiwissenschaft, -dienst und -wesen. Berlin: Kameradschaft, 1913–1933.

Zanck. *Wegweiser durch das polizeiliche Gross-Berlin*. Berlin: S. Gerstmann's Verlag, 1922. [Important basic outline.]

HISTORIES

Assessor. "Die Berliner Polizei," In Hans Ostwald, ed. *Groszstadt-Dokumente*. Berlin, 1907.

Albert Ballhorn. *Das Polizeipräsidium zu Berlin*. Berlin, 1852.

Lothar Danner. *Ordnungspolizei Hamburg. Betrachtungen zu ihrer Geschichte, 1918 bis 1933*. Hamburg: Verlag Deutsche Polizei, 1958.

Willy Feigell. *Die Entwicklung des Königlichen Polizei-Präsidiums zu Berlin in der Zeit von 1809 bis 1909*. Berlin, 1909.

Dieter Fricke, *Bismarcks Prätorianer. Die Berliner politische Polizei im*

Kampf gegen die deutsche Arbeiterbewegung, 1871–1898. Berlin: Rütting & Loening, 1962.

E. Hölldorfer. *Die geschichtliche Entwicklung des Begriffes der Polizei nach deutschem Strafecht.* Diss. Tübingen, 1899.

Paul Kampffmeyer. *Geschichte der modernen Polizei im Zusammenhang mit der allgemeinen Kulturbewegung.* Berlin, n.d.

Emil Klingelhöller, *Der Verband Preussischer Polizeibeamten in seinem Werden und Wirken.* Berlin: Deutsche Polizeibuchhandlung und Verlag, 1926.

Das Königliche Polizeipräsidium in Berlin. *Die innere Front.* Berlin: A. Jandorf, 1917.

Helmuth Koschorke, ed. *Die Polizei—einmal anders!* Munich: Zentralverlag der NSDAP, 1937.

Walter Obenaus. *Die Entwicklung der preussischen Sicherheitspolizei.* Berlin, 1940.

Paul Riege. *Kleine Polizeigeschichte.* Lübeck: Verlag für polizeiliches Fachschrifttum, 1954.

Paul Schmidt. *Die ersten 50 Jahre der Königlichen Schutzmannschaft zu Berlin.* Berlin: Ernst Siegfried Mittler & Sohn, 1898.

Roland Schönfelder, ed. *15 Jahre deutsche Polizei-Sportbewegung.* Berlin: Freiheitsverlag, 1936.

———. *Vom Werden der deutschen Polizei.* Leipzig: Verlag von Breitkopf & Härtel, 1937.

POLICE THEORY, RULES, REGULATIONS, AND LAWS

Ernst van den Bergh. *Der Polizeigedanke einst und jetzt.* Frankfurt a.M.: Heinrich Reinhardt, 1948.

Ernst van den Bergh, Karl Fahr, Friedrich Wolfstieg. *Die Preussischen Polizeibeamtengesetze nebst Ausführungsbestimmungen und Ergänzungsgesetzen.* Berlin: Carl Heymann & Kameradschaft, 1929.

Bill Drews. *Preussisches Polizeirecht. Ein Leitfaden für Verwaltungsbeamte.* Berlin: Carl Heymann's Verlag, 1927. [By the President of the Prussian Oberverwaltungsgericht.]

W. R. Hermann, *Was ist Beamtentum?* Berlin: Kameradschaft Verlagsges., 1925.

Albert Horst. *Der Dienstvorgesetzte als Lehrer.* Berlin, 1927.

Walter Katschke and Albert Schmid. *Das Recht des Wachgewerbes. Kommentar zur Novelle der Gew.O. vom 7. Februar 1927 (RGBl. I.S. 57).* Berlin: Carl Heymann, 1929.

Hans Kehrl. "Die Polizei," in *Die Verwaltungs-Akademie. Ein Handbuch für den Beamten im nationalsozialistischen Staat.* Vol. II. Berlin: Industrieverlag Spaeth & Linde, 1938 [?].

Erich Klausener, Christian Kerstein, and Robert Kempner, eds. *Das Polizeiverwaltungsgesetz vom 1. Juni 1931. Textausgabe mit Quellenmaterial und kurzen Erläuterungen.* Berlin: Verlag für Recht und Verwaltung C. A. Weller, 1931.

Heinrich Müller. *Ueber Präventivpolizei. Diss.* Zurich, 1937.

Neese, ed. *Das Lehrbuch für die Polizeischulen.* Berlin: Verlag für Politik und Wirtschaft, 1921.

Schaeffer. *Allgemeines Polizeirecht in Deutschland.* Leipzig, 1929.

Wilhelm Troitzsch. *Die Polizeipflicht in politisch bewegten Zeiten. Eine juristische Studie.* Königsberg: Gräfe & Unzer Verlag, 1933.

Walter Drobnig. *Der Mitteldeutsche Aufstand 1921. Seine Bekämpfung durch die Polizei.* Lübeck. Deutscher Polizeiverlag, 1929.

Wilhelm Hartenstein. *Der Kampfeinsatz der Schutzpolizei bei inneren Unruhen.* Berlin-Charlottenburg: Verlag Offene Worte, 1926.

———. *Die Führung und ihre Mittel beim Kampfeinsatz der Schutzpolizei.* Berlin: Verlag Offene Worte, 1933.

Karl Kübler. "Aufbau, Organisation, Gliederung und Stärke der Schutzpolizei in der Weimarer Republik in vergleichender Gegenüberstellung zu heute." Semesterarbeit, 12. Polizeiratsanwärter-Lehrgang, Polizeipräsidium Stuttgart, 1956. [Available at Police Institute Hiltrup.]

Karl von Oven. *Strassenkampf/Gedanken zur Polizeiführerausbildung/ Die Tätigkeit der Polizeikommandos bei der Vorbereitung des grossen Aufsichtsdienstes/Vorausdisponieren in Kampfverhältnissen.* 4th ed. Berlin and Lübeck: Deutscher Polizeiverlag, 1931.

Hans Roden, *Polizei greift ein—Bilddokumente der Schutzpolizei.* Leipzig: Breitkopf & Härtel, 1934 [?].

Bernhard Weiss, ed. *Die Polizeiverordnungen für Berlin.* Berlin: C. A. Weller, 1931.

Max Weiss, ed. *Die Polizeischule. Systematische Darstellung und Erläuterung des deutschen Polizeirechts.* 3d ed. Dresden: Verlag der Polizeischule, 1920 2 vols.

SCHUTZPOLIZEI

Anonymous. *Volk und Schupo.* Cologne: Gilde Verlag 1929 [?].

Ernst van den Bergh and Karl Fahr, eds. *Das preussische Schutzpolizei-*

beamten-Gesetz vom 16. August 1922. 2d ed. Berlin: Kameradschaft Verlagsges., 1925.

1. *Berufspflichten des deutschen Soldaten. Vom 2. März 1922.* 2. *Polizei und Wehrmacht. Vom 30. April 1921.* 3. *Vorschrift über den Waffengebrauch des Militärs und seine Mitwirkung zur Unterdrückung innerer Unruhen. Vom 19. März 1914.* Berlin: Reichsdruckerei, 1926.

Gustav Schmitt. *Waffentechnisches Unterrichtsbuch für den Polizeibeamten: Die Waffen. Der Schiessdienst. Das Handgranatenwerfen.* 4th ed. Berlin: Verlag R. Eisenschmidt, 1925.

———. *Strassenpanzerwagen: Die Sonderwagen der Schutzpolizei.* Berlin: Verlag R. Eisenschmidt, 1925.

———. *Der Einsatz der Schutzpolizei im Aufruhrgebiet.* 3d ed. Berlin: Verlag R. Eisenschmidt, 1929.

Fritz Tejessy and Albrecht Bähmisch, eds. *Beamtenausschüsse der Schutzpolizei.* Berlin: Kameradschaft Verlagsges., 1929.

Vorschriften für die staatliche Polizei Preussens (V.f.d.P.). *Die Körperschulung beim Vollzugsdienst (K1. KS).* 2d ed. Berlin: Kameradschaft Verlagsges., 1931.

———. *Vorschrift für die Waffenausbildung der Schutzpolizei.* Teil II. Berlin: Kameradschaft Verlagsges., 1932.

DETECTIVE FORCE

Frank Arnau. *Das Auge des Gesetzes. Macht und Ohnmacht der Kriminalpolizei.* Düsseldorf and Vienna: Econ Verlag, 1962.

Kurt Daluege. *Nationalsozialistischer Kampf gegen das Verbrechertum.* Munich: F. Eher, Verlag, 1936. [In collaboration with Liebermann von Sonnenberg.]

"Das Spiel ist aus—Arthur Nebe. Glanz und Elend der deutschen Kriminalpolizei," in *Der Spiegel,* Hannover, 3. Jhg., Sept. 29 to Dec. 29, 1949.

Willy Gay. *Die preussische Landeskriminalpolizei. Ihre Errichtung, ihre bisherige und beabsichtigte Entwicklung, ihre Aufgaben.* Berlin: Kameradschaft Verlagsges., 1928.

Willy Gay and Max Julier. *Wie kann die vorbeugende Tätigkeit der Polizei bei Bekämpfung des Verbrechertums ausgebaut und erfolgreicher gestaltet werden?* Berlin: Kameradschaft, 1925.

Hans Bernd Gisevius. *Wo ist Nebe?* Zurich: Doemer, 1966.

Menzel. "Die Entstehungsgeschichte der deutschen Kriminalpolizei." [Lecture delivered at police school in Berlin-Spandau, May 2, 1957.

MS available in Kripo department of police school, Berlin-Spandau, Nr. 3/57.]

Middeldorf. "Das kriminalpolizeiliche Fahndungswesen," [MS available at Kripo department of police school in Berlin-Spandau, Nr. 2/54.]

Alfredo Niceforo. *Die Kriminalpolizei und ihre Hilfswissenschaften.* Gross-Lichterfelde-Ost: Langenscheidt, 1909. [See introduction by Heinrich Lindenau with brief description of the Berlin detective force under the Empire.]

Hans Schneickert. *Einführung in die Kriminaltechnik. Leitfaden für den Unterricht in den Polizeischulen.* Berlin: Nauck, 1921.

———. *Eignungsprüfungen für den Kriminaldienst.* Berlin, 1923.

Wilhelm Stieber. *Praktisches Lehrbuch der Kriminalpolizei unter besonderer Berücksichtigung der Kriminologie und Kriminaltaktik.* 2d rev. ed. Potsdam: A. W. Hayn, 1921.

Wolfgang Ullrich. *Verbrechensbekämpfung. Geschichte, Organisation, Rechtssprechung.* Berlin-Spandau: Luchterhand Verlag, 1961. [Important.]

CRIMINALITY IN BERLIN

Albert Amend. *Die Kriminalität Deutschlands, 1919 bis 1932.* Munich, 1937.

Karl S. Bader. *Soziologie der deutschen Nachkriegskriminalität.* Tübingen, 1949.

Ernst Engelbrecht. *15 Jahre Kriminalkommissar.* Berlin-Schöneberg: Peter J. Oestergaard, 1927.

———. *In den Spuren des Verbrechertums.* Berlin-Schöneberg: Peter J. Oestergaard, 1930 [?].

Ernst Engelbrecht and Leo Heller. *Berliner Razzien.* Berlin: Hermann Paetel, 1924.

———. *Kinder der Nacht. Bilder aus dem Verbrecherleben.* Berlin: Hermann Paetel, 1925.

Franz Exner. *Krieg und Kriminalität.* Leipzig, 1926.

Wilhelm Flitner. *Der Krieg und die Jugend.* [Wirtschafts- u. Sozialgeschichte des Weltkrieges, ed. by Carnegie Endowment for Int. Peace.] Stuttgart and Berlin, 1927.

Erich Frey. *Ich beantrage Freispruch. Aus den Erinnerungen des Strafverteidigers Prof. Dr. Dr. Erich Frey.* Hamburg, 1959. [Not always accurate.]

Hugo Friedländer. *Interessante Kriminal-Prozesse.* Berlin, 1912.

Emil Julius Gumbel. *Zwei Jahre Mord.* 4th ed. Berlin: Neues Vaterland, 1921.

————. *Vier Jahre politischen Mord.* 1922.

————. *Verschwörer.* Vienna: Malik, 1924.

————. *Verräter verfallen der Feme.* 1929.

————. *Lasst Köpfe rollen.* 1932

————. *Vom Fememord zur Reichskanzlei.* Heildelberg: Lambert Schneider, 1962.

Robert Heindl, ed. *Archiv für Kriminologie.* Leipzig: F. C. W. Vogel, 1925–1932.

Friedrich Karl Kaul. *Justiz wird zum Verbrechen. Der Pitaval der Weimarer Republik.* Berlin: Das Neue Berlin, 1953. [East German publication.]

————. *Verdienen wird gross geschrieben. Der Pitaval der Weimarer Republik.* Berlin. Das Neue Berlin, 1954.

Kriminalistische Monatshefte. Zeitschrift für die gesamte Kriminalistische Wissenschaft und Praxis. Berlin-Charlottenburg: Bali Verlag Berger & Co., 1927 to 1933.

Hans Langemann. *Das Attentat. Eine kriminalwissenschaftliche Studie zum politischen Kapitalverbrechen.* Hamburg: Kriminalistik, 1956.

Ernst Liebermann von Sonnenberg and Otto Trettin. *Kriminalfälle.* Berlin: Universitas, 1934.

Ingenieur Nelken. *Publikum und Verbrechen.* Berlin, 1927.

————. *Verbrechen und Versicherung.* Berlin, 1928.

Ulrich Possehl. *Moderne Betrüger.* Berlin: Bali Verlag Berger & Co., 1928.

Paul Reiwald. *Die Gesellschaft und ihre Verbrecher.* Zurich: Paul-Verlag, 1948.

Richter. *Der Kampf gegen Schund- und Schmutzschriften in Preussen.* Berlin: R. von Decker Verlag, 1929.

Wilhelm Sauer. *Kriminalsoziologie.* Berlin and Leipzig: Verlag für Staatswissenschaften und Geschichte, 1933.

Franz von Schmidt. *Vorgeführt erscheint. Erlebte Kriminalistik.* Stuttgart: Verlag Deutsche Volksbücher, 1955.

Hans Schneickert. *Einführung in die Kriminalsoziologie und Verbrechensverhütung.* Jena: Gustav Fischer, 1935.

Paul Schweder. *Die grossen Kriminalprozesse des Jahrhunderts. Ein deutscher Pitaval.* Hamburg: Kriminalistik, 1961.

K. A. Tramm. *Brandstiftung und Brandursachen. Die Technik ihrer Ermittlung.* Kiel: Verlag der Landesbrandkasse, 1933.

Erich Wulffen. *Verbrechen und Verbrecher.* Berlin: Hanseatischer Rechts-
und Wirtschaftsverlag, 1925.

Georg A. Zinn. "Der politische Mord," in *Süddeutsche Juristenzeitung. III.*
Heidelberg, 1948. 141 ff.

POLITICAL POLICE

Eugen Ernst. *Polizeispitzeleien und Ausnahmegesetz, 1878–1910.* Berlin:
Vorwärts, 1911.

Karl Frohme. *Politische Polizei und Justiz in monarchischem Deutschland.* Hamburg: Auer, 1926. [Introduction criticizes the police and judiciary of the Weimar Republic.]

*Die Geheime Staatspolizei. Ihre geschichtliche Entwicklung und Organi-
sation. Ihre Beamten und deren Rechtsstellung im Gesetz zu Artikel 131
GG und im Regierungsentwurf des Bundesbeamtengesetzes. Denkschrift
des Bundes Deutscher Polizeibeamten e.V.* Kassel, 1953.

Hennig. "Das Wesen und die Entwicklung der politischen Polizei Berlins,"
in *Mitteilungen des Vereins für die Geschichte Berlins,* 43. Jhg. (1925),
Nr. 7–9.

Paul Kampffmeyer. "Die politische Polizei," in *Sozialistische Monatshefte,*
35. Jhg. (1929), Heft 1.

Bernhard Weiss. *Polizei und Politik.* Berlin: Gersbach & Sohn Verlag,
1928.

BOOKS BY LEADING OFFICIALS

Emil Eichhorn. *Meine Tätigkeit im Berliner Polizei-Präsidium und mein
Anteil an den Januar-Ereignissen.* Berlin: Verlagsgenossenschaft "Freiheit," 1919.

Ferdinand Friedensburg. *Die Weimarer Republik* Berlin, 1946. [Friedens-
burg was Deputy Police President of Berlin, 1925-27.]

Albert C. Grzesinski. *Inside Germany.* Trans. Alexander S. Lipschitz. New
York: E. P. Dutton, 1939.

Carl Severing. *Mein Lebensweg.* Cologne: Greven Verlag, 1950. 2 vols.

Bernhard Weiss. "Der frühere Vizepräsident der Berliner Polizei erzählt
aus seinen Erfahrungen," in *Berliner Forum* (RIAS-Berlin, Jan., 1950).

Index